SEMEIA 49

THE APOCRYPHAL JESUS AND CHRISTIAN ORIGINS

Guest Editor:
Ron Cameron

©1990
by the Society of Biblical Literature

SEMEIA 49

Copyright © 1990 by the Society of Biblical Literature

All rights reserved. No part of this work may be reproduced or transmitted in any form or by any means, electronic or mechanical, including photocopying and recording, or by means of any information storage or retrieval system, except as may be expressly permitted by the 1976 Copyright Act or in writing from the publisher. Requests for permission should be addressed in writing to the Rights and Permissions Office, Society of Biblical Literature, 825 Houston Mill Road, Atlanta, GA 30329, USA.

ISSN 0095-571X
ISBN 1-58983-222-1

Printed in the United States of America
on acid-free paper

CONTENTS

Contributors to this Issue iv

Introduction
    Ron Cameron 1

Proverbs as Sayings of Jesus in the *Epistula Apostolorum*
    Julian Hills 7

"What Have You Come Out To See?" Characterizations of John and Jesus in the Gospels
    Ron Cameron 35

"Easter Faith" and the Sayings Gospel Q
    John S. Kloppenborg 71

"Time to Murder and Create": Visions and Revisions in the *Gospel of Peter*
    Arthur J. Dewey 101

The Youth in the *Secret Gospel of Mark*
    Marvin W. Meyer 129

Thoughts on Two Extracanonical Gospels
    John Dominic Crossan 155

All the Extra Jesuses: Christian Origins in the Light of the Extra-Canonical Gospels
    Burton L. Mack 169

CONTRIBUTORS TO THIS ISSUE

Ron Cameron
  Department of Religion
  Wesleyan University
  Middletown, CT 06457

John Dominic Crossan
  Department of Religious Studies
  DePaul University
  2323 North Seminary Avenue
  Chicago, IL 60614

Arthur J. Dewey
  Theology Department
  Xavier University
  3800 Victory Parkway
  Cincinnati, OH 45207

Julian Hills
  Theology Department
  Marquette University
  Milwaukee, WI 53233

John S. Kloppenborg
  Faculty of Theology
  University of St. Michael's College
  81 St. Mary Street
  Toronto, Ontario M5S 1J4
  Canada

Burton L. Mack
  School of Theology at Claremont
  1325 North College Avenue
  Claremont, CA 91711

Marvin W. Meyer
  Department of Religion
  Chapman College
  Orange, CA 92666

INTRODUCTION

Ron Cameron
Wesleyan University

The writing of gospels lies at the heart of early Christian reflective activity. During the past two decades, scholars have witnessed an explosion of intense study of gospel literature, necessitating a reorientation of our perspectives about Jesus and the beginnings of Christianity. This explosion can be gauged by the outburst of books and articles treating the gospels of the New Testament; and it can be calibrated, to a certain degree, by noting the increased attention given in various quarters to some of the apocryphal gospels. It is still the case, however, that the New Testament is frequently investigated in isolation, without reference to those texts not included in the canon. The majority of the other gospels are rarely considered seriously, being routinely regarded as of lesser importance, and assumed to be dependent on or influenced by the New Testament. The purpose of this *Semeia* volume is to help rectify such an unhappy situation by taking up for forthright investigation a set of apocryphal gospels which, if taken seriously, make a difference in the way we (are to) understand the beginnings of Christianity.

The challenge of the apocryphal Jesus is nothing less than a call to see early Christianity in a fresh light, not as something given but as itself an unsettled issue to be investigated by all students of the New Testament as historians of religion in antiquity. The essays in this volume provide alternative reconstructions of Christian beginnings by selecting five extracanonical moments of Christian reflection that produced a written legacy, and by subjecting those writings to critical, disciplined, exegetical scrutiny. The gospels analyzed in this volume are the *Secret Gospel of Mark*, the *Gospel of Peter*, the Synoptic Sayings Gospel Q (with material reference to the *Gospel of Thomas* for purposes of comparison), and the *Epistula Apostolorum*. Our objective is to present close readings of choice texts often rejected and long neglected by scholarship. No attempt has been made to restrict our inquiries to the usual, tired question of the relationship of these gospels to the writings of the New Testament. Instead, each text is investigated as a document worthy of study in its own right.

Both sayings and narrative gospels are taken up for examination. In the former, the employment of sayings traditions in narrative contexts is systematically explored, primarily in terms of rhetorical concerns and, incipiently, in terms of social contexts. And in the latter, the drama of discipleship and the narratives of the passion are explored, in part, through the employment of the techniques of form, redaction, and genre criticism. In all cases, discrete differences in language, audience, and logic are noted that indicate specific traditions, settings, or groups. These essays thus form a set in terms of their emphasis on literary composition and exegetical interpretation. Their larger challenge, however, concerns the critical task of historical reconstruction. Our ultimate goal is to achieve a deeper understanding of early Christianity by sifting through the other gospels which were written and probing the circumstances that produced them. And though every essay is concerned chiefly with a single apocryphal gospel, each contains implications for the very genesis of those gospels that came to be included in the New Testament. In the final analysis, therefore, this volume forms a set by virtue of its focus on the task of redescription, calling for a reassessment, of the beginnings of Christianity.

The initial essay by Julian Hills sets the frame of reference for our analysis of sayings traditions employed in narrative contexts. The topic of discussion is the function of proverbs as sayings of Jesus in the post-resurrection discourses and dialogues of the *Epistula Apostolorum*. Four proverbs are assessed as test cases to determine the nature and authority of proverbial speech. Hills demonstrates that the authority of these proverbs is independent of and antecedent to that of Jesus as the risen revealer. They function, in fact, essentially as elaborations in a rhetorical argumentation, to urge understanding, establish paradigms, supply a precedent, and create the conditions for the author's appeals for acceptance of the directives recommended in his gospel handbook. Both the literary context in which the proverbs are embedded and the communal setting which they reflect are thus indispensable to the persuasive task which the proverbs render for the community counseled by the text.

My essay addresses more explicitly the function of rhetoric in the composition of the gospels. The purpose of this paper is to clarify the ways in which John the Baptist and Jesus were characterized by means of a close reading of Q (and the *Gospel of Thomas*) and a comparison with contemporaneous modes of description in the literature of the Greco-Roman world. How John and Jesus were characterized, why they came to be related, the ways those characterizations were developed thematically in Q through the literary composition of a speech, and the means by which that speech served the needs of the Q community are my central interpretative concerns. Rhetorical criticism indicates that sayings characterizing John and Jesus were forged in the context of creating a speech, composed according to the pattern of elaboration of the chreia worked out in Greco-Roman schools, and designed to vindicate that group which produced them in the name and under the authority of Jesus. This speech thus reflects a considerable degree of self-consciousness about what its group was doing. Created in the process of early Christian mythmaking, the elaboration addresses the problem of how to incorporate the apocalyptic imagery secondarily ascribed to its founders with the full consciousness that John and Jesus did not really appear apocalyptic. Neither John nor Jesus was remembered as an apocalyptic preacher. And though an apocalyptic idiom is entertained in the text to make sense of a perceived social crisis, apocalyptic assumptions never did become constitutive even for the community of Q. The essay will show that the conceptual concerns characterizing the entire pericope are governed by a wisdom way of viewing the world, not an apocalyptic vision. Accordingly, the analysis calls for the necessity to reconsider the beginnings of the Jesus tradition in light of the secondary character of apocalyptic imagination.

The Synoptic Sayings Gospel Q is examined more systematically in John S. Kloppenborg's essay. He does not present a rhetorical analysis of the text, however, but explores the ramifications of the thesis that Q was a gospel, composed of sayings, which served as the guiding theological statement of an identifiable community. The seemingly curious fact that Q does not characterize Jesus in terms of the kerygmatic significance of the cross (and resurrection) is confronted head-on. Since the wisdom story of the persecution and vindication of the righteous one forms the generic pattern of the passion narratives in both the New Testament and the *Gospel of Peter*, Kloppenborg endeavors to identify any components of that story which may appear in Q. He concludes that, though several Q sayings might seem to cohere with certain elements of the wisdom story, those generic components are nowhere gathered together or plotted narratively in Q. In addition, Kloppenborg establishes that the earliest stages in the formation of Q betray no influence of an individualizing interpretation of the wisdom story or of its specific application to Jesus. Rather, Q interprets Jesus' death corporately within the framework of a deuteronomistic understanding of prophetic activity. Kloppenborg has thus demonstrated that there is no need to appeal to a theology of the cross in order to imagine the origins of Christianity. For Q itself documents an alternative rationale sufficient to account for its beginnings, and cites a prophetic paradigm as a mythic precedent to reflect upon its subsequent social history. Persecution is simply the occupational hazard of those who are envoys of Wisdom; and vindication is guaranteed by the sayings themselves, arising out of the characterization of Jesus' speech as words intrinsic to Wisdom.

The wisdom story of the persecution and vindication of the righteous one is discussed in more detail in Arthur J. Dewey's essay. His analysis concerns the *Gospel of Peter*, a fragmentary narrative gospel that contains a story of Jesus' crucifixion, an epiphany story, a story of the empty tomb, and the introduction to a resurrection story. Employing the techniques of form, redaction, and genre criticism, Dewey proposes that four distinct, written layers can be identified in the text, which he delineates as follows. The original layer narrates Jesus' crucifixion according to the generic pattern of the wisdom story. A second layer expands upon that original unit by appending a miraculous epiphany story as its supplement. A third layer, made up of narrative fragments and editorial glosses attached to each of the first two layers, fills out the contours of that account by depicting individuals as specific characters in a more historicizing scheme, breeding dissension between the people and the leaders of the Jews, and drawing lines of demarcation between Jewish and Christian groups. The final redactional layer, added sometime after those Christians identified themselves with the apostle Peter and became alienated from their Jewish matrix, was composed after the fall of Jerusalem, contemporaneous with the writing of the Gospel of Mark. Dewey's principal thesis, that the *Gospel of Peter*'s original layer contains within it the generic seeds of all subsequent passion narratives, deserves serious consideration. His ultimate conclusion is more significant still: even at that initial stage we have not an historical report, but an imaginative attempt to discern the Wisdom of God.

The final essay by Marvin W. Meyer utilizes more exclusively the method of redaction criticism to analyze a series of episodes within a narrative gospel. The topic of his investigation is the story of the youth in the *Secret Gospel of Mark*. Arguing that the canonical Gospel of Mark is an abridgment of the *Secret Gospel of Mark*, Meyer advances the thesis that the youth serves as a paradigm to dramatize a vision of discipleship which, though presented in a truncated form in canonical Mark, is exemplified most graphically in that longer version composed of the fragments found in *Secret Mark* together with their canonical gospel counterparts. This drama of discipleship is recounted as a subplot in five episodes: the youth refuses to follow Jesus; the youth is raised from the dead and baptized; the youth's family is not received at Jericho; the youth flees naked from Gethsemane; and the youth appears in the empty tomb. Meyer's suggestion that the role of this youth for Mark is comparable to that of the Beloved Disciple in John should be taken seriously. The clear implication of this analysis is very important indeed, for Mark's use of a narrative sequence treating the theme of discipleship indicates that this gospel was read and re-read as a mythic document for social self-definition.

Two responses conclude the volume. John Dominic Crossan's response is restricted to the essays by Dewey and Meyer, which propose alternative redactional analyses of the *Gospel of Peter* and the *Secret Gospel of Mark* based on critical debate with his own published work. Burton L. Mack's response is directed primarily to the essays by Hills, Kloppenborg, and me, which engage issues and methods with which he is concerned in his most recent work. Both responses seek to encourage us and our colleagues to push beyond the accepted boundaries of biblical scholarship into promising new frontiers. The call is to take up the challenge of the apocryphal Jesus, and reconsider the beginnings of Christianity.

Proverbs as Sayings of Jesus in the *Epistula Apostolorum*

Julian Hills
Marquette University

ABSTRACT

Among the words of Jesus in the *Epistula Apostolorum* (*Ep. apost.*) are several proverbs or proverb-like sayings. The presence of these discrete sayings in the midst of discourse and dialogue naturally raises the question of their history: whence they derive, and in what source or sources the author of the *Ep. apost.* came by them. But there is a second and equally important question, which concerns the nature and authority of proverbial speech: In what sense is a proverb authoritative, and how in this document can its authority enhance or complement that of the risen revealer? The answer to this second question depends less on tradition-historical findings than on what can be learned from two settings: the literary context into which each saying is introduced, and the communal setting which the writing as a whole reflects and to which it responds. Analysis of four sayings suggests that the proverb, as observed in the *Ep. apost.* and as pondered in modern discussion, is inherently suited to its particular persuasive task within the community of the *Ep. apost.*

0.   Introduction

0.1   The *Epistula Apostolorum* is a remarkable survivor among the NT apocrypha. No part of the original Greek has been preserved either in manuscript or in quotation, yet so far as can be determined the work has been copied and read within the Ethiopian Church from that Church's beginnings to the present day. For decades catalogues of Ethiopic manuscripts in the great European libraries had referred to an apocryphal work appended to the Ethiopic version of the 5th century church order, the *Testamentum Domini*, but the *Epistula* as an independent writing was all but unknown to western scholars until 1895. In that year Carl Schmidt announced his discovery of a Coptic codex containing an "Epistle of the Apostles," and gave a preliminary account of its contents. Montague Rhodes James subsequently identified the work with the latter part of the Ethiopic "Testament," a critical edition of which was being prepared by Louis Guerrier. Guerrier's edition and translation appeared in 1913, Schmidt's in 1919.

0.2   The wait for Schmidt's apocryphon had been long. In some quarters high expectations were deemed to have been disappointed (Bardy: 110–11). Others welcomed the text as an extraordinary find, "comparable with the Didache or the Odes of Solomon for its additions to our knowledge of the second century" (so Lake: 16; cf. Deissmann: 44). In any case, so thorough was Schmidt's review of the major introductory questions (e.g. the date and place of writing) that his judgments quickly established themselves as a virtually unchallenged consensus, for example in the standard reference works. The *Ep. apost.* was regularly appealed to as a mid-2d century witness to particular ideas or traditions (e.g. the often quoted 'creed' at the end of chap. 5), but it was not until Manfred Hornschuh's investigation that the attempt was made afresh to explore the writing's own setting and purpose. Even today our knowledge of this writing and of its author's circle is slight compared, for instance, with what has been learned of the writings with which Kirsopp Lake favorably compared it sixty-five years ago. However, comparative materials (e.g. the Nag Hammadi writings) are now plentiful, the *Epistula*'s genre is better understood, and it may be that new questions can yield new insights into this text. In particular it may reasonably be hoped that some progress will be made in the central interpretive issue, namely the hermeneutics of literary dialogue between the risen Lord and the disciples.

0.3   The dialogue which forms the greater part of the *Ep. apost.* is inaugurated at the time of the post-resurrection appearance of the Lord (chaps. 9–12) and concluded at the ascension (chap. 51). The central importance of the risen Lord's words, not supplementing but rather superseding the words and deeds of the earthly Jesus, is repeatedly stated and implied in the dialogue. The fullest demonstration of this perspective is in chap. 34, where the disciples applaud the source and content of the revelation they have received (*NTApoc* 1. 214):

> "O Lord, such meaningful things you have spoken and preached to us and have revealed to us great things never yet spoken, and in every respect you have comforted us and have shown yourself gracious unto us. For after your resurrection you revealed all this to us that we might be really saved."

0.4   In this speech of the disciples two connected claims may be detected. First, in light of the inclusive time frame (from resurrection to ascension), the record of the Lord's post-resurrection words in the *Ep. apost.* 13–51 is complete. There is no implied gap, in narrative or discourse, which might have allowed additional conversation to go unrecorded. The *Epistula* claims to offer not merely a selection of teachings but the full record of them, as testified by the disciples as a united group. Secondly, this body of teaching is not only complete, it is also uniquely saving. Its content is new ("great things never yet spoken"); what is taught is "revealed" (e.g. chap. 20: "You have revealed all this to us"; chap. 45: "You have revealed everything [to us] well"); and the revelation is hailed as fully salvific ("that we might be really saved"). The saving event *par excellence* is therefore declared to be the transmission of a final revelation in the presence of the leaders of the first Christian community. Its medium and its content are the words of the risen one, who has chosen to deliver his saving gospel only after the resurrection.

0.5   A thorough exploration of the theological presuppositions implied by all this, and of whatever ecclesiastical structure might sustain the authorization of a fresh, post-resurrection revelation, would take us far afield. Among early Christian writings the *Ep. apost.* is not alone in proposing such a temporal setting for saving dialogue (see, for example, the *Apocryphon of James* [NHC 1, 2], the *Apocryphon of John* [NHC 2, 1], and the *Sophia of Jesus Christ* [NHC 3, 4]). The collection and assessment of the contents and claims of the second and third century "revelation dialogues" are a task that is barely begun (see the sound guidelines laid down by Perkins). But these twin features of the *Ep. apost.* just observed, concerning the claimed completeness and the power of these particular post-resurrection words, at once prompt a question with which a beginning may be made of the broader task: In what literary forms does the author permit this revelation to be clothed, especially at what may be judged its decisive moments?

0.6   Given the status already accorded the contents of the "revelation" by its temporal setting, the question of the smaller units' inner coherence and authority might appear a secondary one. But since the prior decision as to genre ("revelation dialogue") will not necessarily have prejudiced the selection of traditional materials, the initial question may stand; indeed, it may be sharpened, as follows: Is *the authority of the revealer* endorsed, complemented, or enhanced (however remotely) by a corresponding *formal authority* inherent in the traditional sayings found in the writing? This is the issue to be investigated here with reference to several proverbs or proverb-like sayings in the mouth of Jesus in the *Epistula Apostolorum*.

0.7   It is well known that from the earliest stages of the Jesus tradition sayings appear which correspond to the various forms of the Jewish *māšāl*. Rudolf Bultmann distinguished three basic types, principles (material and personal), exhortations, and questions (69–73). Numerous examples can be collected from the Synoptic tradition (see the selection in Bultmann: 73–81). So too the 'apocryphal' literature yields its harvest; but apart from the abundance in the *Gospel of Thomas* (NHC 2, 2) it is a relatively modest one. To be sure, sayings conforming to Bultmann's models are many, but the vast majority are exhortations (e.g. in the *Teachings of Silvanus* [NHC 7, 4] and the *Sentences of Sextus* [NHC 12, 1]), and in only a few cases are they attributed to Jesus. The following sample is typical:

> Gos. Thom. 47a (*NHLE* 123):
> "It is impossible for a man to mount two horses or to stretch two bows."
> Gos. Truth (NHC 1, 3) 28.16–17 (*NHLE* 42):
> "He who has no root has no fruit either."
> Gos. Phil. (NHC 2, 3) 52.25 (*NHLE* 132):
> "Those who sow in winter reap in summer."
> Teach. Silv. 88.32–34 (*NHLE* 349):
> "Why do you drink stale water though sweet is available to you?"
> Teach. Silv. 97.18–19 (*NHLE* 352):
> "Have a great number of friends, but not counselors."

To these may be added *Dial. Sav.* (NHC 3, 5) 139.9–11 (*NHLE* 235), where proverbial sayings are summarized. The examples to be studied in the *Epistula* comprise three principles and one question (in fact, a principle in question form).

0.8   The "proverb" has become the focus of considerable scholarly attention of late, and its definition is not yet a matter of consensus. Suffice it to say here that in my judgment the sayings to be dealt with below will bear the designation "proverb" inasmuch as (a) they are short, pithy formulations which (b) may be detached from their context and retain complete sense, but which (c) do not of themselves suggest the application of the truths they enshrine; in addition, (d) these sayings do not imply a religious setting, but purport to relate specific secular or universal insights. (With these criteria compare those established by Fontaine: 74–75.) In each case there are biblical and/or extra-biblical parallels, either in form or in content, which furnish useful controls.

0.9   The four sayings are these (*NTApoc* 1. 197, 208, 213, 225):

chap. 11: "The foot of a ghost or a demon does not join to the ground."
chap. 25: "What has fallen will [arise], and what is lost will be found and what is [weak] will recover."
chap. 32: "Are the fingers of the hand alike or the ears of corn in the field?"
chap. 47: "A blind man who leads a blind man, [both] fall into [a] ditch."

0.10   The examination of each saying will comprise questions concerning (1) the saying's *context*; (2) the saying's *translation* and the relation between the two versions (Coptic [= C.] and Ethiopic [= E.]); (3) the saying's *source* or *origin* and similar sayings in biblical or non-biblical sources; (4) the saying's literary *incorporation* into its context; and (5) the saying's *application* and hence its *function* in the specific discussion of which it is a part. The study will conclude with an assessment of the role of the sayings as bearers of authority in their individual contexts and in the writing as a whole.

1.   Saying 1: *Ep. apost.* 11.8 (*NTApoc* 1. 197):
  C.:   "The foot of a ghost or a demon does not join to the ground."
  E.:   "But a ghost, a demon, leaves no print on the ground."

1.1.1   This saying is found near the end of the writing's post-resurrection appearance scene (chaps. 9–12). The Lord has appeared to the three women (Mary [E.: Sarah], Martha, and Mary Magdalene) at the tomb. He has twice sent one of them to the disciples with news of his resurrection, but they do not believe it. Therefore the Lord himself appears to the disciples, in an account which displays clearly epiphanic features (Hills: 587). To this point the disciples are still "doubting in (their) hearts whether it was possibly he" (chap. 11). The Lord invites three of them to examine his body:
  C.:   "That you may know that it is I, put your finger, Peter, in the nailprints of my hands; and you, Thomas, put your finger in the spear-wounds of my side; but you, Andrew, look at my feet and see if they do not touch the ground."

Thereupon the reason for the last request (only) is given, namely the quoted saying, which is introduced with the formula, "for it is written in the prophet."

1.1.2 The narrative is of course reminiscent of the canonical gospels' post-resurrection accounts, especially those of longer Mark, of Luke, and of John. Indeed, the first glance impression of this account's final section suggests that the *Ep. apost.* presents an extravagant paraphrase of John's 'doubting Thomas' episode. Inasmuch as the presence of three named disciples represents "a tendency to differentiation and individualization," Bultmann could describe the narrative as "characteristic" of "the Apocryphal tradition" (309). But closer inspection will show that there is more at issue than paraphrase, not least the range of comparable materials, of history of religions background, and of editorial intention.

1.2.1 The text of *Ep. apost.* 11.8 in the Coptic version is as follows (IV 9–10 [numbers in this format = paragraph and line in Schmidt, 1919]):

ΟΥΦΑΝΤΑϹΙΑ ΝΔΑΙΜШΝ ΜΑ[ΡΕ]ΡΕΤϤ ΤΟΥΜΕ ϨΙΧΝ ΠΚΑϨ.

1.2.2 It should be noted at once that in speaking of "a ghost *or* a demon" the ET in *NTApoc* 1. 197 must have been misprinted, for the original German translation correctly has "das Gespenst *eines* Daemons" (i.e. "of" for "or"; *NTApok* [= German edition of *NTApoc*]: 1. 132); similarly Hugo Duensing has "Eines Dämonsgespenstes..." (1925: 10; so Schmidt, 1919: 43). For this the Gk. φαντασία δαίμονος (or, in the genitive, φαντασίας δαίμονος) is a probable retroversion. What, then, is a φαντασία δαίμονος? Duensing's rendering, "the ghost of a demon" (= the ET in *NTApoc*), probably overloads the Greek. Contemporary designation of tomb-spirits as δαιμόνιον πνεῦμα (Deissmann: 273–74) may be relevant here, but since φαντασία will be found to mean "apparition," "appearance," or "manifestation" (as opposed to physical reality; see 1.4.1 below), the δαίμων must itself be a "departed spirit" (cf. LSJ: 366a).

1.2.3 The true subject, however, is enclosed within the split habitual form (ΜΑΡΕ- ΤΟΥΜΕ): ΡΕΤ՝, which regularly signifies "foot; lowest part, bottom" (Lambdin, 1983: 261). The full range of Gk. words regularly rendered ΡΕΤ՝ includes ἴχνος, as in Deut 28:35 (RSV "...from the *sole* [LXX ἴχνος] of your foot to the crown of your head"; Crum: 302b). In turn, Gk. ἴχνος embraces such divergent meanings as track, footstep, trace, foot, sole, palm, and route (LSJ: 846b).

1.2.4 A similar uncertainty attaches to the verb, ΤΟΥΜΕ, none of whose regular meanings ("to join, cleave to, be fitting"; Crum: 414a) seems to give quite the sense required. As for ΤΟΥΜΕ with the preposition ϨΙΧΝ, W. E. Crum offers only this passage, giving the meaning "to join, be fixed upon" (415a). There is no difficulty with the last word, καε, whose meaning is virtually coextensive with that of Gk. γῆ.

1.2.5   The text of the Ethiopic version, though showing numerous minor variations in the MSS, is probably secure as follows (56/1–2 [numbers in this format = page and line in Guerrier]):

methata gānēn-sa ʾalbo ʾasara westa medr.

1.2.6   New and better MSS recently made accessible now show that the two nouns with which the saying begins, methat (= C. ⲫⲁⲛⲧⲁⲥⲓⲁ) and gānēn (= C. ⲇⲁⲓⲙⲱⲛ), relate to each other as do their Coptic counterparts. The particle -sa ("indeed, but"; Dillmann, 1970: 321) hardly affects the translation.

1.2.7   Thereafter the Ethiopic becomes less easy to reconcile with the Coptic. The prepositional phrase, westa medr (= C. ⲉⲓϫⲛ̄ ⲡⲕⲁϩ, "on the ground"), is clear enough. But unless the fourth word in the saying, ʾasara, is to be understood as a verb ("to join"; Dillmann, 1970: 747), the only verbal element is the negative possessive, ʾalbo ("he/it does not have..."), which does not at all connote "joining." On balance, however, it is more probable that ʾasara is not verbal, but instead is the accusative of the noun ʾašar ("vestige, trace, footprint"; Dillmann, 1970: 739; the exchange of "s " for "š" is common in Ethiopic MSS). Therefore Isaak Wajnberg's translation is to be followed: "...hat keine Fußspur auf der Erde" (Schmidt, 1919: 42).

1.2.8   Since ʾasar never has the meaning "foot," but is rather the regular Ethiopic for Gk. ἴχνος (a Gk. antecedent already allowed for the Coptic ⲡⲉⲧ´), it is almost certain that behind E. ʾasar and C. ⲡⲉⲧ´ stood Gk. ἴχνος. In light of the uncertainty about the original verb, it is not possible to say whether the intended meaning was "foot" or "footprint." The second is more likely, since ἴχνος as "foot" is almost exclusively a poetic usage (e.g. in Euripides Bacchae 1133–34). We arrive at the following literal readings:
  C.: "The foot of a departed spirit's apparition does not join the ground."
  E.: "A departed spirit's apparition does not have/leave a footprint on the ground."

1.3.1   Several proposals have been made as to the saying's source or origin. Adolf Harnack, commenting on Schmidt's preliminary account of the text, conjectured that the saying reflects Wis 18:17 (RSV "Then at once apparitions [φαντασίαι] in dreadful dreams greatly troubled them"; Harnack: 8). Guerrier cited Dan 14 (= Bel):19–20, where Daniel remarks to Cyrus, "Behold now the pavement, and mark well whose footsteps are these [τίνος τὰ ἴχνη ταῦτα]" (56 n. 1). A. A. T. Ehrhardt's hypothesis, that the saying comes from "a midrash on the story of the witch of Endor" in 1 Samuel 28 (362 n. 1), is worthy of mention but presently incapable of verification. Nearer in thought would seem to be a phrase in Job 11:7 LXX: ἴχνος κυρίου εὑρήσεις; ("Do you perceive the trace [or: track] of the Lord?"). But even here the implications are quite different, and we are a long way from speaking of a source.

1.3.2   Unless the author composed the saying, perhaps (as Schmidt believed) on the basis of Luke 24:39 (RSV "See my hands and my feet, that it is I myself; handle me, and see; for a spirit [πνεῦμα] has not flesh and bones as you see that I have"), it is a reasonable presumption that he found it, as he says, "written in the prophet," i.e. in a writing now lost.

1.3.3   Three further parallels must be brought into the discussion, however. The first is Ignatius *Smyrn.* 3.2, an independent witness to the tradition found in Luke 24:39 (so Lightfoot: 1/1. 11 and 2/2. 296–97; Koester, 1957: 47–50; Cameron: 49–51; Schoedel: 226–27):

> "And when he came to those with Peter he said to them: 'Take, handle me and see that I am not a phantom without a body [δαιμόνιον ἀσώματον].'"

The second, deriving from Lucretius *De rerum natura* 1.304, is a saying employed twice by Tertullian in arguing for the corporeality of the risen Jesus (*De anima* 5; *Adv. Marc.* 4.8):

> Tangere enim et tangi, nisi corpus nulla potest res.
> "For nothing can touch or be touched, except body."

Even more interesting is the saying, which James (488 n. 1) took to be a probable quotation from *Ep. apost.* 11.8, in Commodian *Carmen apologeticum* 559–68. As in the *Epistula,* the proverbial saying occurs in the midst of a post-resurrection appearance account. Jesus addresses Thomas as follows:

> "I am not a shade/shadow [*umbra*], such as are the dead:
> 'A shade [*umbra*] does not make a footprint [*vestigium*].'"

1.3.4 A further group of comparable materials comes into view if, rather than the formal saying, the *topos* of 'the search for a phantom's footprint' is considered. Familiar from early Christian literature is a passage in the *Acts of John* 93, where John reports (*NTApoc* 2. 227):

> "I often wished, as I talked with him (Jesus), to see his footprint [ἴχνος] in the earth, whether it appeared...and I never saw it."

To this should be added Philostratus *Heroicus* 13.2, where the venerable Vinedresser relates his meeting with an athletic spirit (de Lannoy: 14; cf. also the report about Poseidon in Homer *Iliad* 13.68–72, and the discussion in Dölger: 115 n. 4):

> "As he ran by you could not see his footprint [ἴχνος], nor did his foot make any mark upon the ground."

1.3.5 The special religious dimensions of the term ἴχνος have been well documented. In antiquity footprints are found, among other things, "as votive-offerings indicating the presence of a god" (LSJ: 846b; for evidence see Dow and Upson; Castiglione). The footprint is also specified in an intercessory appeal for a just man, in *Apoc. Elij.* 5.12 (Rosensthiel: 111):

> "Where now is the footprint of a righteous person, that we should worship you? or where is our teacher, that we might appeal to him?"

1.3.6 Thus the issue of the saying's original referent is other than the identification of a canonical prototype. None of the canonical accounts prepares us for Andrew's assignment in the *Epistula*, whereas a variety of interpretive possibilities is seen to be raised by a wider review of contemporary sources. Not least is the saying's integrity maintained against the view that it is the mere invention of the author.

1.4.1 The incorporation of the saying about the footprint of an apparition is already anticipated at the start of chap. 11. The disciples, having now been summoned by the Lord himself, still do not yet believe, because

C.: "We thought it was a ghost [ⲟⲩⲫⲁⲛⲧⲁⲥⲓⲁ], and we did not believe it was the Lord."

E.: "He came before us like a ghost [*methat*] and we did not believe that it was he."

At first sight this remark is patently tautologous, each half amounting to the same thing. But in fact it is of the greatest importance to the author that a distinction be observed between *two* issues: the identity of the risen one (as the disciples' teacher), and the nature of the risen body (as corporeal). And it is through the use of the proverbial agraphon that the two issues are made to stand apart from each other. This is confirmed by the fact that the charge to Peter and to Thomas has only one stated purpose: "That you may know that it is I"; the charge to Andrew, on the other hand, is justified by the explicitly anti-docetic potential of the prophetic saying.

1.4.2   That an anti-docetic argument is the true goal of the account is made certain by the disciples' confession in chap. 12:

> "But we [touched] him that we might truly know whether he [had risen] in the flesh, and we fell on our [faces] confessing our sin, that we had been [un]believing."

Confession of former unbelief in the nature of the resurrection body is alone sufficient warrant for the Lord's new invitation, "Rise up."

1.5.1   The precise application of the saying therefore becomes clear. The second—and for this author, decisive—question posed by the resurrection is resolved by a prophetic "proof-text." But *how* does the proof-text prove? The key here is the fact that in the context of wider contemporary ἴχνος ("footprint") speculation the saying purports to offer the litmus test of daimonhood: what is a daimon, and what is not. It therefore has nothing intrinsically to do with the *Christian* "post-resurrection appearance" and "demonstration [of the risen body]" complex into which it has now been absorbed.

1.5.2   With this observation the difference among the sayings quoted in 1.3.2 and 1.3.3 above becomes apparent. Ignatius *Smyrn.* 3.2 has its saying thoroughly personalized: *"I am not* an incorporeal demon." Similarly Luke 24:39 has: "A spirit has not flesh and bones, *as you see that I have."* But in the case of Tertullian and Commodian it is a completely impersonal saying. The authority in each of the latter cases comes as it were from outside, from the realm of common knowledge, but also of wisdom, and of proverb. This is exactly the situation also in *Ep. apost.* 11.8. By supplying the additional authority ("written in the prophet"; cf. chaps. 19, 33, 35, 43, 47, 49) the author adds a further interpretive dimension, which must be addressed later.

2. Saying 2: *Ep. apost.* 25.8 (*NTApoc* 1. 208):
 C.: "What has fallen will [arise], and what is lost will be found and what is [weak] will recover."
 E.: "Now what has fallen will arise, and what is ill will be sound."

2.1.1 The saying's context is a long section which began in chap. 21 with the Lord's statement that "as my Father awakened me from the dead, in the same manner you also will arise in the flesh." But the issue raised by this prediction is not taken up into the dialogue of questions and answers until chap. 22, when the disciples ask:

> "O Lord, is it really in store for the flesh to be judged (together) with the soul and spirit, and will (one of these) really rest in heaven and the other be punished eternally while it is (still) alive?"

2.1.2 It is striking that although these chapters have earned the description, "an apologetic treatise *De resurrectione*" (Koester, 1971: 203), there is in fact no sustained discussion of this topic at all. When the dialogue in chaps. 21–26 is inspected speech by speech, it becomes evident that three virtually independent subjects hold the stage: (a) the process of dialogue, explored through many expressions of what may be termed the rhetoric of the dialogue genre; (b) ethical teachings, of themselves irrelevant to the theoretical issue of resurrection; and (c) the resurrection of the flesh. When those speeches alone are examined which concern resurrection, it becomes clear that until the quoted proverb the Lord's only response is to declare not *how* but simply *that* the resurrection of the flesh will happen. Yet it is equally clear in chap. 24 that it is precisely the *how* question that the author wishes to articulate and answer:

> "O Lord, is it then possible that what is dissolved and destroyed [i.e. the body] should be whole?"

2.2.1 The Coptic text of *Ep. apost.* 25.8 is as follows (XX 1–3):

ⲁⲣⲁ ⲡⲉⲧⲁϩϩⲉⲉⲓⲉ ϥⲛⲁ[ⲧⲱⲛⲉ ⲁ]ⲟⲩ ⲡⲉⲧⲥⲁⲣⲙⲉ ⲥⲉⲛⲁϭⲛ̄ⲧϥ ⲁⲟⲩ ⲡⲉⲧϭⲟ[ⲟⲃⲉ ϥⲛ]ⲁⲟⲩϫⲉⲓ̈.

2.2.2 The reconstructions, though made by Schmidt before he had access to the Ethiopic text, clearly stand the test of comparison. The term with which the saying is introduced, ⲁⲣⲁ, will be discussed below with its

Ethiopic counterpart (-kē). Only a few additional remarks need be made. The verbs in the third line of the Coptic, 6BBE and ⲞⲨⲰϪⲈⲒ̈, like those in lines one and two, are of course complementary. The first has only two standard Gk. equivalents: ἀσθενεῖν ("to be weak, sick") and δειλιᾶν ("to be fearful"; Crum: 805a). The second verb, however, expresses the full breadth of possibilities summarized by Crum as "to be whole, safe, sound" (511b; e.g. Gk. σώζεσθαι and compounds; ὑγιάζειν; ἰᾶσθαι), and in specifically religious discussion is regularly rendered "to be saved." Duensing's "recover" (in *NTApoc* 1. 208) is thus only one option, but probably the right one (so also James: 494).

2.2.3   A second observation concerns the tense of the main verb in each clause. Each is a future, relating the reversal of the state of affairs expressed in the relative forms. To the extent that the saying as a whole may be considered proverbial, the possibility of an original Gk. 'gnomic' future must be borne in mind. The Ethiopic offers no help in this, for its imperfect tenses also allow but do not require such a sense.

2.2.4   Finally it may be noted that the gender of the subject is masculine. Coptic lacks a distinct grammatical neuter (as does Ethiopic), and therefore the forms translated "What..." in this context might in another have been rendered "He who...." At least it needs to be pointed out that the gender is not feminine (cf. Gk. σάρξ, "flesh," in the previous sentence).

2.2.5   The Ethiopic witnesses are united in the following reading (68/7–8):

> za-wadqa-kē yetnaššaʾ wa-za-dawaya yaḥayyu.

2.2.6   The range of Ethiopic *ḥaywa* is similar to that of Coptic ⲞⲨⲰϪⲈⲒ̈. In this context "recover" suits both versions well. (The same Ethiopic form occurs in chap. 39 opposite C. ⲰⲚϨ, "to live" [XXIX 4; 82/3]; on the other hand, C. ϤⲚⲀⲞⲨⲰϪⲈⲒ̈ is found once elsewhere in the *Epistula*, in chap. 47 opposite E. *yedexxen*, "he will be saved" [XXXIX 11; 88/9].)

2.2.7   Two issues remain. The first is the stark fact that in the Coptic the saying has three lines, in the Ethiopic only two. Given the antiquity of the single Coptic witness (over 600 years older than the earliest Ethiopic MS), its longer reading cannot summarily be dismissed. But the line "and what is lost will be found" is nevertheless suspect. Form-critical considerations suggest that the Coptic version is an original "double-stranded mashal" expanded by "analogous formation" (for this principle see Bultmann: 82, 85). In addition, the statement "What is lost will be found" contradicts the grim prediction in chap. 39, that "the lost will be lost eternally."

2.2.8   Finally we must consider the word with which the Coptic version begins, ⲁⲣⲁ, and its Ethiopic parallel, -kē. Their presence here is of more than purely philological interest. In Coptic, ⲁⲣⲁ is regularly the transliterated Greek *interrogative particle* (= ἆρα, with circumflex accent), used to introduce direct questions (Lambdin, 1983: 359). Thus in *Ep. apost.* 39.9 (XXIX 14; *NTApoc* 1. 219) Schmidt and Duensing translate as a question a speech of the Lord beginning with ⲁⲣⲁ: "Does not every man have the power to live and to die?" As it happens, the parallel Ethiopic in 39.9 shows that the author instead wrote the Gk. "inferential (illative) particle" (= ἄρα, with acute accent; BAG: 103); in fact the Coptic simply transliterates the common inferential phrase, ἄρα οὖν (E. *nāhu-kē*; Dillmann, 1970: 630, 812): "So then...." It is precisely this inferential ἄρα that is found, here without οὖν, in the present saying in *Ep. apost.* 25.8. (The position of ἄρα as the first word in its clause, if this was the case in the original Greek, is unclassical but attested, e.g. in Luke 11:48; cf. Matt 17:26, where Jesus' pronouncement is introduced with ἄρα γε: "*Then* the sons are free" [RSV].)

2.2.9   In light of the above, this ⲁⲣⲁ (= E. -kē) in *Ep. apost.* 25.8 draws attention to the saying as shaping a *conclusion*: there is resurrection, the flesh falls, *therefore* the flesh rises. But ἄρα, being "more subjective than οὖν," is further used "in announcing the discovery or correction of an error" (LSJ: 232; Smyth § 2795; as an extension of this, BDF can point in the NT to "a classical use of ἄρα" with the meaning "as they say" [1 Cor 15:15 = Gk. εἴπερ ἄρα: "if, *as they say*, it is true that..."; BDF § 452.2, accepted by Barrett: 348]). The particle proves to be most appropriate as an introduction to a saying both drawing a conclusion and reporting proverbial wisdom: "as they say."

2.3   There has been no satisfactory suggestion as to the saying's origin. A double-stranded *māšāl* in Jer 8:4 has as its first line, in question form, what we find in *Ep. apost.* 25.8:

Jer 8:4 LXX   Μὴ ὁ πίπτων οὐκ ἀνίσταται;
ἢ ὁ ἀποστρέφων οὐκ ἐπιστρέφει;
"Does not he who falls arise?
or he who turns away, does he not return?"

2.4   Aside from the verb "to rise," nothing in the saying about rising and recovering is foreshadowed in the discussion which precedes it. The Lord's recent question, "[What is it] then [that pa]sses away? Is it [the flesh] or the spirit?" does not even bring "falling" into the discussion. The question and answer simply ensure that "the flesh" will be understood as the antecedent to the saying's "*What* has fallen...." On the other hand, the saying is editorially tied to its context by what is appended to it:
C.:   "...that in what is thus done [may be revealed] the glory of my Father."
E.:   "...that my Father may be praised therein."
With this may be compared a redactional phrase found twice elsewhere (in chaps. 19 and 36): "...that he who sent me may be glorified."

2.5.1   As became clear from a consideration of the introductory ἆρα, the saying is signaled as a conclusion or conclusive principle. More precisely, it permits, even recommends, a deduction from the facts of the matter as the author presents them. Granted that there is resurrection (that is, "rising" of some sort), and granted that of the flesh and the spirit only the former seems liable to dissolution (and hence to "falling"), the resurrection must *ipso facto* be a resurrection of the flesh. Only the disciples' recognition that it is the flesh that falls establishes this point, for the saying itself does little more than secure the general principle of rising again.

2.5.2   A. H. C. van Eijk has traced the use in early Christian literature of what in the *Epistula* is the first line of this two-line saying. In Justin Martyr's treatise *De res.* frg. 109 (preserved in John of Damascus), what is only implied in the *Epistula*, that the spirit does not fall, is explicitly stated: "The resurrection concerns the flesh that has fallen, for the spirit does not fall" (van Eijk: 518). Van Eijk points to Justin's use here of πνεῦμα rather than ψυχή as evidence that a tradition is involved, because elsewhere Justin always prefers the dichotomy ψυχή ("soul")-σάρξ ("flesh"). Following Justin, Tertullian remarks that "Nothing will expect to rise again, except that which has previously succumbed" (*De res.* 18.5; cf. 57.3), and that "Nothing rises except that which has fallen" (*Adv. Marc.* 5.9.4). Van Eijk notes that in the *Epistula*, in Justin, and in Tertullian, "the formula serves as an argument against the heretical (gnostic) assertion of a purely spiritual resurrection" (522).

2.5.3   Later writers, for example Methodius, Origen, Aphraates, and Augustine, apply the saying about falling and rising to the individual εἶδος ("form, shape, nature") of the deceased, rather than to the flesh. It is Methodius, according to van Eijk (525), who first explicitly introduces the text from Jeremiah 8 quoted above. However, the first line of the *Epistula*'s saying is far closer to Jer 8:4 than it is to van Eijk's "formula." And in addition it is striking that the standard, almost formulaic, use of Jer 8:4 in the early church is in connection not with resurrection but with forgiveness, and more specifically with penitential discipline (as in Tertullian *De paen.* 8; Cyprian *Test.* 114; Ps.-Ignatius *Eph.* 10.1-2; *Didascalia* 6; *Const. apost.* 2.14). Therefore it need not be supposed that the *Epistula* is quoting an established proof of the resurrection, nor, for that matter, that its author intended to establish such proof himself. In this case he does not even appeal to the authority of "the prophet" (Jeremiah, for example) as he did in *Ep. apost.* 11.8. Instead, the verification offered by the saying comes from outside both the biblical tradition and the stock of proof-texts for the resurrection (such as Psalm 3, quoted in full in chap. 19). The reason for this strategy will be discussed below.

3. Saying 3: *Ep. apost.* 32.2 (*NTApoc* 1. 213):
E.: "Are the fingers of the hand alike or the ears of corn in the field?"

3.1 The saying's context is a discussion of mission, specifically mission to Israel and to the gentiles. In chap. 30 the Lord gives the mission charge: "Go you and preach to the twelve tribes and preach also to the Gentiles and to the whole land of Israel from [sunrise] to sunset and from [South to] North." The disciples' initial reticence ("Who will believe us...?") is answered by the Lord's assurance that they will be given the power for effective preaching, so that their successors may "teach the other nations." There follows a chapter devoted to a prediction of the conversion of Paul and his instruction by the twelve; it is he, says the Lord, who "will be for the salvation of the Gentiles." The question which prompts the proverbial response comes at once, at the start of chap. 32: "O master, do we have together with them one hope of the inheritance?" i.e. are the disciples and their successors to share the same hope as the gentiles who are to be won by the ministry of Paul?

3.2.1 *Ep. apost.* 31-37 are extant only in Ethiopic, but the page numbers of the Coptic codex show that these chapters were present also in the earlier version. The text of 32.2 is as follows (74/6):

ʿerruy-nu weʾetu ʾaṣbaʾta ʾed wa-sabl-ni ba-westa garāht.

3.2.2   Both phrases depend upon the adjective ʿerruy: "equal, the same [as]" (from ʿarraya, "to be level, equal"; Lambdin, 1978: 378). The translation of the first pair of nouns is secure. As for the second pair, *sabl* (a singular or collective noun) may be better rendered "heads of wheat," according to American usage, than "ears of corn" (*sabl* = Gk. στάχυς; Dillmann, 1970: 335). If this is done, the parallelism is properly observed: fingers/heads of wheat; hand/field.

3.3   No specific source has been identified. Guerrier remarked (74 n. 3) that the proverb is still alive in modern Arabic, as "All the fingers of the hand are not equal."

3.4   Nothing in the saying is hinted at in the previous chapters. While the vocabulary items "fingers" and "hand" are used (the former in chap. 12 [in C.; E. = "hand"], the latter six times before chap. 32), the human and arboreal metaphors are not prepared for other than by the preceding question's "one" ("*one* hope," italicized in *NTApoc* 1. 213); this "one" looks forward to the proverb's "alike" and "the same." Clearly, then, it is the one-ness that is at issue (rather than the possibility of hope or inheritance).

3.5   Yet the application is not as clear as at first sight appears. The proverb looks like a rhetorical question, expecting silent assent to a clear-cut Yes or No. (The Ethiopic question form, unlike that of Greek, does not regularly offer the hearer or reader an implied answer; the particle *-nu* indicates that the sentence is a question, but "the interrogative clause receives no definite colouring"; Dillmann, 1974: 513.) But what follows immediately upsets this expectation. Quite apart from the Lord's own expansion of the saying, the disciples' first remark after hearing it shows that all is not clear: "O Lord, are you speaking again in parables (E. *messālē* = Gk. παραβολαί or παροιμίαι) to us?" It seems that it is the disciples who are asking the rhetorical question. The additions to the initial proverb must be explored.

3.5.1   The additions consist of two questions, whose effect is to emphasize the difference between members of different orders, first implicitly and then explicitly (74/7):

"Or do fruit-bearing trees give the same fruit?
Do they not bring forth fruit according to their nature?"

The second of these questions gives the impression of being a pedantic restatement of the first, designed to remove every shadow of ambiguity.

The first, on the other hand, looks like a generalized version of a figure widespread in antiquity: A cannot come from B, or Can A come from B? The following are well known NT examples:

> Luke 6:44 (= a question in Matt 7:16):
> "Figs are not gathered from thorns, nor are grapes picked from a bramble bush."
>
> John 1:46:
> "Can anything good come out of Nazareth?"
>
> Jas 3:11–12:
> "Does a spring pour forth from the same opening fresh water and brackish? Can a fig tree, my brethren, yield olives, or a grapevine figs?"

3.5.2   The example from James 3 is especially instructive. The point the author wishes to establish is that which is made by the proverbial questions: One source, one product. The communal evidence with which James is actually dealing, however, is the fickle human tongue, "setting on fire the cycle of nature" (3:6) in its ability both to curse and to bless (3:10). Indignant at the travesty, he declares: "My brethren, this *ought not* to be so," and by way of proof offers the natural law of the quoted proverbs. The example from Q, on the other hand, part of a "cluster" of five aphorisms in Luke 6:43–45 (Crossan: 158), has three stages of explication: (a) the proverb proper, in Luke 6:44b (cf. Matt 7:16b; *Gos. Thom.* 45a); (b) a statement of the principle supported by the proverb, still retaining the arboreal model but generalized to "no good tree...a bad tree...each tree," in Luke 6:43–44a (cf. Matt 7:17–18; Ignatius *Eph.* 14.2); and (c) an ethical principle now made more explicit with reference to "the good man," in Luke 6:45a (cf. *Gos. Thom.* 45bc).

3.5.3   Numerous extra-biblical examples of this figure are cited by Johann Jakob Wettstein (1. 697 and 2. 673). It is striking that in every case a saying that is genus-specific (e.g. fig, olive, grape) precedes or follows the generalization; indeed, in some cases the latter is not stated at all. The impression is fostered that in the *Ep. apost.* there is preserved *only* the latter, i.e. only the kernel of the principle, the husk of a specific example being absent. There is even some minor MS evidence that the scribal tradition sensed the lack, for two good witnesses (MSS B and K) read ʾaskāl ("grape, cluster, vine"; Dillmann, 1970: 378) for the quoted reading's ʾakāl ("body, substance, nature"; Dillmann, 1970: 782). In any case, the first of the explanatory questions, "Do fruit-bearing trees give the same fruit?" is seen by the author of the *Epistula* to require further explanation. Such a tendency to commentary is found elsewhere with this type of figure (see Beardslee, 1972: 99, 102). In *Gos. Thom.* 45 the statement that "Grapes are not harvested from thorns, nor are figs gathered from thistles" is elucidated with the sober comment, "for they do not produce fruit." Similarly in the Nag Hammadi *Apoc. Pet.* (NHC 7, 3) 76.4–8 (*NHLE* 342) the saying, now personalized, is expanded with a common sense aside: "People do not gather figs from thorns..., *if they are wise*, nor grapes from thistles."

3.5.4   However, in the *Epistula* the explanatory questions turn out to be no substitute for a plain answer to the disciples' question. It is arguable that they eliminate reflection and even contradict one possibility as to the meaning of the original saying. That there is a great deal at stake here is evident from the use of two "Amen" sayings, in 32.4 and 5. The sparing use of this formula elsewhere in the *Ep. apost.* suggests that special emphasis is being placed on speeches introduced with it. Here the resolution amounts to a promise to the disciples of a status as 'first among equals.' The principal proverb seems, therefore, to be a vehicle for the gentle assurance that the inclusion of the nations, authorized by the Lord himself, results in no lessening of divine favor towards the disciples and their successors (= the author's circle of Jewish-Christians).

4.   Saying 4: *Ep. apost.* 47.4 (*NTApoc* 1. 225):
C.:   "But a blind man who leads a blind man, [both] fall into [a] ditch."
E.:   "For a blind man who leads a blind man, both will fall into a ditch."

4.1.1   This familiar saying occurs in the final part of the *Ep. apost.*, a section concerned to a special degree with relations between members of the community the writing was intended to serve. Chaps. 41–42 deal with the authorization of mission to those outside, and with the incorporation of the obedient into the author's group. Chaps. 43–45 comprise a dialogical expansion of the story of the wise and foolish virgins, amounting to a definition of the author's community. Now in chaps. 46–50 attention is turned to inner-community regulation.

4.1.2   The logic of chap. 47 is somewhat more complicated than that of the earlier contexts discussed. The chapter's content up to and including the saying may be summarized as follows: (1) If A falls beneath his burden (the burden = sin against B), B must admonish A for the sake of the good that A has (previously) done to B; (2) when B has rebuked A and A returns, A will be saved and B will have eternal life; (3) but if B sees A (who has

Hills: Proverbs in *Epistula Apostolorum* 25

previously done good to B) sinning, and encourages A in sin, B will suffer a great judgment; (4) this is in accord with the saying, "A blind man who leads a blind man...." The instruction as a whole is reminiscent of Matt 18:15-17; Gal 6:1-2; Jas 5:19-20; 1 John 5:16; and, among the Qumran writings, CD 9.1-3 and 1QS 5.25-6.1.

4.2   The Coptic (XL 1-3) and Ethiopic (89/1-2) texts are as follows:
  C.:   ογβλλε δε εϥϭωκ ⲛ̄ογβλλε ⲥⲁⲣογ²εειε ⲛ̄ⲡ[ⲥⲛⲟ] ⲁⲉ.ⲡ[ⲏⲓ̈ ⲁⲩ]²ⲓⲉⲓⲧ.
  E.:   ʾesma ʿewer ʿewera za-yemarreh kelʾēhomu westa gebb yewaddequ.

4.2.1   There are no translation problems here. Two points emerge from a comparison of the Coptic reading with Matt 15:14 and *Gos. Thom.* 34. First, *Ep. apost.* 47.4 in both versions lacks an explicit conditional sense ("if"). Secondly, although the basic vocabulary is common to all three texts, the saying in the *Epistula* shows no conclusive sign of assimilation to the canonical version (but see 4.4 below).

4.3   Clearly the most likely source of this saying is Matt 15:14. Though the metaphor of the blind leader of the blind is well attested prior to the first century (Wettstein: 1. 422-23), the figure stated together with this consequence—falling into the pit—is rare. The closest non-biblical parallel is probably *Test. Reub.* 2.9: "[The spirit of procreation] leads the young person like a blind man into a ditch and like an animal over a cliff."

4.4   At the beginning of the chapter, the sinner is said to have "fallen" under his burden. This choice of analogy probably looks forward to the use of the saying about the blind. More immediately each version attaches the saying with a connecting particle: the Ethiopic has ʾesma (= Gk. γάρ, "for"), the most natural connective in this context; the Coptic, on the other hand, has ⲇⲉ (= Gk. δέ), which looks suspiciously like an assimilation to Matt 15:14 (cf. the Coptic text in Schrage: 85).

4.5   This proverb had a long and lively career in early Christian literature. Bultmann suggested that an "original meaning" is irrecoverable (99). But it is worthwhile to survey the range of contexts in which the proverb is made to serve. Apart from *Gos. Thom.* 34, where any specificity can be deduced only with difficulty, the saying is found in a variety of settings. In Luke 6:39 the implied meaning is, "how canst thou set thyself up for a judge, who art thyself blind!" (Bultmann: 99). In Matt 15:14 the Pharisees as "blind guides" are the referent. Thereafter the dominical proverb is applied to heretics, to Judaizers, to hypocritical teachers, to the deluded mind of whoever rejects the rule of faith (for the latter, Tertullian *Adv. Marc.* 4.36), and to those who indiscriminately welcome the lapsed (so Cyprian *Ep.* 43). But in extant texts, nowhere other than in the *Epistula* is the proverb used to support an author's recommendation for dealing with a fellow believer's sin. This suggests for *Ep. apost.* 47.4 what was claimed for 25.8, that this writer was choosing neither to appeal to a traditional *topos* (here as a disciplinary threat), nor to introduce a known dominical word so as to establish such a threat; indeed, there is no implication of coercion at all. Instead the saying works as an *ad hoc* and external verification of the correctness (perhaps better, the reasonableness) of chap. 47's communal instructions.

5.   The Proverbs' Function in the *Ep. apost.*

5.1.1   Now that the four proverbial sayings have been examined, it remains to assess their function as bearers of authority in the *Ep. apost.* At the beginning of this study the quest for a precise definition of proverb was set aside and a four-element working delineation of these particular sayings adopted. The related issues of function and authority must now be taken up in light both of the findings above and of recent discussion of the proverb in biblical and related literature.

5.1.2   It has recently been urged by James G. Williams that in formal terms the proverb and the aphorism cannot be sharply distinguished (80; Crossan: 19). Williams opts instead for a distinction in terms of implied origin, between collective voice (= proverb) and individual voice (= aphorism). The former regularly presents ancient, collective wisdom, the latter the subjectivity of the individual. This observation is of importance for an assessment of the sayings in the *Ep. apost.* Analysis of the individual units has already suggested that the "voice" behind them is not, at least not in origin, that of the *Epistula*'s revealer figure. Nor is it the voice of simple corroboration. It is a voice of a third kind, determining not only the appropriate terms of reference (the 'grammar' of each subject matter, as it were) but also the decisive principle (or 'law') under which the particular matter at hand can be resolved (or rather, already has been resolved; see further, 5.3 below). It is to be suggested that here proverb is *precedent*, albeit precedent of a special kind. But this conclusion will depend on discussion of two issues: first, the nature of the subject matter to which these proverbs are related as compared, for example, with the proverbs in the Synoptic gospels; second, the kind of truth to which proverbs in general, and these proverbs in particular, lay claim.

5.2   In an important article on "Uses of the Proverb in the Synoptic Gospels" William Beardslee has suggested that all wisdom sayings, however apparently general, have "an element of confrontation" (1970: 66). The Synoptic sayings, while including instances of "a rather general folk wisdom," more characteristically have the confrontational challenge "immensely concentrated and intensified." Beardslee collects examples of proverbial sayings exhibiting paradox (e.g. Mark 10:31 par.: "Many that are first will be last") and hyperbole (e.g. Matt 8:22 par.: "Leave the dead to bury their dead"), and summarizes the evidence as follows (1970: 69):

> [T]he proverb does have a distinctive usage in the Synoptics in which paradox and hyperbole challenge the typical proverbial stance of making a continuous project of one's life, but a usage which paradoxically views this challenge as itself the way of life.

So while it is to be recognized that many of the Synoptic proverbs "simply represent the widespread tradition of practical wisdom," the proverbs' characteristic intensification works "to jolt the hearer...into a new judgment about his own existence" (1970: 70–71). This existential aspect of the Synoptic proverbs, it may be claimed, is directly related to a radical call to new understanding and life present, in varying degrees, throughout the Synoptic tradition. In other words, the overall character and intention of the proverbs' host traditions (or writings) are not incidental to the character and authority discovered in the sayings themselves, both inherent and as conferred by context (see Beardslee, 1972: 101; Kirschenblatt-Gimblett).

5.2.1 Compared with an agenda of existential decision, the demand made of its reader by the *Epistula* is of a less dramatic sort. This writing is not a gospel, at least not one of the Synoptic type. (Ehrhardt described it as "a gospel which was current in Egypt" [360].) Its audience is more self-consciously defined as the author's community, and the communal understanding it seeks to achieve is precisely that, recognition by *the* community (i.e. the author's) of the basic structure of salvation in Jesus Christ (see, for example, the author's stated purpose in chaps. 1–2). The subject matter to which the four proverbs are attached may be considered highly theoretical, on the one hand, or merely practical, on the other: the nature of the resurrected body, the inclusion of the gentiles, and communal casuistry. The writing's communal self-consciousness raises the issue of authority in a manner precisely the reverse of the challenge of the Synoptics. There the implied hearer is regularly outside, called to be inside (granted that these are relative terms). Here the implied hearer is safely within—safe but for the threat of false teachers. This stance is reinforced again and again by a sharp distinction between the author's "us" and the opponents' "them" (see for example the exclusiveness evident in chap. 34, quoted in 0.3 above). How, then, is a community such as this to be corrected, reformed, or newly enlightened?

5.2.2   For the most part the only necessary authority is that of the Lord himself. With great regularity the Lord's speeches are introduced with the phrase, "He [± answered and] said to us," and there is no question that in general this is sufficient support for what is taught. But at several decisive moments—decisive, it seems, for the reconstruction and maintenance of the community—even the "He said" of the risen Lord is not enough. It is as if the community and its revealer make up something of a closed system: new insights will require other and external warrant. The spokesperson for a community that is to "love one another and obey each other" (chap. 18) will need an alien wisdom to penetrate the charmed circle of present understanding and action. Such is the wisdom of proverb, introduced to secure the insights upon which, from the author's point of view, the community's future depends.

5.3   The question of authority turns upon the nature of this wisdom. As noted in 0.7 above, the *Epistula*'s proverbs are all "principles," three statements and one question. Their immediate role is to urge not action, but understanding. They pretend to establish "laws" or, more accurately, "paradigms" (Collins: 6), each of which, though recognized at its appearance, has to be invoked. The role of the one who invokes them is clearly an important one; but the proverbial sayings themselves seek less to qualify their utterer than to supply a context for the hearer's decision about a subject matter that ultimately is external to both speaker and hearer. This context can only be implied, as that in which the proverb 'makes sense'; it is the implied parallel to the new topic, to which the proverb corresponds as precedent.

5.3.1   A glance back at the *Epistula*'s sayings strengthens these impressions. The principles stated are of a conditional kind, whatever their formal or rhetorical boast. (Contrast the first three examples quoted in 0.7 above.) It would have to be admitted, for instance, that it was a matter of some debate in antiquity whether in fact a "daimon" can leave a footprint (see Dölger, referred to above, 1.3.4); similarly, what has fallen will not *necessarily* arise, nor what is weak recover; the fingers of the hand and the ears of wheat are both unlike *and* alike (comparable with snowflakes, perhaps); a blind man with a stick, or traveling a familiar route, may well avoid a fall both for himself and for his companion. (The modern English proverb discussed by Crossan [12–13], "A stitch in time saves nine," has both form and content to commend it to us; but the principle embodied in it is not universal, nor can its future congeniality be guaranteed—cf. Aldous Huxley's memorable contribution to the genre, "Ending's better than mending" [33].) The sayings in the *Epistula* are true to their host genre, the dialogue; in the final analysis they invite assent but not surrender.

5.4   There is one further element of persuasion. It was seen above that the first of the three sayings is introduced with the formula, "for it is written in the prophet." Within the *Ep. apost.* itself there are two clues to the interpretation of this phrase. The first is the assertion, a commonplace in 2d and 3d century Logos (Word) theology, that when the prophets spoke their words were those of Jesus Christ. So in chap. 19 the full text of Psalm 3, quoted as "the prophecy [of the] prophet David," is commented on as follows (*NTApoc* 1. 204):

> "But if all the words that were spoken by the prophets are fulfilled in me—for I was in them—how much more will what I say to you truly happen."

A second and related clue has to do with the nature of the prophetic message. According to *Ep. apost.* 3 the prophets spoke *ba-ʾamsāl* (*NTApoc* 1. 192 = "in parables"; so Wajnberg, "in Gleichnissen" [Schmidt, 1919: 28]). Now, whereas E. *messālē* (already quoted from chap. 32 in 3.5 above) is the regular equivalent of Gk. παραβολή in the NT, E. ʾamsāl has a broader range: likeness, proverb, similitude, and enigma, as well as parable (Dillmann, 1970: 171); hence Duensing's translation, "in Bildern" (1925: 6). Justin, an author probably contemporary with the *Epistula*, writes of the prophets' words and deeds being "veiled *in parables and types* (παραβολαῖς καὶ τύποις)" (*Dial.* 90.2 [ANF 1. 244]; cf. *De res.* frg. 3 [ANF 1. 300]). Similarly Hippolytus refers to the prophets as speaking "*in parables and dark sayings* (διὰ παραβολῶν καὶ αἰνιγμάτων)" (*De antichr.* 29 [ANF 5. 210]; cf. Clement *Prot.* 2 [ANF 2. 174] and *Strom.* 5.8 [ANF 2. 457]). Indeed, the whole program of revelation fulfilled by the risen Lord in the *Ep. apost.* may be said to answer a prophetic promise. With chap. 34 (in 0.3 above) compare Jer 33:3:

> "Call to me and I will answer you, and will tell you great and hidden things which you have not known."

5.5   Thus for this writer the proverbial style is anticipated as prophetic, and the prophetic word is claimed to prefigure the dominical.

This does not mean that the issue of authority and assent is foreclosed. On the contrary, it has already been seen that these proverbial sayings, whatever their source, appeal to an external, antecedent voice. In the *Epistula* they claim to establish, among other things, that the followers of Simon and Cerinthus (chaps. 1, 7) do not have reason on their side; and they claim to demonstrate that in defying the logic proffered by the proverbs' collective voice, these "false apostles" are also defying the prophetic and dominical word. The dialogue genre, evoking as it does the "school" with its teacher and students, encourages in its readers the realization that there are facts of salvation that may be learned, and rules of community life that are to be mastered. For these special tasks of communal discipline the proverbs of Jesus have become an authoritative mnemonic.

WORKS CONSULTED

ANF   See Roberts, Donaldson, and Coxe

BAG   See Bauer

Bardy, Gustave
1921   Review of Carl Schmidt, 1919. *RB* 30: 110–34.

Barrett, C. K.
1971   *The First Epistle to the Corinthians.* 2d ed. BNTC. London: Black.

Bauer, Walter
1979   *A Greek-English Lexicon of the New Testament and Other Early Christian Literature* [= BAG]. 2d ed. Rev. Frederick W. Danker. Trans. William F. Arndt and F. Wilbur Gingrich. Chicago/London: University of Chicago Press.

BDF   See Blass and Debrunner

Beardslee, William A.
1970   "Uses of the Proverb in the Synoptic Gospels." *Int* 24: 61–73.
1972   "Proverbs in the Gospel of Thomas." Pp. 92–103 in *Studies in New Testament and Early Christian Literature: Essays in Honor of Allen P. Wikgren.* Ed. David E. Daube. NovTSup 33. Leiden: Brill.

Blass, Friedrich, and Albert Debrunner
    1961   *A Greek Grammar of the New Testament and Other Early Christian Literature* [= BDF]. Trans. and rev. Robert W. Funk. Chicago: University of Chicago Press.

Bultmann, Rudolf
    1976   *The History of the Synoptic Tradition.* Rev. ed. New York: Harper & Row.

Cameron, Ron
    1984   *Sayings Traditions in the Apocryphon of James.* HTS 34. Philadelphia: Fortress.

Castiglione, L.
    1970   "Vestigia." *Acta Archaeologica Academiae Scienciarum Hungaricae* 22: 95–132.

Collins, John J.
    1980   "Proverbial Wisdom and Yahwist Vision." *Semeia* 17: 1–17.

Crossan, John Dominic
    1983   *In Fragments: The Aphorisms of Jesus.* New York: Harper & Row.

Crum, W. E.
    1939   *A Coptic Dictionary.* Oxford: Clarendon.

Deissmann, Adolf
    1980   *Light from the Ancient East.* Reprint of 1922 ed. Grand Rapids: Eerdmans.

Dillmann, C. F. A.
    1970   *Lexicon Linguae Aethiopicae.* Reprint of 1865 ed. Onasbrück: Biblio Verlag.
    1974   *Ethiopic Grammar.* Reprint of 1907 ed. Amsterdam: Philo.

Dölger, Franz Joseph
    1922   *Die Eucharistie nach Inschriften frühchristlicher Zeit.* Münster: Aschendorff.

Dow, Sterling, and Frieda S. Upson
    1944   "The Foot of Serapis." *Hesperia* 13: 58–77.

Duensing, Hugo
    1925   *Epistula Apostolorum.* KlT 152. Bonn: Marcus and Weber.

Ehrhardt, A. A. T.
1964 "Judaeo-Christians in Egypt, the Epistula Apostolorum and the Gospel to the Hebrews." Pp. 360–82 in Vol. 2 of *Studia Evangelica* 3. Ed. F. L. Cross. 2 vols. TU 88. Berlin: Akademie-Verlag.

van Eijk, A. H. C.
1971 "'Only that can rise which has previously fallen': The History of a Formula." *JTS* 22: 517–29.

Fontaine, Carol R.
1982 *Traditional Sayings in the Old Testament*. Sheffield: Almond.

Guerrier, Louis
1913 "Le Testament en Galilée de notre Seigneur Jésus-Christ." PO 9/3: 1–96.

Harnack, Adolf
1897 "Ein jüngst entdeckter Auferstehungsbericht." Pp. 1–8 in *Theologische Studien Bernhard Weiss zu seinem 70. Geburtstag dargebracht*. Göttingen: Vandenhoeck & Ruprecht.

Hennecke, Edgar, ed.
1963-65 *New Testament Apocrypha* [= *NTApoc*]. Rev. Wilhelm Schneemelcher. Trans. ed. R. McL. Wilson. 2 vols. Philadelphia: Westminster. Original German edition: *Neutestamentliche Apokryphen* [= *NTApok*]. 3d ed. Rev. Wilhelm Schneemelcher. Tübingen: Mohr-Siebeck, 1959–64.

Hills, Julian
1986 "The *Epistula Apostolorum* and the Genre 'Apocalypse.'" Pp. 581–95 in *Society of Biblical Literature 1986 Seminar Papers*. Ed. Kent Harold Richards. SBL Seminar Papers 25. Atlanta: Scholars.

Hornschuh, Manfred
1965 *Studien zur Epistula Apostolorum*. Patristische Texte und Studien 5. Berlin: De Gruyter.

Huxley, Aldous
1968 *Brave New World*. First published in 1932. New York: Bantam.

James, Montague Rhodes
  1924 *The Apocryphal New Testament*. Oxford: Clarendon.

Kirschenblatt-Gimblett, Barbara
  1973 "Toward a theory of proverb meaning." *Proverbium* 22: 821–27.

Koester, Helmut
  1957 *Synoptische Überlieferung bei den apostolischen Vätern*. TU 65. Berlin: Akademie-Verlag.
  1971 "One Jesus and Four Primitive Gospels." Pp. 158–204 in *Trajectories through Early Christianity*. Ed. James M. Robinson and Helmut Koester. Philadelphia: Fortress.

Lake, Kirsopp
  1920 "The Epistola Apostolorum." *HTR* 14: 15–29.

Lambdin, Thomas O.
  1978 *Introduction to Classical Ethiopic (Ge'ez)*. HSS 24. Missoula: Scholars.
  1983 *Introduction to Sahidic Coptic*. Macon, GA: Mercer University Press.

de Lannoy, Ludo, ed.
  1977 *Flavii Philostrati heroicus*. Leipzig: Teubner.

Liddell, Henry George, and Robert Scott
  1940 *A Greek-English Lexicon* [= LSJ]. Rev. Henry Stuart Jones. Oxford: Clarendon.

Lightfoot, J. B.
  1981 *The Apostolic Fathers*. 2 parts in 5 vols. Reprint of 1889–90 ed. Grand Rapids: Baker.

LSJ   See Liddell and Scott

NHLE   See Robinson

NTApoc,
NTApok See Hennecke

Perkins, Pheme
  1980 *The Gnostic Dialogue*. New York: Paulist.

Roberts, Alexander, James Donaldson, and A. Cleveland Coxe, eds.
1926 *The Ante-Nicene Fathers* [= ANF]. American Reprint of the Edinburgh Edition. 10 vols. New York: Scribner's.

Robinson, James M., ed.
1977 *The Nag Hammadi Library in English* [= *NHLE*]. San Francisco: Harper & Row.

Rosensthiel, Jean-M.
1972 *L'Apocalypse d'Élie*. Paris: Geuthner.

Schmidt, Carl
1895 "Eine bisher unbekannte altchristliche Schrift in koptischer Sprache." *SPAW*: 705–11.
1919 *Gespräche Jesus mit seinen Jüngern nach der Auferstehung*. With the collaboration of Isaak Wajnberg. TU 43. Leipzig: Hinrichs.

Schoedel, William R.
1985 *Ignatius of Antioch*. Hermeneia. Philadelphia: Fortress.

Schrage, Wolfgang
1964 *Das Verhältnis des Thomas-Evangeliums zur synoptischen Tradition und zu den koptischen Evangelienübersetzungen*. BZNW 29. Berlin: Töpelmann.

Smyth, Herbert Weir
1956 *Greek Grammar*. Rev. Gordon M. Messing. Cambridge: Harvard University Press.

Wettstein, Johann Jakob
1962 *Novum Testamentum Graecum*. 2 vols. Reprint of 1751–52 ed. Graz: Akademische Druck- und Verlagsanstalt.

Williams, James G.
1981 *Those who Ponder Proverbs: Aphoristic Thinking and Biblical Literature*. Sheffield: Almond.

"WHAT HAVE YOU COME OUT TO SEE?"
CHARACTERIZATIONS OF JOHN AND JESUS IN THE GOSPELS

Ron Cameron
Wesleyan University

ABSTRACT

This paper endeavors to clarify the ways in which John ("the Baptist") and Jesus were characterized by means of a close reading of select portions of Q and the *Gospel of Thomas* and a comparison with contemporaneous modes of description in the literature of the Greco-Roman world. Critical analysis demonstrates that the earliest Christian references to John present him not as a biblical prophet but as a recognizable Cynic. That characterization is developed in Q through a series of comparisons and contrasts between John, Jesus, and the community of Q. Rhetorical criticism indicates that those comparisons and contrasts were forged in the context of creating a speech, composed according to the pattern of elaboration of the chreia worked out in Greco-Roman schools, and designed to vindicate that group which produced the tradition in the name and under the authority of Jesus. The chreia elaboration in Q is fundamentally an exercise in wisdom speculation, which sought to ally Jesus and John as envoys of Wisdom, founders said to be vindicated along with their followers despite being rejected by their contemporaries. The implications of this study include the need to investigate other instances in which chreiai have been used to compose larger units of narrative and discourse in the gospels, and the necessity to reassess the origins of the Jesus tradition in light of the secondary character of apocalyptic imagination.

0. *Introduction*

One of the most pressing problems in the study of the New Testament is to clarify the various characterizations of its principal figures. Studies of the gospels' portraits of Jesus, for example, have typically been preoccupied with various christological titles applied to him (Hahn, 1969). Although a certain amount of information can be gathered through such investigations, all too frequently the analysis has suffered from a lack of scope, being conceptually limited to canonical texts and titular attestations, and overlooking the broader perspectives gained by a comparative analysis with the literature of the Greco-Roman world. The purpose of this paper is to come to a better understanding of the characterization of John (commonly called "the Baptist") and Jesus by means of a close reading and comparative analysis of select portions of the earliest Christian sayings gospels, Q and the *Gospel of Thomas* (*Gos. Thom.*). I have selected Q and *Gos. Thom.* for this investigation in part because they provide independent textual attestations of certain characterizations of John and Jesus that are often overlooked in our concern for the way(s) in which the canonical gospels have used such traditional materials in the composition of their narratives. As such, these sayings gospels offer excellent examples for an analysis that would take seriously the intersection of textual history and social history in a (re)construction of the beginnings of Christianity.

This paper will unfold in four parts. In the first I will present reasons for my selection of which texts from Q and *Gos. Thom.* are to be treated. In the second I will provide an overview of the formal features of the texts, and I will concentrate my exegesis on those particular passages which, if read comparatively, make a difference in the way John and Jesus are characterized. In the third I will introduce a different model for analyzing those texts in Q, namely, the pattern of the chreia elaboration that was worked out in Greco-Roman schools. And in the fourth I will suggest that the text of Q 7:18–35[1] was in fact composed according to this rhetorical pattern, and I will offer a reading of the text based on that model. Throughout this paper the triple focus of my concerns will be the careful collection of data, their accurate description, and their critical assessment.

1. Selection of Texts to be Treated

The principal texts to be treated are Q 7:18–19, 22–23, 24–28, 31–35; and *Gos. Thom.* 46, 78. These are the parallel passages in which, together with Q 16:16 (see below), John is unequivocally mentioned in Q and/or *Gos. Thom.* Although some interpreters might begin their investigation with the opening sections of the Synoptic Sayings Gospel in Q 3, which traditionally are designated (1) the coming of John the Baptist (Luke 3:1–4 ‖ Matt 3:1–6), (2) John's preaching of repentance (Q 3:7–9), (3) John's preaching of the Coming One (Q 3:16–17), and (4) the baptism of Jesus (Luke 3:21–22 ‖ Matt 3:13–17), such attempts are problematic. In the first place, Luke 3:1–4, 21–22 par. are of uncertain attestation in Q. "The principal grounds for tracing" vss 1–4 back to Q are, according to the recent collation of *Q Parallels* by John S. Kloppenborg, "(1) the necessity of positing some sort of introduction for Q 3:7–9, (2) the Matthew-Luke agreements against Mark [1:2] in the omission of the Malachi [3:1] quotation and in the relative order of the Isaiah [40:3] quotation and introduction of John, and (3) the 'minor agreement' 'the region about the Jordan' [cf. Mark 1:5]" (Kloppenborg, 1988: 6). However, "the agreements of Matthew and Luke against Mark are slight and can be explained without recourse to a Q *Vorlage*.... The large amount of Markan material present in this section as well as the likelihood of Lukan redaction in [his vss] 1–2 render it unwise to include [these verses] in Q" (6). Moreover, though there are also "some Matthew-Luke agreements against Mark" in vss 21–22, principally "(a) the use of a participial form of 'to baptize,' (b) ἀνοίγω ['to open'] instead of σχίζω ['to split, tear apart'], (c) the use of ἐπ' αὐτόν ['on him'] in place of εἰς αὐτόν [literally: 'into him'], and (d) the placement of καταβαίνω ['to descend'] before ὡσ(εὶ) περιστεράν ['like a dove']," here too "the extent of Matthew-Luke agreements is too slight to posit a Q *Vorlage* and all of the 'minor agreements' are easily explained as redactional modifications of Mark [1:9–11]" (16; see the redactional analysis in Kloppenborg, 1987a: 85 n. 157). In the second place, Q 3:7–9, 16–17 do not explicitly mention John by name. Although the embedded contexts of these verses in Matthew and Luke identify the speaker as John (the Baptist), the extant text of Q does not make that identification explicit. Methodologically, therefore, we are obliged to turn our attention first to those passages in Q (7:18–19, 22–23, 24–28, 31–35) and *Gos. Thom.* (saying 46) in which John is actually mentioned by name.

Three additional comments about my selection of texts from Q and *Gos. Thom.* are in order. First, I presuppose a minimal text of Q, that is, the text of Q which represents the *literal* agreements of the gospels of Matthew and Luke against Mark. Whereas the text of *Thomas* is secure, that of Q is stable enough not to require an elaborate reconstruction. Second, Q 16:16 will not be considered, in part because its placement in Q is uncertain. Matthew places this verse at 11:12–13, i.e., after Q 7:28, where the connection between John and Jesus makes sense thematically and does not serve obvious Matthean theological interests (which are introduced in 11:14–15; see Lührmann, 1969: 27–28). However, since the context that Luke gives for this saying is far more difficult, and since there is no apparent reason for Luke to have moved this verse to chapter 16, it seems best to conclude either that both Matthew's and Luke's settings are secondary or that the saying's original setting in Q is irrecoverable (see Kloppenborg, 1988: 56). If I may anticipate the argument for the composition of Q 7:18–35 that I will give below, Q 16:16 does not fit the rhetorical pattern employed in the composing of this chapter. This observation corroborates the suggestion that this verse did not appear after Q 7:28. Third, I include *Gos. Thom.* 78 in my discussion, even though John is not mentioned there by name, because it furnishes the only independently attested parallel to John's description in Q 7:24–25.

2. Formal Features and Cynic Characterizations of John and Jesus

Q 7:18–35 is widely regarded as a composite piece. At least three distinct pericopae (7:18–23, 24–28, 31–35) make up this unit, thematically bound together by references to John and Jesus. Two main indicators of redaction separate the text into these three basic sections: (1) Q 7:24a joins (with a genitive absolute) the statements made about John in vss 24b–28 with Jesus' answer to the question of John's disciples in vss 18–23; and (2) Q 7:31 introduces a new theme ("this generation") and a new form (the parable, vss 31–32), which are related to the context of John and Jesus by the addition of vss 33–34 (see M. Dibelius, 1911: 6–8; Bultmann, 1976: 23, 164–65, 172; Lührmann, 1969: 25).

Q 7:18–23 is usually identified as a pronouncement story or apophthegm, a saying (vss 22–23) artificially set in a narrative context (vss 18–19). Although Rudolf Bultmann surmised that this saying could be an authentic word of Jesus that circulated independently of its context (1976: 23, 110, 126, 128, 151), it is more likely that the entire scene is a Christian product, since the story seems to infuse "the title ['the one who is to come'] with specifically Christian content" (Kloppenborg, 1987a: 107; so also Kraeling, 1951: 127–29; Vögtle, 1971: 219–42). The response attributed to Jesus is drawn from a series of texts from Isaiah, to the effect that with Jesus' activity the time of peace has arrived. Note that, though there is a clear ranking of Jesus over John in this passage, "there is no polemic here" (Kloppenborg, 1987a: 108). Any notions of an anti-Baptist polemic are imported into the text from (a misreading of) the context, possibly inspired by Luke's own editing, whose interest in exalting Jesus above John is betrayed most conspicuously in the two main elements of redaction in this pericope: the repetition of John's question (Q 7:19) by his disciples (Luke 7:20) and the reference to Jesus' miracles in the summary report of Luke 7:21, which betrays Luke's concern for seeing and hearing (1988: 52; see also Wink, 1968: 24 n. 4; Vögtle, 1971: 220).

The midsection (Q 7:24–28) is clearly composite, preserving at least two discrete sayings (vss 24–26, 28) and a quotation from scripture (vs 27) which, in their Q context, are addressed to the crowds with reference to John (vs 24a). Q 7:24–26 is constructed of a series of three questions and answers. As the threefold asking of the question itself intimates, Q's emphasis is on the identity of the one in the "wilderness" (ἔρημος, vs 24b), on *what* it is that one went out to see. This indicates that one should not take the interrogative τί ("what?") to mean "why?" (= διὰ τί; see Bauer, 1979: 819; Blass and Debrunner, 1961: sec. 298–99) and punctuate the

Greek text to make the verb part of the answer. Each of the answers is formulated as a rhetorical question; the last two questions, however, are qualified with statements. Those modifications are important. They indicate not only that the initial answer may be a ploy—John is surely not a reed shaken by the wind. They also intimate that even these last two answers are equally insufficient, requiring additional characterizations to explain how John is neither a person clothed in soft garments nor (merely) a prophet. Indeed, the concluding description of John as more than a prophet seems to invite even further explication (Kloppenborg, 1987a: 109), as the "commentary words" (so Wanke, 1980: 215) appended in Q 7:27, 28 confirm.

The first (vs 27) is a quotation from scripture (Mal 3:1, influenced by the wording of Exod 23:20) that is found independently in Mark 1:2. The second (vs 28) is a saying that is found independently in *Gos. Thom.* 46. The quotation in vs 27 gives one explanation of what "more than a prophet" might mean when, in stating that the messenger was sent before "your" (i.e., Jesus', not God's) face, it "explicitly identifies John as the precursor of Jesus and implicitly identifies him with Elijah *redivivus*" (Kloppenborg, 1987a: 109). The saying in vs 28a offers a rather different, more exalted explanation: none is greater (μείζων) than John among those born of women. As the text now stands, there is a stacking up of epithets attributed to John, from a prophet to something more, from an identification with Elijah *redivivus* to the claim that no human being is greater than he. Nevertheless, these two verses rest somewhat uncomfortably in their context. On the one hand, "Q 7:27 tries to qualify in prophetic terms what is said in 7:26b, namely, that John does not fit into the usual categories, even that of prophet." On the other hand, Q 7:28 "does not comment on 7:27 as its position might suggest, but relates back to 7:26b" as well. "It is connected to the cluster of sayings not because of any attraction to 7:27, but because of the affinities of [the comparative adjectives] μικρότερος/μείζων ['lesser'/'greater'] in 7:28 with περισσότερον ['more'] in 7:26b" (110).

Recognizing that both vss 27 and 28 provide comments on vs 26 may well be important for the compositional history of this passage. One might note parenthetically that codex Bezae saw this too, and placed vs 28a *before* the scriptural quotation in vs 27. However, that placement only recognizes but does not resolve the problem, since one must then explain why two adjoining verses are each introduced with λέγω ὑμῖν ("I tell you" [vss 26b, 28a]). At the very least, whatever the relative stages of compositional history may be reflected in vss 27–28, explicit identifications of John with Elijah "are found only in later levels of tradition" (Kloppenborg, 1987a: 110; cf. Mark 9:11-13; Matt 11:14-15;

17:13; Luke 1:17). There is no evidence that Elijah was imagined as the precursor of the *Messiah* in pre-Christian Judaism (so Fitzmyer, 1981: 671–73; against Moore, 1966: 357; Schürer, 1979: 515; Mowinckel, n.d.: 299)—that notion is first attested in Justin's *Dialogue with Trypho* 49.1–7; cf. 8.4. The reference to the coming of a prophet along with the messiahs of Aaron and Israel in the *Rule of the Community* (1QS 9.11), moreover, is too isolated and indeterminate to permit the conclusion that the Qumran community itself—to say nothing of Jewish society in general— "focused much hope on an expectation of such a prophet" (Horsley, 1985: 441; against Cullmann, 1959: 13). Accordingly, when one considers that there is "very little evidence for any Jewish expectation of an eschatological prophet prior to the early Christian communities' interpretation[s] of Jesus" and John (Horsley, 1985: 437), the identification of John as a prophetic precursor should be recognized as a secondary Christian attempt to augment earlier characterizations of him in the tradition.

The final section of this unit (Q 7:31–35) contains a parable (vss 31–32), to which an interpretation has been appended (vss 33–34), and which is concluded by a summarizing proverb (vs 35). It is the addition of the interpretation which brings the parable into the context of a discussion of John and Jesus. Indeed, whereas the parable seems so opaque, the examples used in the interpretation are intelligible on their own; but since these examples seem to fit the parable "so artificially" (Kloppenborg, 1987a: 111), many scholars regard them as "commentary words" (Wanke, 1980: 216) that were added because the ambiguity of the parable invited explication.

Precisely how the parable (which compares the situation of "this generation" to that of children in the agora) and its application (which relates the lifestyles of John and Jesus to that parabolic situation) are to be understood is far from clear (see Zeller, 1977: 252–57; Fitzmyer, 1981: 678–79; Cotter, 1987: 294–95). Are the uncooperative children those addressed by John and Jesus? Or do the children represent "this generation," calling unsuccessfully to John and Jesus? Does "this generation" represent *two* groups of children, each calling to the other yet refusing to respond? Or are John and Jesus identified with one group which calls, and "this generation" with another which rejects their summons? An interpretation that enjoys wide acceptance regards John and Jesus as the announcing "children" (παιδίοις) and "this generation" as the unresponsive audience. It should be noted, however, that this identification is supported mainly by the concluding proverb, which characterizes John and Jesus as Wisdom's "children" (τέκνα), her envoys or representatives who proclaim God's message to an unrepentant people (see Suggs, 1970: 38–58). Indeed, only on the basis of this proverb, with its appeal to "the deuteronomistic motif of Sophia's sending of the prophets to call Israel to repentance," are John and Jesus portrayed even remotely as *"preachers;* the rejection of the two in [vss] 33–34 is apparently not based upon their preaching, but upon their respective life styles" (Kloppenborg, 1987a: 111).

The observations that John and Jesus are juxtaposed throughout this entire unit of Q 7, and that they are described in vss 33–34 in terms of distinctive lifestyles, compel us to raise anew the question of their characterization in this passage. Since scholars have usually focused their attention upon the identification of John as a prophet (vs 27) and even more (vs 26b), it seems best to begin our (re)assessment with the description that is presented in the midsection of the text. It has been customary to interpret these verses in moralistic terms. The following quotation from Martin Dibelius (1911: 11) is representative:

> Only foolish or absurd expectations could be disillusioned by John. But whoever is inspired to move out to the wilderness with different intentions, whoever cherishes the legitimate hope to encounter a prophet in the ancient abode of revelation, such a person will not be disillusioned, for he has found something greater than a prophet.

This quotation fails to persuade because it does not clarify why certain terms are used in the text or explain how they are imagined to be related to the context. Precisely what is the connection between the description of John as even more than a prophet and his characterizations as neither a reed shaken by the wind nor a person clothed in soft garments? How does this characterization, which begins at the level of a natural phenomenon (a reed, vs 24) and apparently concludes in terms of a classical religious and political figure of Israelite history (a prophet, vs 26), work rhetorically (see Vaage, 1987: 552–71)? Recall that, when discussing this passage above, we noted that of the three responses given to the identification of John, the last two were glossed with qualifying statements. The lack of a comment on the possibility that one might actually go out to the desert to see a reed shaken by the wind suggests that everyone would probably agree: it would be "not really worth so long a trip" (Fitzmyer, 1981: 673–74). And the comment that John is even more than a prophet indicates that everyone might also agree: "prophets" did draw people into the desert. The issue, however, is whether John actually corresponds to such an expectation. The descriptions in Q 7:24–26 suggest that the prospect of seeing a prophet in John amounts to a wholly inappropriate expectation (Vaage, 1987: 555, 561). Accordingly, in order to clarify the characterization of John, and to understand the rhetorical edge of this passage, one needs to turn to the intervening description and comment (vs 25), for they are "the logical fulcrum" that makes the transition from the characterization of John as a shaken reed to something more than a prophet persuasive (552–53, 565–66).

Leif Vaage has shown that the combination of soft clothing (μαλακός) and royal or palatial life gives Q 7:25 its particular edge and characterization. Although the apparent characterization of John in terms of soft clothing and, specifically, "the opposition of John to those persons dressed in soft clothing at [a] royal dwelling" seem anomalous within the gospel tradition, such an opposition is a frequent "feature of the polemic of Greco-Roman Cynics against their contemporary culture" (556–57). Cynics, of course, were popular moral "philosophers" who "flourished in the Roman Empire" during the first century C.E., adopted an "independent life-style," and strove for that form of "self-sufficiency (αὐτάρκεια)" which allowed one "to be satisfied with the simplest diet and personal furnishings." They exhibited a "rejection of the claims of society by repudiating the state, marriage, and the accepted sexual [and social] mores" of the day, and they sought "to convert [people] by bringing them to their senses...by means of bold speech (παρρησία)," insisting on "the individual's ability to free himself from the yearning for fame, riches, and pleasure that shackles [humankind]" (Malherbe, 1976: 201, 203). For the purposes of comparison, the most pertinent examples of a Cynic opposition to the "soft" life can be selected from the writings of the Cynics themselves, those Cynic *Epistles* which come chiefly "from the Augustan age" (Malherbe, 1977: 2), are written in the name and under the authority of the Cynic heroes of the past, "appear to have been written as propaganda pieces, and are a prime source for our understanding of Cynicism" (1976: 202).

In pseudo-Crates's *Epistle* 19 ("To Patrocles") there is a polemic against Odysseus who, in contrast to Diogenes, was falsely called by some "the father of Cynicism because once he put on the garb of the Cynic." The critique turns on the contention that "the cloak does not make a Cynic, but the Cynic the cloak." The principal charge against Odysseus is that he was the "softest" (μαλακώτατον) of all his companions, a softness exemplified by the fact that he put pleasure (ἡδονήν) above all else, always succumbed to sleep and to food, and praised the sweet (ἡδύν) life (1977: 68–69). It is important to recognize that this description of Odysseus "is an epitome of the Homeric epic, which records the effort of Odysseus to return to his royal palace and Penelope" (Vaage, 1987: 558). As such, the "soft" life which is criticized is implicitly placed in the context of the palace. Parenthetically we might note that other Cynic *Epistles* appealed more positively to the figure of Odysseus, using his erstwhile Cynic garb as evidence that sanctions the Cynic lifestyle (e.g., pseudo-

Diogenes *Epistle* 7 ["To Hicetas"], citing Homer *Odyssey* 13.434–38; see Malherbe, 1977: 10, 98–99; 1978: 50–51). In those cases in which Odysseus is nobly regarded, his clothing is then described as fit admirably for kings (e.g., pseudo-Diogenes *Epistle* 34 ["To Olympias"]), since it is precisely the attire worn by every sensible person, including those Cynics who shun despots no less than slanderers in the agora (1977: 142–45).

In pseudo-Diogenes's *Epistle* 29 ("To Dionysius") the tyrant Dionysius is addressed in the second person singular, criticized for seeking security by surrounding himself with bodyguards and citadels, and offered a Cynic pedagogue to "turn [him] away from softness" (μαλακίας). Such "softness" is identified as the "sacred sickness…called tyranny," and it is characterized as a life surrounded by sycophants who seek personal gain, make off with the tyrant's possessions, and corrupt the standards of his household. Although "cutting, cautery and medication must be employed" to relieve the infectious putrefaction, Dionysius is pictured as refusing the rigors of a Cynic panacea and choosing rather, in the manner of children (παιδία), to feed his insatiable disease (1977: 126–29).

In pseudo-Crates's *Epistle* 29 ("To Hipparchia") the Cynic life is characterized as robust endurance (ὑπομένειν), which others cannot bear on account of their "softness" (μαλακίαν; 1977: 78–79). In pseudo-Diogenes's *Epistle* 28 "the so-called Greeks" are the object of Cynic invective because they "pretend to everything, but know nothing." In particular, the denunciation charges that they envy one another when they see someone else wearing clothing which is a little "softer" (μαλακώτερον ἱμάτιον; 1977: 120–21). Similarly, in pseudo-Diogenes's *Epistle* 12 ("To Crates") the masses (οἱ πολλοί) are criticized for seeking a short cut to happiness (εὐδαιμονίαν); they fail, unable to lead a life of austerity on account of their "softness" (μαλακίαν; 1977: 106–7). All of these examples, which could easily be multiplied (see Vaage, 1987: 557–61), indicate that opposition to the "soft" life, characterized by luxurious clothing or palatial dwellings, was a feature of the Cynic critique of culture. The characterization of John in Q 7:24–26 suggests that his place in the history of religions corresponds to these contemporary, Cynic critics of Greco-Roman civilization. It is for this reason that John is said here to be more than a prophet. The attempt to identify John as Elijah *redivivus* in Q 7:27 notwithstanding, "John does not fit into the usual categories, even that of prophet" (Kloppenborg, 1987a: 110). For this stage of Q, John is rather like the Cynic in pseudo-Diogenes's *Epistle* 21 ("To Amynander"), a "prophet of indifference" (ὁ τῆς ἀπαθείας προφήτης) who speaks plain words in opposition to the deluded life (Malherbe, 1977:

114–15; cf. Lucian *Philosophies for Sale* 8; and see also Vaage, 1987: 561–64, 571 n. 35).

Our analysis has indicated that the midsection of Q 7:18–35 has its focal point in the characterizations of John in vss 24–26, 27, 28. In these verses John is characterized primarily as a Cynic; only secondarily is he designated the greatest of humans and, aided by interpreting a precedent from scripture, identified as the Elijanic precursor of Jesus. The two sayings which frame Q's quotation from scripture are also found in *Gos. Thom.* Since our analysis has been centered on Q 7:24–26, I will discuss only its parallel in *Gos. Thom.* (saying 78) at this time. In so doing, I hope to provide some control to our investigation as well as test the results of our findings.

Q 7:24b–25 is paralleled in *Gos. Thom.* 78:

> Jesus said, "Why have you come out to the countryside? To see a reed shaken by the wind? And to see a [person] clothed in soft garments [like your] kings and your princes? They are clothed in soft [garments] and cannot recognize truth."

This version of the saying contains only one question, introduced with the interrogative ⲈⲦⲂⲈ ⲞⲨ (= διὰ τί, "why?"), to which two responses are given. Each response is a rhetorical question; the second is elaborated with a comparison which, once again, associates "softness" with royal or princely life. The comment that those clothed in soft garments cannot recognize truth need not be taken in a specifically gnostic sense (against Fitzmyer, 1981: 673; Gärtner, 1961: 241–42), since the phrase to "know the truth" is used elsewhere (e.g., John 8:32; cf. 1 John 2:21; 2 John 1) to mean to be cognizant of true "reality" or divine "revelation" (see Bultmann, 1964: 239, 245–47; 1971: 434–36; Dodd, 1968: 171–72, 176–78, who compares Plato *Republic* 508D–509A).

Perhaps the most conspicuous feature of *Thomas*'s version of this saying is, for those who know Q, the lack of an obvious reference to John. This apparent absence is variously explained as an accidental omission or intentional deletion (e.g., Schrage, 1964: 161; Haenchen, 1961: 57–58; Quispel, 1967: 80), despite the well-known tendency to expand the tradition by the addition of names of people and places. But is there any reason to think that John is being referred to here in *Thomas*? It is Jesus who is the speaker; conceivably he or his followers are implicitly being characterized. Note that *Gos. Thom.* 78 asks *why* certain persons have come out to the "countryside" (ⲤⲰϢⲈ). Whereas Q's emphasis is on the identity of the one in the wilderness, on *what* it is one went out to see, the single question in *Thomas* probes one's reasons for seeking truth, away from cities or towns, out in the country. The cultural critique of "soft" clothing has already been traced in the tradition. What about the metaphor of the reed blown by the wind and the statement about failing to know truth?

A clue to their usage may be found in the sustained attack on the philosophical schools, especially the Stoics, in Lucian of Samosata's *Hermotimus* (written between 160 and 180 C.E.). In this, his longest work, Lucian presents himself in the role of the interlocutor Lycinus, criticizing the Stoic student Hermotimus for aligning himself with one school of thought, instead of first seeking to ascertain truth (ἔγνωσται τἀληθές) and then inquiring if any school has discovered it (*Hermotimus* 66). The search takes an entire lifetime; there are never any short cuts. For even if one seems to have found truth and chosen which school has as well, one must then select the right teacher with care, lest he be not genuine but counterfeit. Failing to make the right choice, Hermotimus is told, means "that nothing will save you from being dragged by the nose...or from following a leafy branch in front of you as sheep do; you will be like water spilt on a table, running whithersoever someone pulls you by the tip of his finger, or indeed like a reed (καλάμῳ) growing on a river bank, bending to every breath of wind, however slight the breeze that blows and shakes (διασαλεύσῃ) it" (*Hermotimus* 68; Kilburn, 1959: 389). Yet once one has chosen a teacher, an arbiter would still be required to determine whether that teacher speaks truth or conjures up chimeras—and another arbiter would be required for him. A proverb puts it best: "a great deal of toil and we're where we were" before (*Hermotimus* 69). Only a few persons are brave enough to admit they have been deceived, and to seek to turn others from that snare (*Hermotimus* 75). They are true philosophers. Everyone else, Lycinus says, is an abject coward, fabricating an unreal blessedness in a dreamlike world, as though surrounded by wealth and by kings (*Hermotimus* 75, 71).

This passage from Lucian confirms that the metaphor of the reed shaken by the wind is not used to connote something ephemeral or someone who is unstable (against Fitzmyer, 1981: 674; Bornkamm, 1960: 50). The image is rather one of accommodating pliability, and makes sense in a context that addresses how one lives one's life and where one searches for truth. *Thomas*'s polemic against the "soft" life of kings' courts matches the critique that is found in Q, suggesting that the speaker of this saying is characterized by Cynic modes of speech. Yet there is no mention of John in this passage, nor any reference to the figure of a prophet. Is there any reason to imagine that *Gos. Thom.* might attest to an earlier stage of the tradition, which was further interpreted when it came to be elaborated in its Q context?

3. The Pattern of the Chreia Elaboration in Hermogenes

Q 7:18–35 has all the earmarks of a carefully crafted composition that pairs various characterizations of John and Jesus and exhibits a Cynic mode of description. Several literary features compel us to ask whether and how this entire unit was composed as a block: (1) the text begins with a scene which addresses the relationship of John and Jesus, followed by a beatitude; (2) it next includes a saying that characterizes John in the form of antitheses, preserves a rare (for Q) quotation from scripture, and a statement attributed to Jesus in the first person singular; and (3) it then presents a parable, applies that parable paradigmatically to John and Jesus, and concludes with a proverb. Observing that these sayings are formulated as a series of discrete but interrelated units that concern the characterization of well-known, named figures provides the initial clue to the resolution of our query. But the critical clue is given at the very outset of the text, in the question about Jesus from John. Both a setting and a saying are presented in this scene: a question is raised, a response is given; an identification is sought, and a profile is drawn. Usually described as a pronouncement story, this pericope fits perfectly the definition of a chreia.

According to the classic definition by Aphthonius of Antioch (late fourth-early fifth century C.E.), a chreia is "a [1] concise [2] reminiscence [of a saying or action, ἀπομνημόνευμα] [3] aptly attributed to some [specific] character" and generally "[4] useful [for living]" (Hock and O'Neil, 1986: 225; cf. 23–26; see also Robbins, 1988: 2–4). Its function "was not primarily to offer instruction but to add to the characterization of a well-known figure" (Mack, 1987: 4). And "judging from the very large number of chreiai attributed to Cynics, [the chreia] must have been especially appropriate to [Cynic] philosophy and character" (6; see also Fischel, 1968). Chreiai were frequently elaborated into longer speeches. Such elaborations took considerable skill and practice, and were learned through years of disciplined, graded exercises. The most influential pattern of the chreia elaboration was discussed by Hermogenes of Tarsus (born 161 C.E.) near the end of the second and the beginning of the third century C.E., though Greek theorists and Roman rhetoricians had already worked out the details of the tradition by the first century B.C.E. (Kennedy, 1963: 270; 1984: 12; Mack, 1984: 85; Hock and O'Neil, 1986: 10).[2] Hermogenes emphasized that the chreia could be manipulated through a pattern of elaboration (ἐργασία) to become the basis for rhetorical compositions in written form, and not simply be "a mere elementary exercise designed to help the young student analyze a [given] piece of literature" (Hock and O'Neil, 1986: 163). By comparing the pattern of elaboration which Hermogenes preserves with the order and logic of Q

7:18-35, we will see how this block in Q was composed, and be able to identify its distinctive features, determine its mode of argumentation, and clarify the essentials of its characterization.

Hermogenes *On the Chreia* (Hock and O'Neil, 1986: 177):

But now let us move on to the chief matter, and this is the elaboration (ἐργασία). Accordingly, let the elaboration be as follows: (1) First, an encomium, in a few words, for the one who spoke or acted. Then (2) a paraphrase of the chreia itself; then (3) the rationale.

For example: *Isocrates said that education's root is bitter, its fruit is sweet.*

(1) Praise (ἔπαινος): "Isocrates was wise," and you amplify the subject moderately.

(2) Then the chreia (χρεία): "He said thus and so," and you are not to express it simply but rather by amplifying the presentation.

(3) Then the rationale (αἰτία): "For the most important affairs generally succeed because of toil, and once they have succeeded, they bring pleasure."

(4) Then the statement from the opposite (κατὰ τὸ ἐναντίον): "For ordinary affairs do not need toil, and they have an outcome that is entirely without pleasure; but serious affairs have the opposite outcome."

(5) Then the statement from analogy (ἐκ παραβολῆς): "For just as it is the lot of farmers to reap their fruits after working with the land, so also is it for those working with words."

(6) Then the statement from example (ἐκ παραδείγματος): "Demosthenes, after locking himself in a room and toiling long, later reaped his fruits: wreaths and public acclamations [cf. Demosthenes *On the Crown* 58]."

(7) It is also possible to argue from the statement by an authority (ἐκ κρίσεως). For example, Hesiod said [*Works and Days* 289]:

"In front of virtue gods have ordained sweat."
And another poet says [Epicharmus frg. 287]:
"At the price of toil do the gods sell every good to us."

(8) At the end you are to add an exhortation (παράκλησιν) to the effect that it is necessary to heed the one who has spoken or acted.

So much for the present; you will learn the more advanced instruction later.

Although this is not the place to present a full-scale exegesis of Hermogenes's pattern of elaboration of the chreia, a few remarks will be necessary at this point for us to understand how the rhetorical argumentation works in the literary composition of a speech. (For a fuller explication, on which I am heavily dependent in the discussion that follows, see Mack, 1984: 93–99; 1987: 15–28.)

Hermogenes's list of eight items may appear simple and unsophisticated, but a "closer reading shows...that each item was carefully chosen, the composition creative and the logic of the whole persuasive" (1987: 22). The chreia selected as the example is a saying aptly attributed to Isocrates, "a founder figure with whom the practice of rhetoric and the formation of the Hellenistic school were combined" (1984: 94). It is a well-attested saying in antiquity (see Hock and O'Neil, 1986: 325–26) about education (παιδεία):

"Isocrates said that education's (παιδείας) root is bitter, its fruit is sweet."

The elaboration begins with a word of (1) *praise* ("Isocrates was wise [σοφός]"), which could be amplified as appropriate. "This corresponds to the introduction of a speech" (Mack, 1984: 94) and helps establish the ethos and authority of Isocrates, makes it clear that the person "performing the elaboration is not the speaker of the chreia," and provides an "opportunity for linking the character of the speaker of the chreia with the theme of the chreia in keeping with the standard notion about matching character with speech" (1987: 23).

The (2) *chreia* is then (re)cited ("he said thus and so"), frequently by means of a paraphrase, in order to present the saying "as a statement of the thesis to be elaborated" (23). Such an amplification of the "presentation" (ἑρμηνείαν) enables one to enhance the chreia's "meaning" significantly.

The (3) *rationale* ("for the most important affairs generally succeed because of toil [πόνων], and once they have succeeded, they bring pleasure [ἡδονήν]") is of critical importance, for it restates the chreia propositionally "in the form of an assertion which can be argued" (1984: 95). "To make this move, the student would need to determine the 'issue' embedded within the chreia and to find a generally valid proposition that addressed the issue. In this case the 'issue' was the *relationship* between the 'bitter root' and the 'sweet fruit,' a relationship left vague by the chreia's metaphor" (1987: 23). The rationale which Hermogenes gives, moreover, translates the "bitter root/sweet fruit" metaphor "into the sequence 'labor first/then rewards'" (23). In so doing, the technical terms of "toil" (πόνος) and "pleasure" (ἡδονή) are introduced into the discussion and will serve as the guiding metaphors for the elaboration that is to follow. The emphasis on the labor or toil requisite to success was axiomatic in the culture. The clever reference to pleasure is also telling, for it alludes to one of the "final categories" or "chief ends" (ἡδύς, "pleasant") used in deliberative rhetoric, expressing one of the conventional values of the society (1984: 88, 95). As such, the rationale is making "a claim...for the validity of the thesis in terms of a conventional value" (1987: 24).

The (4) *statement from the opposite* ("for ordinary affairs [τὰ τυχόντα] do not need toil [πόνων], and they have an outcome that is entirely without pleasure [ἀηδέστατον]; but serious affairs [τὰ σπουδαῖα] have the opposite outcome") tests the validity of the thesis dialectically by inverting the terms of the rationale. If "the opposite is recognized as true" then "the proposition gains in credibility" (24). In this particular case, the terms for toil and pleasure given in the rationale are reiterated, but recast in terms of the new contrast between ordinary and serious affairs. Whereas the former connotes "happenstance" and chanciness, the latter denotes "excellence with earnestness.... Thus, one detects a stacking [up] of connotations with good affairs defined by purpose, toil and pleasure on the one side, and chance affairs defined by happenstance and unhappiness on the other" (24).

The (5) *statement from analogy* ("for just as it is the lot [δεῖ] of farmers to reap their fruits after working [πονήσαντος] with the land, so also is it for those working with words") "by definition...was to be taken from the world of common experience.... The analogy pointed to a common phenomenon regarded as an instance of a universal principle" (24). This particular analogy is telling not only because it picks up on the agricultural metaphors explicit within the chreia but also because it defines παιδεία specifically as "working with words." In keeping with the proposition stated in the rationale, moreover, "the point is made in the analogy that the cultivation of the land must precede the harvesting of the fruit" (25). And since the metaphorical image of agricultural endeavor, especially that of sowing seed, was used as a standard instructive analogy for the inculcation of παιδεία ("teaching, culture") in the Greek and Roman periods (see Cameron, 1986: 21–23; Mack, 1988b: 159–60), the sequence of "effort/produce" is seen to be "constitutive in all arenas": the natural, the agricultural, and the rhetorical (Mack, 1984: 96).

The (6) *statement from example* ("Demosthenes, after locking himself in a room and toiling [μοχθήσας] long, later reaped his fruits: wreaths and public acclamations") "by definition...[was] to be taken from the arena of history and be about some well-known person. Its function is to show that the general principle at issue has been actualized in a particular instance" (97). Selecting Demosthenes, the famous rhetor "who actually worked with words" (1987: 26), referring to his hours of toiling and resultant acclaim, and alluding eruditely to his "famous oration 'On the Crown' [58]...would not have damaged the argument at all." In addition, "the clever inclusion of an allusion to the canons of literature is a special touch, introducing as it does the next category of argumentation" (1984: 97).

The (7) *statement by an authority* ("for example, Hesiod said [*Works and Days* 289]: 'In front of virtue [ἀρετῆς] gods have ordained sweat.' And another poet says [Epicharmus frg. 287]: 'At the price of toil [πόνων] do the gods sell every good to us'") was intended "to confirm the truth of the developed proposition by showing that recognized authorities had said much the same thing" (97). A pertinent quotation from Hesiod on the subject of work would surely have helped clinch the argument, not least because it specifies "the necessity of labor [as] grounded in the ordinance of the gods" and indicates that "the pleasurable goal" attained by toil "is none other than ἀρετή itself, the mark par excellence of the highest human achievements" (98). The additional quotation by Epicharmus, a Sicilian writer of comedy of the fifth century B.C.E., reinforces the fact that it is the gods who have ordained labor, and sums up the argument with the pairing of the terms "toil" and "good."

The (8) *exhortation* ("it is necessary to heed the one who has spoken or acted") forms a concluding period, given "as a call to respond" to Isocrates, "the author of the chreia" (1987: 27), because the argument won in the process of the elaboration "has confirmed the truth of his saying" (1984: 98).

4. *The Pattern of Elaboration in Q 7:18–35*

We have noted that the opening scene of Q 7:18–35 fits the description of a chreia perfectly, and we have observed that this entire unit is composed of sayings which feature the relationship of John and Jesus. Using the pattern of the elaboration of the chreia discussed by Hermogenes as our guide, let us take a fresh look at the composition of the text and at its characterizations of John and Jesus. Naturally we should not expect the elaboration pattern to be employed in a wooden way, since Q is neither a student's literary assignment nor a teacher's classroom exercise. Moreover, the presence of parallels in *Gos. Thom.* to certain sections of Q 7 indicates that this unit has not been created out of whole cloth by the author of (this stage of) Q. Traditional materials have been utilized in the composition of the text. However, should we discover the pattern of elaboration actually operative in the text, that should alert us to reconsider (our understanding of) this unit in light of the rhetoric being employed.

The pattern of elaboration in Q 7:18–35 may be displayed as follows:
(1) Praise: *vacat*
(2) Chreia: 7:18–19, 22
(3) Rationale: 7:23

(4) Statement of the Opposite: 7:24–26
(7) Statements by an Authority: 7:27, 28
(5) Statement from Analogy: 7:31–32
(6) Statement from Example: 7:33–34
(8) Concluding Periodization: 7:35

(1) Since we are dealing with a composition in Q that also forms part of Matthew's and Luke's narratives, an initial word of *praise* to introduce the speaker would not be appropriate and should not be expected. We begin with the chreia itself.

(2) A *chreia*, it will be recalled, is "a [1] concise [2] statement or action which is [3] attributed with aptness to some specified character" (Hock and O'Neil, 1986: 83 [Theon]; cf. 66–67). Because the pattern of elaboration in Q 7:18–35 is so developed, forming the longest continuous unit in the Synoptic Sayings Gospel, the initial problem facing the interpreter is to reconstruct the original chreia. It is clear that a question (vs 19) is raised to which an answer was given. But two responses are presented as answers in the text (vss 22, 23); isolating which response most likely was the primary is the issue. The first clue to the reconstruction of the text is to see that, though neither rejoinder really answers the question directly, the references to scripture in the initial response (vs 22) fit the developing portraits that are made in the elaboration pattern which follows. The next clue comes from a comparison of the question with the rather curious beatitude preserved as the second response (vs 23). A comparison of that question and this beatitude reveals that three contrasts are made and aligned:

Question (vs 19):
Are you / the one who is to come / or should we expect another?
Rejoinder (vs 23):
Whoever / is not offended by me / is blessed.

Note that the question asked of Jesus ("are you?") is immediately redirected to address someone else ("whoever"). In addition, an eschatological identification for Jesus ("the one who is to come") is countered with an appeal ("is not offended by me") which suggests that appearances are deceiving, that such an equation may be a trap. Finally, the concluding query ("or should we expect another?") is juxtaposed with a pronouncement ("is blessed") that vindicates both Jesus and the other person(s). Although this rejoinder might appear to answer the question affirmatively, a closer look reveals that the identification presupposed by the inquiry is countered with a response that questions such an expectation. In fact, a conclusion is subtly drawn which inverts the sense of that inquiry. The logic of this rejoinder thus rides on the insinuation that the questioner has not interpreted Jesus' role correctly. The response succeeds on account of its shrewdness: Jesus' activity is legitimate, and so, whoever is with him is too.

The question and this rejoinder would make a fine chreia. "The response turns the tables" on the conventional wisdom of a challenging question "by means of a clever rejoinder that picks up on the assumptions underlying the challenge and [that] frustrates them by means of another consideration" (Mack, 1988b: 62). The fact that this second response (vs 23) is so thoroughly aligned to contrast with the question, whereas the initial response (vs 22) seems created to serve the subsequent argumentation, suggests that the original chreia comprised this question and that second response. Paraphrasing, the reconstructed original most likely read as follows:

> When asked, "Are you the one who is to come or should we expect another?" Jesus replied, "Whoever is not offended by me is blessed."

The last clue in the text confirms this reconstruction, for it shows how the chreia, once created, came to be reworked and elaborated in the process of transmission at a later stage of the tradition. With the crafting of a new response for Jesus (vs 22), the original response (vs 23) was retained but recast to fit a new rhetorical function. Whereas the original response succeeded on account of its shrewdness, in its new function that response will be used as a topic for persuasion, to provide the rationale for the elaborated argument to follow. That amplification occurred, I suggest, when the chreia was selected as a theme for elaboration, in order to clarify the characterizations of John and Jesus and to vindicate the Q group which appealed to them for authorization. The elaboration will turn on a series of comparisons and contrasts between and among those persons. The issue will concern expectations.

We must now ask why the chreia was created in the first place, for that answer will provide both the situation in and the occasion for which Q came to elaborate various characterizations of John and Jesus into a single, coherent argument. Since the eschatological orientation presupposed by the chreia question was judged to be incorrect, the chreia seems designed to counter such an expectation by presenting a profile of Jesus' character distinguished by clever, invitational speech. The chreia thus originated in a group situation in which deliberations were taking place in response to contrasting claims about the identity of Jesus and the legacy of a community. Apocalyptic language was entertained on that occasion to reflect upon the rationale of the group's character. Bringing John into the discussion presented the opportunity to meditate on Jesus' sagacity by using John's activity as a foil. Nevertheless, to inquire into the titular identification of some "one who is to come" (ὁ ἐρχόμενος, vs 19) is really rather curious. Introduced without explanation in Q 3:16 at the second stage of composition of the text, this title will be redactionally inserted later in the Synoptic Sayings Gospel in 13:35b (see Kloppenborg, 1987b). The elaboration in Q 7:18–35 is entrusted with the task of assessing the appropriateness of such a designation for Jesus by comparing it thematically with a contrasting set of characters, developing that theme literarily through the composition of a speech, and calling into question the expectations (προσδοκᾶν, vs 19) of others in keeping with the issue posed by the chreia. Accordingly, the rhetorical problem facing this stage of the redaction of Q is how to incorporate the apocalyptic imagery secondarily ascribed to its founders and members with the full consciousness that Jesus and John did not really appear apocalyptic. By invoking an apocalyptic idiom without fully appropriating its assumptions (see Kloppenborg, 1987c), Q seeks to integrate a panoply of portraits into a mythic characterization of its origins.

The original chreia took a position on the question of Jesus' identity and activity. When that chreia was effaced by transferring the response to a subsequent place in the argumentation, another response was substituted to explicate the implications of the original question, yet provide a thematic contrast for a different mode of characterization. John and his "disciples" were introduced into the narrative at precisely this point in order to align—and then undermine—underlying expectations and "prophetic" precedents.

The newly created chreia that is found in Q 7:18–19, 22 is a classic example of a responsive (ἀποκριτική) sayings chreia. According to the classification system developed by Aelius Theon of Alexandria, a rhetorician from apparently the mid- or late first century C.E. who compiled a teachers' handbook for guiding students in their first lessons in rhetorical education (the *Progymnasmata*, or "preliminary exercises"), sayings chreiai were frequently formulated as responses to an inquiry (Hock and O'Neil, 1986: 85, 87; cf. 29). This passage from Q illustrates Theon's description beautifully:

> When John sent some of his disciples (vs 18) to Jesus, saying, "Are you the one who is to come or should we expect another?" (vs 19), Jesus is said to respond with a virtual pastiche from Isaiah (26:19; 29:18–19; 35:5–6; 42:6–7, 18; 61:1) in Greek: "Go and tell John what you see and hear: the blind receive their sight, the lame walk, lepers are cleansed, and the deaf hear, the dead are raised up, the poor have good news preached to them" (vs 22).

Although some interpreters have regarded the situation that is depicted in this chreia as historical (e.g., Kümmel, 1957: 109–11; Scobie, 1964: 143–44; Schütz, 1967: 100, 103–4), it must be understood that chreiai were not designed to provide historical information or offer instruction (see Hock and O'Neil, 1986: 41–46). Their function was rather "to add to the characterization of a well-known figure and to explore the application" of a particular religious or "philosophical position to some situation in life" (Mack, 1987: 4). That is why the essence of the chreia can be described as speech-in-character, for each chreia "combined speaker, speech, and circumstance" (1984: 86). A character is named, a question is posed, a response is given. The task for the hearer was to "catch the point" of the chreia and "match the [particular religious or] philosophical position implied with the character [who is] named" (1987: 4).

John's question "is it *you*...?" poses the issue of identification; the designation "the one who is to come" suggests an eschatological orientation (cf. Mal 3:1; 4:5; Dan 7:13; Hab 2:3; Q 3:16; 13:35b; and see Klostermann, 1927: 94; Laufen, 1980: 407–9). But Jesus' response only appears to provide an answer. It selects an aspect of the question with which apparently to agree, citing passages from Isaiah predicting the coming time of peace. But those citations do not trade in "messianic" expectations, and are chosen from the perspective of the "miraculous" in view (Kloppenborg, 1987a: 107–8). Q 7:18–19, 22, therefore, is deliberately enigmatic; we should not be surprised to discover that this question is not directly answered even in the new response. In fact, the elaboration that follows will deflect the issue from an eschatological identification to a rather different characterization (ἠθοποιία). Precisely how such characterizations are made will be the subject of the elaborated argument. But the naming of John as well as Jesus indicates that they will be intertwined thematically throughout the development of that argument. And as the reference to what John's disciples see and hear in vs 22 intimates, the figures named in the chreia will be distinguished by action no less than by speech.

(3) The beatitude in Q 7:23, which constituted the response in the original chreia, functions now as the *rationale*, serving to restate the new chreia in the form of a thesis to be argued. In the process of elaboration this beatitude was too clever to be discarded altogether, and so was retained here as an emphatic assertion. Note that the beatitude consists of a single statement without either a ὅτι ("because") or motive (γάρ, "for") clause, which would customarily express the reason for one's being blessed. As such, this really is a "propositional" statement. The issue still concerns underlying expectations, but now, based on the allusions to Isaiah introduced into the response (vs 22), the implicit critique of the

original chreia is specified in terms of more explicit anticipations. Those allusions, moreover, permit "Jesus" to construct an argument that turns not simply on a saying attributed to him, but on a chreia that makes reference to a known, biblical authority. Such a learned maneuver is wholly in keeping with the rhetorical tradition of Hermogenes, which produced theses selected from chreiai of well-known authors. In addition, the inclusion of those allusions raises the question of the utility of biblical precedents for an exploration of characterization. That issue will be explored in subsequent sections of the argument.

Two other features of this beatitude should be noted. First, the relative pronoun ὅς ("who") with the particle ἐάν (= ἄν, i.e., "the one who, whoever") is "intended to be generic" (Fitzmyer, 1981: 668; against Dupont, 1961: 952–54), and refers not (only) to John but to any person not offended by Jesus. In redirecting the question from Jesus' identity to his blessing of another person's legitimacy, the rationale thus sets the stage for an explication that will focus not only on Jesus and his activity but also on the acceptance or rejection of the Q community. That shift was prepared for in the preceding response ("what *you* see and hear" [vs 22]), and will be encountered again in the succeeding rhetorical questions ("what have *you* come out to see?" [vss 24, 25, 26]). Second, astute observers may have noted the play on words suggested by "taking offense" (σκανδαλίζειν) as "entrapment" (cf. Aristophanes *Acharnians* 687; and see Stählin, 1971: 339–40). To "take offense" hints that when corrective characterizations are introduced in the elaboration, one should not be "bothered" by preconceived notions provisionally broached in the chreia. The rationale is thus interpretative, in that it proposes a thesis to be confirmed and initiates an argument to be developed. At issue is nothing less than a "crisis of classification" (see Green, 1987: 4) for Jesus in Q.

(4) The questions addressed by Jesus in Q 7:24–26 function as the *statement of the opposite*. Unlike the example from Hermogenes, however, this particular statement does not test the thesis simply by inverting the terms of the rationale. Instead, these questions address the problem of characterization by questioning the issue of preconceived expectations, an issue that was broached in the chreia and thematized by the rationale. The statement of "the opposite" actually makes an indirect *contrast* between John and Jesus, not at the expense of one or the other but at the deeper level of presumptions.

One of the striking features of this entire passage should be noted at this time: John and Jesus are compared and contrasted in virtually every unit of the elaboration. Apparent questions asked of one are redirected to the other; seeming characterizations made of one are played off against the other. Accordingly, the change in audience in this scene from John's "disciples" to the "crowd" seems to be a rhetorical ploy (cf. Mark 7:14, 17), designed to shift the discussion from "John's" question about Jesus to "Jesus'" question about John. This corresponds to a statement of the facts (διήγησις) of a case, and provides a contrast between those perceptions held about Jesus and beheld in John.

Two different characterizations of John are contrasted in this passage. On the one hand, he is neither a (mere) reed shaken by the wind nor a person clothed in soft garments. Indeed, the contrast with life in kings' courts indicates that John's lifestyle is the opposite of such luxury. On the other hand, John is not just a (mere) prophet, but "in fact" (ναί, vs 26b; see Berger, 1970: 6–12) is said to be something even (καί) more. The apparent introduction of the title "prophet" is important for it marks the first instance since the chreia in which a title is given in the narrative. Yet even John's identity as a prophet is to be regarded with suspicion. Contemporaneous descriptions from the wider culture indicate that John was really a "prophet of indifference" (Malherbe, 1977: 115), i.e., a recognizable Cynic. Moreover, we have already taken note of the paucity of evidence for an expectation of an eschatological prophet in early Judaism prior to the rise of Christian interpretation. And yet the term "prophet" is significant, for not only are John and Jesus contrasted but their titles are played with as well. Just as the title ("the one who is to come") used in the chreia was directed away from Jesus, so the title ("the prophet") used here in the statement of the opposite is deflected away from John. Why those titles came to be debated is now the question.

The remaining sections of the elaboration pattern are to provide, according to Aphthonius, the corroboration of the thesis (Hock and O'Neil, 1986: 35). The critique of expectations and the ambiguity of designations in Q 7:18–26 do require further exploration, which the balance of the argument is designed to explicate. The elaboration will thus proceed inductively, by means of an arranging of a series of comparisons and contrasts. Since the statement of the opposite is directed primarily toward John, he will remain the principal subject of the subsequent unit. If Jesus is not the coming one as anticipated by the chreia, then perhaps John is—or alternatively, is the messenger made to announce his presence. In any case, the ways John came to be esteemed will now be addressed. The utility of biblical precedents for the clarification of characterization can then be seen. At that time we will finally be able to determine why John and Jesus were juxtaposed throughout the entire elaboration.

(7) The citation from scripture in Q 7:27, introduced with a technical quotation formula (γέγραπται, "it is written"), provides the first *statement*

by an authority. The occurrence of a biblical quotation is striking: apart from the temptation story in Q 4:1–13, which makes up the latest layer of Q, this marks the only passage in the Synoptic Sayings Gospel that cites the Jewish Bible explicitly (cf. γέγραπται in Q 4:4, 8, 10; and see Kloppenborg, 1987a: 247). Note that this statement by an authority stands in the center of the elaboration, indicative of its prominence. The choice of which scriptural passage to quote was an issue of some importance, since the reason for citing authoritative testimony was to provide "supporting arguments" (ἐπιχειρήματα) that demonstrate how previous witnesses had spoken similarly. This quotation, a conflation from Mal 3:1 and Exod 23:20, marks the very first instance in early Christianity in which either of these texts is cited. God's chosen envoy (who is called Elijah the prophet in the appendix in Mal 4:5) is identified as John and linked to the covenant code. The Hebrew epic and prophetic traditions are thus united. To be sure, such an identification virtually scuttles the Cynic characterization made in the statement of the opposite. But it does provide an allusion to the "wilderness" wandering, "a place symbolic of purification and renewal" (Horsley, 1985: 452; see also Funk, 1959: 205–14). And it explains why the "desert" could evoke the imagination enough for people to go out to see.

Notice, however, that the identification of John as a prophet is mitigated somewhat here, even in this quotation from scripture, in that John is designated as an envoy or "messenger" (ἄγγελον). Surely this indicates that "the title 'prophet'" is "to be regarded as an inadequate" epithet for John (Suggs, 1970: 45). Note further that though an identification is made about John ("this is he...") in this passage Jesus' character is still in view: for John is the one sent ahead of Jesus' face, to prepare the way before him. Finally, Q's suggestive usage of κατασκευάζειν ("to prepare") in its citation from scripture is also noteworthy. While differing from the Septuagint text that is quoted, this verb is established both in sapiential contexts to depict Wisdom's embodying herself in envoys whom she "equips" to become "friends of God and prophets" (Wis 7:27), and in exegetical contexts to refer to that education which "shapes" the sage (e.g., Philo *Allegorical Interpretation* 2.93; 3.128; *On Abraham* 48). In addition, attentive observers may have detected a play on words evoked by "preparation" as rhetorical "confirmation" (κατασκευή; see Hock and O'Neil, 1986: 72–73, 95, 107).

The reasons for juxtaposing Jesus and John throughout the elaboration can now be explained. The identification of Jesus presupposed in the chreia was intended not to clarify the "message" of Jesus but to heighten his importance as the eschatological "messenger." The original rejoinder in vs 23 emphasized Jesus' sagacity in extricating himself from such a designation, but the new chreia response in vs 22 seems suited to the needs of a rather different situation. Linking John and Jesus together in the chreia, and identifying John as his predicted precursor, serve to merge Jesus' "wisdom" with John's "prophecy." The new chreia and its elaboration are thus designed to establish Jesus along with John as a founder allied with the prevailing currents of their Jewish heritage. Jesus is positioned with respect to the prophetic tradition, as well as distinguished by his appearance at the beginning of that new movement which the Q community imagined itself to be. This mode of representation is an exercise in wisdom speculation (cf. Wis 7:27; and see Suggs, 1970: 33–55), which saw Israel's history as the negative precedent for the Jesus tradition, whose founders and members will be vindicated like the prophets, despite their rejection by "this generation" (cf. Q 6:22–23; 7:9; 11:47, 49–51; 13:34–35; 16:16; and see Steck, 1967; Jacobson, 1982: 383–89; Mack, 1988a: 616, 625, 628, 630–32). The significance of the rationale suddenly begins to emerge. How one stands in relation to Jesus' vindication makes all the difference for this stage of Q.

The saying attributed to Jesus (introduced with λέγω ὑμῖν, "I tell you") in Q 7:28 provides the second *statement by an authority*. The example given by Hermogenes quoted two approved witnesses, and Q does so as well. The difference is that Q depicts Jesus endorsing the truth of his own chreia. This curiosity may well reflect that, for these Christians, authorities were few and far between, and so were "superimposed upon the elaboration from elsewhere" in a "strictly self-referential" way (Mack, 1987: 38; cf. 1988b: 95, 187, 199). The pattern of elaboration explains why this saying comments on vs 26, and not on the citation in between: Jesus' statement is rhetorically the judgment of an expert, sanctioning the thesis put forth to be argued in the rationale.

Like the rest of the elaborated chreia, Q 7:28 is composed of antitheses. Perceived initially, apropos of humanity, there is no one more highly regarded than John; rationalized programmatically, from the perspective of the community, the "least" in the kingdom is "greater" than he. This seems to be a curious mode of authorization, juxtaposing John and the community of Q. For this reason many have sought to place Jesus in the second half of the saying, identifying him as the "lesser" ranked greater of the two (so F. Dibelius, 1910: 191; Cullmann, 1956: 180; Suggs, 1970: 47). That won't work. The prepositional phrase "in the kingdom" is parallel to "among those born of women," and thus it belongs with the adjective μικρότερος ("lesser, least"), not μείζων ("greater"), in vs 28b. "In this case, 'the least in the kingdom' can scarcely refer to Jesus" (Kloppenborg, 1987a: 109 n. 32). The version of the saying in *Gos. Thom.* 46 confirms this analysis: antithetic parallelism binds both halves of the pronouncement together in terms of the theme "among those born"; and the identity of "the little one" who belongs to the kingdom is clarified by *Thomas*'s express qualification "among you."

The logic of the chreia is thus pressed to its limits, for John's question about Jesus' identity has been completely transposed to the latter's bestowal of another's legitimacy. It is terribly important to see that, by having Jesus himself shift the terms of reference away from John and to the community, this saying serves to advance, not simply sum up, the argument. That is why Q placed the statement by an authority in the middle of the elaboration. Jesus' pronouncement actually authorizes the community's own standing. The reference to the kingdom makes a theological argument that ordains their status as the people of God. Therefore, the elaboration is constructed to support those persons who take no offense at Jesus, arguing that his speech-in-character both is sustained by scripture and ratifies the activity of the group.

(5) The parable about the children in the agora in Q 7:31–32 functions as the *statement from analogy*. A "parable," of course, is a "comparison" (McCall, 1969) "taken from the world of common experience" (Mack, 1987: 24). The rhetorical tradition employed παραβολαί ("parables") as illustrative analogues that provided specific instances of some general principle. Q uses a parable about children as an analogy for what "this generation" is like. We have already seen how ambiguous the terms of the comparison are. Certain features may now become clear.

First, the parable makes reference to two different groups, be they competing groups of children who address one another, or "this generation" which either calls to or is unresponsive to the calls of the children. Whereas the Q group was referred to in the preceding statement by an authority, their competition is introduced here. Second, the curious imagery of the parable may now be explained. Why is this generation depicted as being like children, though they are otherwise described as properly *sitting* in—not impishly running through—the agora and formally *addressing*—not boisterously yelling to—their peers? Wendy J. Cotter has shown that the references to (a) sitting (b) in the agora and (c) calling out are well-attested, formal terms for (a) sitting in judgment (b) at the courts and (c) making speeches (1987: 295–302). Q's use of judicial language in a setting drawn from the marketplace of public opinion is surely significant. The analogy presents a scenario in which the conventional wisdom of the daily round is presumed to govern social codes and principles. A childish complaint is lodged as a charge against another group's activity. The contention that some are not dancing to wedding pipes or mourning at funeral dirges suggests that discordant behavior is thought offensive. The difference between what "this generation" expects and the Q group does provides an analogue to the chreia. As with Q, so with Jesus. An affront to the one gives offense to the other (cf. Q 10:16). Disgruntled detractors who take them to task have misconstrued their rightful identity. In keeping with the point of the rationale, therefore, and in building upon the second statement by an authority, the analogy illustrates the reason for Jesus' pronouncements of his and others' legitimacy: the lifestyle of the Q people is really the cause for taking offense.

(6) The discussion of John's and Jesus' activity in Q 7:33–34 provides the *statement from example*. Such paradigms were by definition to be taken from "the arena of history" (Mack, 1987: 25). Together with the statement from analogy, they served to corroborate the truth of the elaborated thesis. This particular example explicates the general comparison that was depicted in the analogy, illustrating in a concrete case the act of taking offense. Characterization is clearly at issue. John and Jesus, who were already named at the outset in the chreia, are specified as the chosen exempla. Their behavior, characterized in an inverse order from that protested to in the analogy, supports that of the Q people. Consequently, they are denounced in terms of opprobrium ("demons, tax collectors, sinners") for associating with persons thought to lack social standing (cf. vs 22; and see MacMullen, 1974: 140; Stambaugh and Balch, 1986: 77–78; Smith, 1989: 474–86). The appeal to John and Jesus is thus designed to present a negative example of the terms of the rationale. The failure of "this generation" in the past to accept John's role or understand Jesus' identity is indicative of the present difficulties confronted by the Q group in its encounters with its contemporaries.

Asserting that John and Jesus have "come" cleverly alludes to the question posed initially in the chreia, though apocalyptic eschatology is nowhere in view. The language of coming is simply required by the narrative to convey that mode of mythmaking which characterized those enlisted by Wisdom as her emissaries to the world (see Bultmann, 1986: 28). Even the designation of "Son of man" specifically ascribed to Jesus is rendered in a soft, generic hue (cf. Q 9:58; and see Colpe, 1972: 431–32). John and Jesus are both characterized as Cynics: the one "ascetic," the other "hedonistic" (cf. Mark 2:18–19; on these two types see Malherbe, 1982: 49–58), act together to bless the community of Q.

(8) The proverb in Q 7:35 serves not so much as an *exhortation* to heed the speaker, which would be inappropriate in the context of Q. Taking a cue from Aphthonius's elaboration, we should rather designate it the "short epilogue" (Hock and O'Neil, 1986: 225) or *concluding periodization*. The claim is made that the thesis proposed as an argument is valid because Wisdom accredits the speaker. To say that Wisdom is

"justified" by her children bespeaks a forensic vindication (see Schrenk, 1964: 211, 214; Lührmann, 1969: 30). Indeed, the term δικαιοῦν ("to justify") trades on the final category of "what is right" (τὸ δίκαιον) that was employed in forensic rhetorical speech (cf. Aristotle *Rhetoric* 1.3.5), defending people brought forth on charges made against them in the past (Mack, 1987: 12, 18). And to say that Wisdom is acquitted by her "children" invokes the Jewish sapiential tradition (cf. Sir 4:11; Prov 8:32; Wis 7:27). John and Jesus are her paradigmatic envoys, but the Q group is implicated as well (see also Kloppenborg, 1987a: 95). The person who takes no offense at Jesus is said to be the least in the kingdom of God; the one pronounced right by means of the elaboration is blessed with the characterization: Wisdom's child.

And so the Q group is acquitted. Their elaborated thesis is claimed to be valid, based on the very structure of the world: in the presence of Wisdom, that symbol of order, anchored in the fabric of creation itself. She stands for the tenacity of social sanity even at the moment of its apparent lack (see Mack, 1985: 139–50). In appealing to her to validate its thesis, Q lays claim to an old order elaborately characterized as new.

5. Conclusion

What then of the chreia? "Chreiai were not reports but highly crafted anecdotes in the interest of a very selective memory" (1987: 39). The pattern of the chreia elaboration in Q 7:18–35 reflects a considerable degree of self-consciousness about what its group is doing. It is aware of the historical gap separating them from Jesus and John. Yet it claims to be overhearing what they were not really a party to. It asserts, albeit obliquely, that the stories in the past are tales told about them. Taking its cues from a characterization of those "founders," Q says it's like that too.

What are the implications of our analysis? Three issues in particular seem pressing. Since these are the direct result of our investigation of Q 7:18–35, a word of explanation about the formation of Q is in order. Kloppenborg has convincingly demonstrated that the composition of Q may be understood in three phases, beginning as a collection of six similarly structured instructional units: (1) Q 6:20b–49; (2) 9:57–62; 10:2–11, 16; (3) 11:2–4, 9–13; (4) 12:2–7, 11–12; (5) 12:22b–31, 33–34; and (6) 13:24; 14:26–27; 17:33; 14:34–35 (1987a: 342–45).[3] This formative stratum then underwent a secondary literary expansion through the addition of several blocks of prophetic and apocalyptic sayings, as well as polemical materials directed against "this generation" (3:7–9, 16–17; 7:1–10, 18–28; 16:16; 7:31–35; 11:14–52; 12:39–59; 17:23–37). Finally, the temptation story (4:1–13) was placed between the prediction of the "coming one"

(3:16–17) and Jesus' inaugural sermon (6:20b–49), moving Q in the direction of a "biographical" presentation of Jesus' sayings.

Our analysis has been concerned with a block of sayings (Q 7:18–35) composed at the second stage of Q (Q^2). The first order of investigation is to analyze other blocks of Q^2 "speeches," to see whether any of them has also been composed according to the pattern of the chreia elaboration. That would enable us to appraise not only the historical origins of the tradition but also its literary developments. Furthermore, we have discovered that earlier traditions have been utilized in the composition of this unit. Q 7:24–26, for example, is a traditional saying, paralleled in *Gos. Thom.* 78, that has been explicated in Q by the addition of two separate statements by an authority (vss 27, 28). The second order of investigation is to inquire whether and how other traditional (Q^1) sayings have been used in the composition of later (Q^2) units. Such an inquiry might be especially illuminating in clarifying our understanding of those pericopae in which textual history and social history overlap but do not mesh. Finally, we have observed that Q 7:18–35 characterizes John and Jesus not as eschatological preachers but as Cynic figures. That finding is startling, not only because the apparent titles "the one who is to come" and "the prophet" are typically thought of as eschatological, but also because this second stage of Q is generally regarded as apocalyptic. Nevertheless, our analysis has demonstrated that the conceptual concerns sustaining this entire pericope are clearly governed by a wisdom way of viewing the world, not an apocalyptic vision. Accordingly, the third order of investigation is to reassess the origins of the Jesus tradition in light of the secondary character of apocalyptic imagination. Q 7:18–35 may well serve to indicate that both John and Jesus have been recast apocalyptically only at later stages of the tradition.[4]

NOTES

[1] In keeping with current scholarly practice, I shall designate the chapters and verses of Q according to their placement in Luke. Thus, Q 7:18–35 = that Q text which is found at Luke 7:18–35 ∥ Matt 11:2–19.

[2] Cf. pseudo-Cicero *Rhetoric to Herennius* 2.18.28; 2.29.46; 4.43.56–44.57; Cicero *On Invention* 1.34.58–35.61; 1.37.67; Quintilian *Education of the Orator* 5.10.1–125.

[3] See the response by Jacobson, 1987; as well as the contribution of Kloppenborg in this volume. A slight reconfiguration of a few passages initially assigned to Q^1 (e.g., 6:22–23; 12:11–12) but which best fit the profile of Q^2 has been put forward by Mack, 1988a.

4 An earlier draft of this paper was presented at Boston University, the University of Michigan, and the Westar Institute. I am grateful to many colleagues for providing me with helpful comments and critical suggestions, especially Sterling Bjorndahl, Jim Butts, Jon Daniels, John Kloppenborg, Burt Mack, Steve Patterson, Vernon Robbins, David Seeley, and Leif Vaage.

WORKS CONSULTED

Bauer, Walter
    1979   *A Greek-English Lexicon of the New Testament and Other Early Christian Literature.* 2d ed. Rev. Frederick W. Danker. Trans. William F. Arndt and F. Wilbur Gingrich. Chicago/London: University of Chicago Press.

Berger, Klaus
    1970   *Die Amen-Worte Jesu: Eine Untersuchung zum Problem der Legitimation in apokalyptischer Rede.* BZNW 39. Berlin: De Gruyter.

Blass, Friedrich, and Albert Debrunner
    1961   *A Greek Grammar of the New Testament and Other Early Christian Literature.* Trans. and rev. Robert W. Funk. Chicago: University of Chicago Press.

Bornkamm, Günther
    1960   *Jesus of Nazareth.* New York: Harper & Row.

Bultmann, Rudolf
    1964   "ἀλήθεια." Pp. 238–51 in *TDNT.* Vol. 1. Ed. Gerhard Kittel. Trans. Geoffrey W. Bromiley. Grand Rapids: Eerdmans.
    1971   *The Gospel of John: A Commentary.* Philadelphia: Westminster.
    1976   *The History of the Synoptic Tradition.* Rev. ed. New York: Harper & Row.
    1986   "The History of Religions Background of the Prologue to the Gospel of John." Pp. 18–35 in *The Interpretation of John.* Ed. John Ashton. Issues in Religion and Theology 9. Philadelphia: Fortress; London: SPCK.

Cameron, Ron
    1986   "Parable and Interpretation in the Gospel of Thomas." *Forum* 2/2: 3–39.

Colpe, Carsten
1972 "ὁ υἱὸς τοῦ ἀνθρώπου." Pp. 400–477 in *TDNT*. Vol. 8. Ed. Gerhard Friedrich. Trans. Geoffrey W. Bromiley. Grand Rapids: Eerdmans.

Cotter, Wendy J.
1987 "The Parable of the Children in the Market-Place, Q (Lk) 7:31–35: An Examination of the Parable's Image and Significance." *NovT* 29: 289–304.

Cullmann, Oscar
1956 "ὁ ὀπίσω μου ἐρχόμενος." Pp. 177–82 in *The Early Church: Studies in Early Christian History and Theology*. Ed. A. J. B. Higgins. Philadelphia: Westminster.
1959 *The Christology of the New Testament*. London: SCM.

Dibelius, Franz
1910 "Zwei Worte Jesu." *ZNW* 11: 188–92.

Dibelius, Martin
1911 *Die urchristliche Überlieferung von Johannes dem Täufer*. FRLANT 15. Göttingen: Vandenhoeck & Ruprecht.

Dodd, C. H.
1968 *The Interpretation of the Fourth Gospel*. Cambridge: Cambridge University Press.

Dupont, Jacques
1961 "L'Ambassade de Jean-Baptiste (Matthieu 11, 2–6; Luc 7, 18–23)." *NRTh* 83: 805–21, 943–59.

Fischel, Henry A.
1968 "Studies in Cynicism and the Ancient Near East: The Transformation of a *Chria*." Pp. 372–411 in *Religions in Antiquity: Essays in Memory of Erwin Ransdell Goodenough*. Ed. Jacob Neusner. Studies in the History of Religions. Supplements to *Numen* 14. Leiden: Brill.

Fitzmyer, Joseph A.
1981 *The Gospel According to Luke (I–IX)*. Vol. 1. AB 28. Garden City: Doubleday & Company.

Funk, Robert W.
1959 "The Wilderness." *JBL* 78: 205–14.

Gärtner, Bertil
1961 *The Theology of the Gospel According to Thomas.* New York: Harper & Brothers.

Green, William Scott
1987 "Introduction: Messiah in Judaism: Rethinking the Question." Pp. 1–13 in *Judaisms and Their Messiahs at the Turn of the Christian Era.* Ed. Jacob Neusner, William Scott Green, and Ernest S. Frerichs. Cambridge: Cambridge University Press.

Haenchen, Ernst
1961 *Die Botschaft des Thomas-Evangeliums.* Theologische Bibliothek Töpelmann 6. Berlin: Töpelmann.

Hahn, Ferdinand
1969 *The Titles of Jesus in Christology: Their History in Early Christianity.* New York/Cleveland: World.

Hock, Ronald F., and Edward N. O'Neil, eds. and trans.
1986 *The Chreia in Ancient Rhetoric.* Vol. 1: *The Progymnasmata.* SBLTT 27. Graeco-Roman Religion Series 9. Atlanta: Scholars.

Horsley, Richard A.
1985 "'Like One of the Prophets of Old': Two Types of Popular Prophets at the Time of Jesus." *CBQ* 47: 435–63.

Jacobson, Arland D.
1982 "The Literary Unity of Q." *JBL* 101: 365–89.
1987 "The History of the Composition of The Synoptic Sayings Source, Q." Pp. 285–94 in *Society of Biblical Literature 1987 Seminar Papers.* Ed. Kent Harold Richards. SBL Seminar Papers 26. Atlanta: Scholars.

Kennedy, George A.
1963 *The Art of Persuasion in Greece.* Princeton: Princeton University Press.
1984 *New Testament Interpretation through Rhetorical Criticism.* Studies in Religion. Chapel Hill/London: University of North Carolina Press.

Kilburn, K., ed. and trans.
1959 *Lucian.* Vol. 6. LCL. London: Heinemann; Cambridge: Harvard University Press.

Kloppenborg, John S.
1987a   *The Formation of Q: Trajectories in Ancient Wisdom Collections.* Studies in Antiquity and Christianity. Philadelphia: Fortress.
1987b   "Formative and Redactional Layers in Q." Paper presented at the One Hundred Twenty-Third Annual Meeting of the Society of Biblical Literature, Boston, MA, 5–8 December.
1987c   "Symbolic Eschatology and the Apocalypticism of Q." *HTR* 80: 287–306.
1988   *Q Parallels: Synopsis, Critical Notes, and Concordance.* Foundations and Facets. Sonoma: Polebridge.

Klostermann, Erich
1927   *Das Matthäusevangelium.* HNT 4. 2d ed. Tübingen: Mohr-Siebeck.

Kraeling, Carl H.
1951   *John the Baptist.* New York/London: Scribner's.

Kümmel, Werner Georg
1957   *Promise and Fulfilment: The Eschatological Message of Jesus.* SBT 23. Naperville: Allenson.

Laufen, Rudolf
1980   *Die Doppelüberlieferungen der Logienquelle und des Markusevangeliums.* BBB 54. Bonn: Hanstein.

Lührmann, Dieter
1969   *Die Redaktion der Logienquelle.* WMANT 33. Neukirchen-Vluyn: Neukirchener Verlag.

McCall, Marsh H., Jr.
1969   *Ancient Rhetorical Theories of Simile and Comparison.* Cambridge: Harvard University Press.

Mack, Burton L.
1984   "Decoding the Scripture: Philo and the Rules of Rhetoric." Pp. 81–115 in *Nourished with Peace: Studies in Hellenistic Judaism in Memory of Samuel Sandmel.* Ed. Frederick E. Greenspahn, Earle Hilgert, and Burton L. Mack. Scholars Press Homage Series. Chico: Scholars.
1985   *Wisdom and the Hebrew Epic: Ben Sira's Hymn in Praise of the Fathers.* Chicago Studies in the History of Judaism. Chicago/London: University of Chicago Press.

1987 "Anecdotes and Arguments: The Chreia in Antiquity and Early Christianity." The Institute for Antiquity and Christianity Occasional Papers 10. Claremont: Institute for Antiquity and Christianity.

1988a "The Kingdom That Didn't Come: A Social History of the Q Tradents." Pp. 608–35 in *Society of Biblical Literature 1988 Seminar Papers*. Ed. David J. Lull. SBL Seminar Papers 27. Atlanta: Scholars.

1988b *A Myth of Innocence: Mark and Christian Origins*. Philadelphia: Fortress.

MacMullen, Ramsay
1974 *Roman Social Relations: 50 B.C. to A.D. 284*. New Haven/London: Yale University Press.

Malherbe, Abraham J.
1976 "Cynics." Pp. 201–3 in *The Interpreter's Dictionary of the Bible: Supplementary Volume*. Ed. Keith Crim. Nashville: Abingdon.

1977 *The Cynic Epistles: A Study Edition*. SBLSBS 12. Missoula: Scholars.

1978 "Pseudo Heraclitus, Epistle 4: The Divinization of the Wise Man." JAC 21: 42–64.

1982 "Self-Definition among Epicureans and Cynics." Pp. 46–59, 192–97 in *Jewish and Christian Self-Definition*. Vol. 3: *Self-Definition in the Greco-Roman World*. Ed. Ben F. Meyer and E. P. Sanders. Philadelphia: Fortress.

Moore, George Foot
1966 *Judaism in the First Centuries of the Christian Era: The Age of the Tannaim*. Vol. 2. Cambridge: Harvard University Press.

Mowinckel, S.
n.d. *He That Cometh*. New York/Nashville: Abingdon.

Quispel, G.
1967 *Makarius, das Thomasevangelium und das Lied von der Perle*. NovTSup 15. Leiden: Brill.

Robbins, Vernon K.
1988 "The Chreia." Pp. 1–23 in *Greco-Roman Literature and the New Testament: Selected Forms and Genres*. Ed. David E. Aune. SBLSBS 21. Atlanta: Scholars.

Schrage, Wolfgang
1964   Das Verhältnis des Thomas-Evangeliums zur synoptischen Tradition und zu den koptischen Evangelienübersetzungen. BZNW 29. Berlin: Töpelmann.

Schrenk, Gottlob
1964   "δίκη." Pp. 178–225 in *TDNT*. Vol. 2. Ed. Gerhard Kittel. Trans. Geoffrey W. Bromiley. Grand Rapids: Eerdmans.

Schürer, Emil
1979   *The History of the Jewish People in the Age of Jesus Christ (175 B.C.-A.D. 135)*. Vol. 2. Rev. and ed. Geza Vermes, Fergus Millar, and Matthew Black. Edinburgh: T. & T. Clark.

Schütz, Roland
1967   *Johannes der Täufer*. AThANT 50. Zurich/Stuttgart: Zwingli.

Scobie, Charles H. H.
1964   *John the Baptist*. Philadelphia: Fortress.

Smith, Dennis E.
1989   "The Historical Jesus at Table." Pp. 466–86 in *Society of Biblical Literature 1989 Seminar Papers*. Ed. David J. Lull. SBL Seminar Papers 28. Atlanta: Scholars.

Stählin, Gustav
1971   "σκάνδαλον." Pp. 339–58 in *TDNT*. Vol. 7. Ed. Gerhard Friedrich. Trans. Geoffrey W. Bromiley. Grand Rapids: Eerdmans.

Stambaugh, John E., and David L. Balch
1986   *The New Testament in its Social Environment*. Library of Early Christianity. Philadelphia: Westminster.

Steck, Odil Hannes
1967   *Israel und das gewaltsame Geschick der Propheten: Untersuchungen zur Überlieferung des deuteronomistischen Geschichtsbildes im Alten Testament, Spätjudentum und Urchristentum*. WMANT 23. Neukirchen-Vluyn: Neukirchener Verlag.

Suggs, M. Jack
1970   *Wisdom, Christology, and Law in Matthew's Gospel*. Cambridge: Harvard University Press.

Vaage, Leif Eric
   1987   "Q: The Ethos and Ethics of an Itinerant Intelligence." Ph.D. diss., Claremont Graduate School.

Vögtle, Anton
   1971   "Wunder und Wort in urchristlicher Glaubenswerbung (Mt 11,2–5/Lk 7,18–23)." Pp. 219–42 in *Das Evangelium und die Evangelien: Beiträge zur Evangelienforschung*. Düsseldorf: Patmos.

Wanke, Joachim
   1980   "'Kommentarworte': Älteste Kommentierungen von Herrenworten." *BZ* NS 24: 208–33.

Wink, Walter
   1968   *John the Baptist in the Gospel Tradition*. SNTSMS 7. Cambridge: Cambridge University Press.

Zeller, Dieter
   1977   "Die Bildlogik des Gleichnisses Mt 11 16f. / Lk 7 31f." *ZNW* 68: 252–57.

"EASTER FAITH" AND THE SAYINGS GOSPEL Q

John S. Kloppenborg
University of St. Michael's College

ABSTRACT

If Q functioned like the intracanonical gospels, serving as the guiding theological statement of a particular community or group of communities, it is necessary to ask what significance the Sayings Gospel attached to Jesus' death and resurrection. Like the other gospels, Q provides a framework for comprehending Jesus' death, but interprets his death corporately, by relying on the framework of the deuteronomistic understanding of prophetic activity. In keeping with the typicalities of Q's sapiential genre, vindication of the speaker is not comprehended as narratible "resurrection" event, but as immanent in the sayings themselves. If one wishes to speak of Easter at all, one must say that what the Markan and post-Markan Easter traditions localize and particularize by narration, Q assumes to have always been a characteristic of Jesus' words as the words of Sophia.

0. Introduction

It has been three decades now since Heinz Eduard Tödt in a few pages precipitated the collapse of the hitherto prevailing opinion that Q was a predominantly paraenetic or catechetical work functioning in the theological shadow of the passion kerygma (Tödt, 1956; 1959; 1963[2]; ET: 1965). Since that time it has become quite usual to speak of "the community of Q" as a definable and autonomous group within primitive Christianity and to assume that the Q document reflects in some important way the theology of a "second sphere" of primitive Christianity uninfluenced by the kerygmatic assertion of the saving significance of Jesus' death and resurrection. Implicit in this is the suggestion that Q represents the main and guiding theological statement of a particular community or group of communities. Or to put matters more succinctly, Q served as a "gospel."

Tödt's work represented an important correction of earlier estimations of the function of Q as purely catechetical or paraenetic, a view which found a major exponent in Martin Dibelius. Reasoning on the basis of Paul's mainly paraenetic usage of the Jesus tradition, Dibelius concluded that words of Jesus were collected and transmitted not, in the first place, for biographical ends or to aid in the articulation of a soteriology, but for hortatory purposes (Dibelius, 1935: 241–46). Only later was the biographical potential of some of the Q sayings exploited. But even so, the theological heart of the tradition was never found within Q. In England, B. H. Streeter and T. W. Manson took similar positions. Q circulated in communities in which the redemptive significance of the passion of Jesus was the central theological assertion. As Manson puts it, "the central thing is the Cross on the Hill rather than the Sermon on the Mount" (Manson, 1949: 9). In such a context, Q could only serve the theologically subservient role of ethical or catechetical supplement to the passion kerygma (Manson, 1949: 16; Streeter, 1924: 292). Thus Q was circumscribed both theologically and hermeneutically by non-Q tradition, and its *Sitz im Leben* accordingly restricted. This view, incidentally, is perpetuated in Werner Georg Kümmel's most recent edition of his monumental *Introduction*:

> ...we must consider that in the Palestinian community in which Q must have originated...the passion kerygma repeated by Paul [1 Cor 15:3–5] was formulated at a very early date and that it attests the redemptive significance of the death of Jesus. In that case the collecting of the words of Jesus could not have taken place in conscious disregard of this basic confession. (Kümmel, 1975: 73)

This misconstrual of the nature of Q was due in part to the pervasive assumption that the passion kerygma was for all practical purposes as old as Easter and therefore self-evidently part of all early Christian preaching. And in part it derived from an overvaluation of hortatory portions of Q at the expense of other portions. Against this Tödt observed that if indeed the passion kerygma was the decisive theological presupposition, then it is curious that Q nowhere alluded to the kerygma. Moreover, Tödt noted that Manson's characterization of Q rested, at least in part, on his assertion that "[a] striking feature in Q is the exceedingly small quantity of polemical matter" and the overwhelming bulk of "positive religious and moral teaching" (Manson, 1949: 16; Tödt, 1965: 244). This, however, simply ignores the significant sections of Q which are sharply polemical (e.g., Q 11:14–26, 29–32)[1] and which display no strong paraenetic or catechetical interest at all. Far from being a catechetical document, Q should be understood as the renewed preaching of the kingdom and as a theological statement in its own right (Tödt, 1965: 241–51).

1. Catechesis and Missionary Preaching in the "Second Sphere"

The thesis that the tradition of the sayings of Jesus emanated from a "second sphere" of primitive Christianity was propounded at somewhat greater length by Ulrich Wilckens (1967:1–20). Whereas in Pauline usage, the sayings tradition was employed paraenetically and presented either anonymously, or as words of the exalted Lord, or as words of the apostle acting with the authority of the exalted Lord or the Spirit, the Palestinian Jesus-tradition was always presented as sayings and deeds *of Jesus*. In the Pauline and hellenistic missionary spheres, the center of theological gravity was the kerygma of the crucified and risen Lord who had become the eschatological mediator, and the few sayings of Jesus that had infiltrated this sphere served only as paraenetic sentences. Wilckens' explanation of this neglect of the Jesus-tradition was a simple one: This form of Christian theologizing had its origins in the circle of Stephen which had had no contact at all with the pre-Easter Jesus-traditions and which was soon separated from those persons who had. By contrast, the "second sphere" of Christian tradition—which was chronologically in fact the first—was represented by the Jerusalem community which continued the preaching of the earthly Jesus. For this circle, the resurrection was not understood as exaltation of the eschatological mediator, but as God's according of eschatological confirmation to Jesus and his proclamation (Wilckens, 1967: 13).

The *Sitz im Leben* of the Jesus-tradition, according to Wilckens, was the didactic activity practiced in Christian synagogues (1967: 12). But at this point Wilckens was unwilling to follow the direction indicated by Tödt. If the Jesus-tradition was transmitted by those who, unlike the Hellenists, claimed continuity with the pre-Easter Jesus, it is unthinkable that the tradition of the death and resurrection of Jesus could be separated from the tradition of his sayings (and deeds). Thus Wilckens argued that the entire Jesus-tradition derived from the Jerusalem community, which employed an early version of the Synoptic passion narratives in the context of cultic recital and the sayings tradition in a halakic context (Wilckens, 1967: 14; 1968: 72).

The presence of the passion narrative alongside the Q material was also assumed by Ernst Käsemann although he rejected Wilckens' characterization of Q as halakic. As long as we "think in terms of the mutual edification of the community or of Christian instruction, it remains absolutely inexplicable why what is undoubtedly the most important element for all time—the narrative of Passiontide and Easter—was omitted" (Käsemann, 1969: 119). The solution, according to Käsemann, was to regard Q as guidance for mission. It was for such a purpose that sayings concerning discipleship and provision for mission in Q 10 were taken up, and that the oracles of Christian prophets came to be transmitted alongside mission sayings in Q. Odil Hannes Steck and Paul Hoffmann took the same view. For Steck, Q was a sayings collection for the instruction of missionaries to Israel, containing pieces of prophetic preaching (e.g., Q 6:20–21), paraenetic materials for the converted, sayings such as Q 6:22–23 and Q 12:10 transmitted for the consolation and exhortation of the missionaries themselves, and woe oracles and threats to be used against the impenitent (e.g., Q 10:13–15; 11:29–32, 39–52). Nevertheless, it was to be assumed that the passion and resurrection stories were also known to the tradents of Q (Steck, 1967: 288).

Hoffmann defends in greater detail the view that Q was a collection used by "wandering charismatics" in their preaching to Israel (Hoffmann, 1975: 333–34), although he parts company with those who hold that it presupposed either a salvific interpretation of Jesus' death or knowledge of the passion stories (Hoffmann, 1970: 64–65). The principal bases for positing a missionary *Sitz* are the character of the collection as a whole and, in particular, the perspective of Q's mission instruction (Q 10:2–16). Hoffmann draws attention to the relatively numerous admonitions to repent, to be prepared and to accept Jesus' sayings, and detects an anti-zealot tone in the beatitudes (Q 6:20–23), the admonition to love one's enemies (Q 6:27–28) and in the greeting of peace (Q 10:5). He also notes the similarities in the description of travelling missionaries in Q and in 2 John 10–11 and the *Didache* 11–13. Each relates stereotypically the actions of coming (Q 10:5; 2 John 10; *Did*. 11.1; 12.1), reception into a house (Q 10:5–7; 2 John 10; *Did*. 12.1–4; 13.1) and greeting (Q 10:5; 2 John 10). The difference in Q's perspective, however, is decisive. Whereas the *Didache* and 2 John give regulations for churches in regard to the reception of travelling missionaries, Q's instructions are for the missionaries themselves (Hoffmann, 1971: 52; 1975: 333). All this, according to Hoffmann, suggests that Q was employed by a Jewish Christian group [*Gruppe*] (rather than a community [*Gemeinde*]) engaged in missionary preaching to the Jewish people.

While Hoffmann's anti-zealot thesis has not commended itself widely, he is undoubtedly correct in noting the signs of itinerancy in Q.[2] Gerhard Dautzenberg, for example, has observed that Q's virtual equation of the hospitality shown to itinerants (Q 10:10–11, 16) with the reception of what they have to proclaim (10:9) betrays a proximity to the actual situation of preaching that Mark, whose kerygma is formulated rather abstractly (Mark 1:14–15), lacks (Dautzenberg, 1979: 22). But what Hoffmann neglects is the fact that Q's mission speech shows signs of redactional reformulation from an ecclesial perspective. Its addressees have been changed from the itinerant preachers to a community responsible for the commissioning and support of those missionaries. Dieter Zeller has persuasively argued, for example, that the prayer to the "Lord of the harvest" (Q 10:2) which introduces the more specific mission instructions (Q 10:3–11) "is not directed at those sent out in vs 3 but at Christians who might be imagined to be gathered for prayer prior to the commissioning, as in Acts 13:1–3" (Zeller, 1982: 404). To this observation we might add that Q 10:7 ("for the laborer is worthy of his reward"), which like Q 10:2 refers to missionaries as workers (ἐγράται), is not aimed at itinerants but at the communities from which they can expect support.[3] In his 1984 Bern dissertation, Migaku Sato even suggests that the whole of Q 9:57–10:24 has been formulated from the perspective of the liturgical commissioning of missionaries, and hence reflects an ecclesial perspective (1984: 444, 454).

Thus it is not simply a matter of Q's containing both mission instructions and sayings directed at a commissioning community. Rather, mission instructions have in the course of redaction been enveloped and bracketed literarily by sayings which reflect a broader ecclesial *Sitz*. The original mission instructions are now enclosed on one side by two (or perhaps three) chriae dealing with discipleship (Q 9:57–58, 59–60, 61–62?) and the community-directed exhortation to pray for missionary preachers (Q 10:2), and on the other by the so-called Johannine thunderbolt (Q 10:21–22) and the appended beatitude (Q 10:23–24). These framing materials serve not to buttress the activity of the itinerants but to undergird and legitimate the existence of the community itself as the privileged recipient of revelation.

Similarly, Q 12:22b–31, 33–34 perhaps contains admonitions which were originally used as counsel for itinerant missionaries, as Zeller (1977: 93) and Heinz Schürmann (1982: 158) suggest. However, in its present literary form the admonitions against anxiety in the face of material want end with the more general admonition to "seek the kingdom and these things will be added to you" (Q 12:31). There is no reason to restrict this saying to wandering preachers—for whom it would be more appropriate to say not "seek the kingdom" but "preach the kingdom." Instead, it is directed more generally to an audience which has adopted (or is encouraged to adopt) a way of life free from material cares.[4] Rhetorically, Q 12:31 belongs with Q 6:20, where the indicative "blessed are the poor" implies an imperative to refuse the customary evaluation of the poor life. Likewise, "to 'seek his kingdom' in 12:31 is not to seek what human cultures typically seek (12:29–30a). Rather, to 'seek his kingdom' is to seek that father, who in 12:30b is said to know the needs of the poor, whose sufficient supply has already been exemplified in the nurture of the ravens (12:24) and the thriving lilies (12:27)" (Vaage, 1986: 7). Nothing here suggests a specifically missionary *Sitz*.

The saying that concludes this cluster, Q 12:33–34, similarly addresses not penniless missionaries, but those sedentary members of the community for whom the temptation to material acquisition is a real one. Hence, while it is true that Q, like Mark (6:6b–13), contains mission instructions, these are now presented within a much more comprehensive framework aimed not exclusively at wandering preachers, but at a community responsible, among other things, for the support and commissioning of such missionaries.

2. The Synoptic Passion Narratives and Q

None of this, of course, addresses the main issue raised by Käsemann, namely, whether or not Q knew and presupposed a cultic recital of a passion narrative. Or, to put the issue a bit differently, if the *Sitz* of Q cannot be restricted either to initial catechesis (to which it is not particularly suited) or mission instructions, and if Q functioned like the intracanonical gospels in the larger context of defining and sustaining the symbolic universe of its addressees, what place did the death of Jesus occupy within the universe of that community?

The assertion that Q knew nothing of the passion stories and accorded no special significance to Jesus' death is sometimes dismissed as an argument *e silentio*. Indeed, Philipp Vielhauer attempts to rebut the suggestion by a *reductio ad absurdum*. While accepting the view that influence of the passion kerygma—understood in the narrow sense of the creedal formula proclaiming Jesus' death and resurrection as a salvific event—is wanting in Q, he observes that so too is it wanting in the Synoptic passion texts (excluding perhaps Mark 10:45 and the words of institution in Mark 14:22–25). But as Vielhauer sees the matter, to follow Tödt would imply not only the necessity of positing a Q community responsible for the transmission of Jesus' words, but the need to posit another community in which Jesus' deeds were related, and yet another which rehearsed the non-Pauline, pre-Markan passion tradition (Vielhauer, 1975: 327). Consequently, like Wilckens, Vielhauer concludes that the passion materials and Q circulated in the same circles, and that Q was employed in the "internal didactic activity" of the community (Vielhauer, 1975: 328).

Plainly the alternatives posed by Vielhauer are not happy ones. But it should be emphasized at once that there is no reason at all to suppose that those responsible for the formulation and transmission of Q were unaware of either the tradition of Jesus' mighty works or of his death. Q takes for granted both Jesus' miracles and exorcisms and those of his followers (7:1–10, 22; 10:9, 13–15; 11:14, 20; 17:6). The only question is whether the Q community thought these events to be worthy of kerygmatic formulation and the answer to this seems to be, No. Vielhauer's argument in regard to the passion stories rests upon the form-critical assumption that the passion traditions circulated prior to Mark as a relatively fixed narrative. Werner H. Kelber states bluntly his objections to this view: "...one cannot speak at all of the 'omission of passion christology' in Q, *as if there had existed a developed text of Jesus' passion prior to Q*" (Kelber, 1983: 192; emphasis added). Apart from a few pericopae such as Mark 14:22–25 (the eucharistic tradition), Mark 14–16 betrays few of the characteristic signs of oral transmission. On the contrary, it represents the convergence of the main Markan *redactional* themes. Thus, according to Kelber, it is not composed from oral units, but from literally hundreds of biblical quotations and allusions (see also Kee, 1975). "Take the scriptural references away, and the story of death has vanished" (Kelber, 1983: 197).

If the Markan passion narrative is a redactional construction (see Donahue, 1976 and Kelber, 1976b), then Vielhauer's dilemma disappears. However, most are unwilling to ascribe such creativity to Mark and, on the basis of the resemblances between Mark and John, posit a pre-Markan passion story. Recently John Dominic Crossan has put forth the hypothesis that imbedded in the *Gospel of Peter* is one such pre-Markan passion story, a narrative which has in fact influenced the composition of the four intracanonical accounts.[5]

If a passion account circulated prior to Mark, the question arises whether Q betrays any significant influence of the theology of the death of Jesus in the pre-Markan narrative(s). If the reconstruction of Q's theology of Jesus' death on the one hand displays no such influence, and on the other, dissents in significant ways from that theology, we could no longer ascribe hermeneutical privilege to those passion stories in respect to Q's theology.

Any reconstruction of a pre-Markan passion account must take into account the frequent quotations of and allusions to texts from the Psalms, especially Psalms 22, 27, 38, 41, 42, 43, 69 and 109. Howard Clark Kee noted over 200 biblical quotations and allusions in Mark 11–16, including 26 from the Psalms in Mark 14–15 alone (1975: 169–71, 183). Most of these texts are used to articulate the motif of the suffering of the righteous one. Allusions to many of the same Psalms appear in the *Gospel of Peter* (Crossan, 1987: 20).

George W. E. Nickelsburg, Jr. has traced the history of the genre of the "wisdom tale" in which the motif of the persecution and vindication of the righteous one came to be expressed (Nickelsburg, 1972: 48–92;

1980: 155–63). This genre, seen in its early stages in the Joseph story (Genesis 37–42), the story of Ahikar, the book of Esther, Daniel 3, 6 and Susanna, is developed further in Wisdom 2, 4–5 and 3 Maccabees. Nickelsburg outlines the salient features of the genre as follows:

> The protagonist is a wise man in a royal court. Maliciously accused of violating the law of the land, he is condemned to death. But he is rescued at the brink of death, vindicated of the charges brought against him, and exalted to a high position...while his enemies are punished.... In the Wisdom of Solomon and the early stages of the tradition that can be extrapolated from it, three important changes occur. 1) The exaltation scene is greatly expanded through the use of materials of Isaiah 13, 14, and 52–53. 2) The protagonist is, in fact, put to death. 3) He is exalted to the heavenly court, where he serves as a vice-regent of the heavenly king. (Nickelsburg, 1972: 170)

The generic pattern may be illustrated from Wisdom 2–5.[6] The actions and professed knowledge of God of the righteous man (2:12–13, 16) prove to be a *provocation* to his opponents who form a *conspiracy* against him (2:12a). That leads to a *trial* and *condemnation* (2:20), resulting in an *ordeal* (2:17, 19) and, eventually, a "shameful death" (2:20). This portion of the story may also depict the *decision* of the hero when faced with the choice of obedience or disobedience to God and his *trust* in God, often framed as a *prayer*. It may also contain a *protest* and mention of *assistance* rendered to the protagonist by helpers. The second main part of the tale relates the *rescue* of the wise man who, in Wisdom, only "appears" to die (3:2–4) but in fact possesses immortality (3:4b). He is *vindicated* in the presence of his persecutors, *exalted* and *acclaimed* (5:1–5) while his enemies react in dismay (5:2) and experience *punishment* (5:9–14).

After a careful consideration of the structure and genre of the Markan passion account, Nickelsburg reconstructs a pre-Markan account on the basis of those elements within Mark 14–15 which are not entirely homogeneous with Markan editorial intention but which accord with the genre of the "wisdom tale" (Nickelsburg, 1980: 182–84). He posits a narrative in which the conflict between Jesus and his opponents had to do with the anti-temple saying (Mark 14:58). The account may have implied Jesus' exaltation at the point of death with Jesus' prayer, expressed in the words of Psalm 22, "followed by an epiphanic sign that marked the fact that God heard him" (Nickelsburg, 1980: 184). The provenance of this account was a group "who understood themselves as a new temple" (1980: 183).

If Nickelsburg is correct, and Q were to presuppose such a narrative, then at least some of the elements of this matrix would doubtless be reflected in Q and some of the motifs characteristic of the putative pre-Markan passion would occur. Of course, Q lacks the narrative format in which the "wisdom tale" is normally expressed and hence cannot provide an emplotted version of the genre of the wisdom tale. There are, nevertheless, several Q sayings which might be seen to cohere with some of the sequences characteristic of the genre.

While there are no elements in Q which express the elements of provocation or conspiracy, the sequences of *trial* and *condemnation* are presupposed. Q 12:11 expressly mentions judicial proceedings, and hostilities and persecution of a more general sort are alluded to in Q 6:22-23; 11:47-51 and 13:34-35. In connection with the judicial proceedings (12:11), the *assistance* of the Spirit plays a role (12:12). *Ordeal* in connection with such proceedings is probably implied by Q 12:4-5 (cf. also Q 6:22-23) and, as in the Wisdom of Solomon, the ignominy of an unjust death is compensated and overcome through the parental care that God exhibits for his own (12:6-7). *Vindication* is expressed variously: the persecuted are, paradoxically, blessed (6:22-23b) and are included in the company of God's prophets (6:23c; 11:49-51; 13:34-35). In spite of opposition, they speak with the voice of Jesus and ultimately, God (10:16), and are the ones who may claim knowledge of God (10:21-22). Both the promise of "reward in heaven" (6:22b; cf. 6:35b) and promise that Jesus' followers will sit on thrones, judging Israel imply vindication and *exaltation* (22:28-30; cf. 13:28-29). Various *acclamations* are present: Jesus and John are identified as Sophia's children (7:35); Jesus' followers are set above the sages because of their superior grasp of revelation (10:21-22); and they are pronounced more blessed than prophets and kings because of what they have witnessed (10:23-24). The predicted *punishment* of the persecutors is evidenced at Q 11:50-51: "The blood shed by all the prophets...will be required of this generation."

It is noteworthy that while Q has many of the elements of the wisdom tale, it consistently deploys these elements in relation to the *collective* experience of the community, which evidently sees itself as continuing the work of the prophets. Apart from Q 7:35, it does not construe any of the elements individualistically with reference to Jesus and even at Q 7:35, John is juxtaposed with Jesus.

Only at the final stage of redaction, with the addition of the temptation story (see Kloppenborg, 1987: 246-62), do elements enter the Q tradition which allow for a privatistic interpretation of persecution, ordeal and vindication, though Q itself does not actualize this option. The devil's challenge "If you are the son of God" (Q 4:3, 9), when seen alongside the provocations of the ungodly in Wis 2:13–18 ("for if the righteous man is God's son, he will help him," Wis 2:18), might be employed in a privatizing interpretation of persecution. Matthew has done precisely this by placing this taunt into the mouths of the soldiers and onlookers at the cross (27:40, 43). But significantly, even at this late stage Q has not actualized the option of an exclusive, personal interpretation of Jesus' death.

While Q shares a few elements with the wisdom tale identified by Nickelsburg, two features of Q stand out. First, the generic components of the wisdom tale that Q does possess are nowhere gathered together or emplotted. This is not too surprising given the genre of Q. Nevertheless, it would be difficult to sustain any argument to the effect that Q's configuration of motifs is due to any influence of a pre-Markan passion story. Even more important is a second observation: The earlier stages of Q betray no influence of the individualizing interpretation of the wisdom tale or its application to Jesus' death. The dominant view of persecution in Q is determined by the deuteronomistic understanding of prophecy and the fate of the prophets (Q 6:23; 11:49–51; 13:34–35), who are treated as Sophia's envoys. As Arland D. Jacobson has amply demonstrated, Q has adopted and adapted deuteronomistic theology as the means by which to comprehend Jesus' and John's preaching, and Israel's rejection of that preaching (Jacobson, 1978; 1982a; 1982b; see also Steck, 1967). Since Q regards both John and Jesus as the children of Sophia (Q 7:35), it seems likely that if Q sees any theological significance in the death of Jesus, it does so through the optic of deuteronomistic theology. On this view, persecution and death are the "occupational hazards" of the envoys of God or Sophia.

As for allusions in Q to the psalms of lament, the evidence is meagre. There is, indeed, in a few Matthean Q texts a slight influence of a complex of motifs deriving especially from Psalms 69 and 109. In Matthew's version of the Q persecution beatitude (Matt 5:11 // Luke 6:22), ψευδόμενοι ("falsely") is appended to καὶ εἴπωσιν πᾶν πονηρὸν καθ' ὑμῶν ("and [when] they speak all evil against you"), perhaps evoking laments such as Ps 68[69]: 5,

> "more numerous than the hairs of my head are those who hate me without cause (οἱ μισοῦντές με δωρεάν), and my enemies who persecute me unjustly have become strong (ἐκραταιώθησαν οἱ ἐχθροί μου οἱ ἐκδιώκοντές με ἀδίκως)"

or Ps 108 [109]: 2,

"for the mouth of the sinner and the mouth of the treacherous opened against me, and they spoke against me with a deceitful tongue (ἐλάλησαν κατ' ἐμοῦ γλώσσῃ δολίᾳ)."

Such "reminiscences" of Psalms 69 and 109, if indeed they be reminiscences, are, however, most likely due to Matthew.[7] The probable wording of Q 6:22b (καὶ ἐκβάλωσιν τὸ ὄνομα ὑμῶν ὡς πονηρόν, "and [when] they cast out your name as evil") recalls not the language of Psalms 69 and 109 but that of Deut 22:14, 19.[8]

In Q's oracle of Sophia (Matt 23:35 // Luke 11:51), Matthew has added to the phrase "the blood of Abel" the qualification "the righteous one" (τοῦ δικαίου) which, as Barnabas Lindars notes, "intended to invite comparison with the Crucifixion of Jesus" (Lindars, 1961: 20). The Q saying itself curiously juxtaposes the killing of the prophets (Q 11:47, 49) and the shedding of their blood (vs 50a) with the mention of Abel and Zechariah (vs 50b) who thus seem to epitomize the righteous who are unjustly murdered. Hence vs 50b introduces into the deuteronomistic complex the motif of the shedding of the blood of the innocent. But as I have argued elsewhere, this conflation occurred not in the Christian redaction of the Sophia oracle, but already in the pre-Christian transmission of it (Kloppenborg, 1987: 145–46). Its presence here cannot be ascribed to influence of a putative pre-Markan passion account.

Although Q 13:34–35 ("behold, your house is forsaken") announces divine judgment on the temple, there is no indication in Q that the community involved thought of itself as a replacement for the abandoned temple. Similarly, while Q indeed speaks of vindication and justification in the face of rejection, it is *Sophia* who is vindicated (ἐδικαιώθη ἡ σοφία, Q 7:35). There is no indication, further, that the locus of vindication is in the death of her envoys.

Thus at precisely the points at which Q might have borrowed motifs from a putative pre-Markan passion account—the motifs of God's vindication of Jesus as the righteous sufferer, the establishment of a temple "not built with hands" and the apologetic use of Psalms 22, 41, 69 and 109—Q does not. Instead, it relies upon the deuteronomistic tradition of the persecution of the prophets, a matrix of ideas which has made only a minor impact on Mark in 12:1–12 (see Steck, 1967: 269–73). It is not simply a matter, then, of Q's *silence* in regard to the pre-Markan passion account (if there ever was one), but of the use of a quite *different explanation* of suffering and the conceptualization of suffering and vindication in corporate terms. In Q we seem to be at a very primitive stage of theologizing the experience of persecution. Jesus' fate evidently was not yet an issue which required special comment. Parenthetically, it might be observed that Q's communal/corporate theologizing is comparable to that posited by Crossan for his "Cross Gospel," although there is no evidence of Q's dependence on the "Cross Gospel" either. Indeed it might be argued that Q's corporate interpretation of suffering is a factor in the "Cross Gospel's" deployment of motifs from the wisdom tale in an inclusive, communal way.

It is tempting to argue that the absence of a specific treatment of Jesus' death in Q is a function of the genre of Q as a sapiential document.[9] Sapiential collections normally do not concern themselves with the death of the teacher. But it must be kept in mind that Q is very far from being "timeless wisdom" like Proverbs. On the contrary, it contains not only chriae which have biographical potential, but its opening sequences in Q 3 and Q 4 impute to the entire collection a biographical cast (see Robinson, 1982: 22; Kloppenborg, 1987: 256–62). Perhaps even more significant is the fact that numerous Q sayings individually, and the collection as a whole, project a "narrative time" which extends from Abel and the beginning of Sophia's sending of the prophets (Q 11:49–51) to the parousia (Q 17:23–24, 26–30, 34–35) and the judgment of Israel (Q 10:13–15; 11:19, 31–32; 22:28–30). Within this extensive temporal framework exists a smaller narrative world defined by the activity of John the Baptist on one side (3:7–9, 16–17; 7:27; 16:16) and the projected missionary activity of Jesus' disciples on the other (10:16; 12:2–12, 22–31; 14:26–27, etc.). To borrow Norman R. Petersen's terms, although Q has only the barest beginnings of "plotted time," it has a rather complete "story time" or "narrative world" (Petersen, 1978: 49–80).[10] Q's narrative world embraces the temporal range in which Jesus' death could be placed. However, Q resists all temptations to plot that particular point on its narrative map. To put matters a bit baldly, Q democratizes Jesus' death by means of deuteronomistic theology, or, more accurately, Q has not yet particularized that death by emplotting it and interpreting it apologetically with motifs drawn from the psalms of lament. There is, in sum, no evidence of Q's acquaintance with the putative pre-Markan theologizing of Jesus' death, and considerable evidence that Q represents a completely independent trajectory of the theologizing of persecution.

3. Resurrection and the Hermeneutical Horizon of Q

The problem of the relation of affirmations of the resurrection of Jesus to Q is perhaps an even more pressing one than that of the "absence" of a salvific interpretation of Jesus' death. Like the death of Jesus, the Easter "events" are not specifically mentioned in Q, either as plotted events, as occur in Matthew, Luke, John and in post-resurrection dialogues such as the *Epistula Apostolorum* and the *Book of Thomas (the Contender)*, or even as events within Q's narrative world, as in the case of Mark's predictions of the appearance of the risen Lord (Mark 14:28; 16:7) or the parousia (13:27).

The significance of Q's silence cannot be dismissed with the simple observation that, as a wisdom document, there is no point at which the resurrection could be thematized. As we have already seen, Q projects a narrative world which compasses the so-called events of Easter. On the other hand, it is hardly imaginable that "Easter" has made no impact on Q, or at least, that the hermeneutic of Q is not determined by some equivalent of what other streams of tradition call "Easter."

It has been repeatedly argued that for Q, Jesus' resurrection was not to be understood as constituting a saving act of God to be thematized in the kerygma. The kerygma for Q still concerns the coming or presence of the kingdom (Q 10:9). But how then is the resurrection understood? Tödt's answer to this is perhaps the clearest and the most widely repeated:

> The resurrection is God's affirmation of Jesus' *exousia* ["authority"]. Thereby the resurrection also is the confirmation before God of the fellowship bestowed by Jesus in his *exousia* on his own. Thus it is comprehensible why Jesus' teaching was taken up again and continued by the community; what Jesus had said had been confirmed by God. (Tödt, 1965: 252)

M. Eugene Boring's work on early Christian prophecy moved this thesis one step further. Boring argued that prophetic and contemporizing forms of speech dominated Q both numerically and hermeneutically. While Q also contained a few historicizing forms, Q is best understood as a "prophetic document from a charismatic community" rather than a wisdom book; it is closer to Jeremiah than it is to Proverbs (Boring, 1982: 180–81). He concludes:

> The historical Jesus was indispensable for the theological understanding of the Q-community. He had been the decisive prophetic messenger of transcendent Wisdom and had been exalted to become the Son of Man. His words, and a few of his deeds, had formed the original nucleus of the Q-materials. But the prophetic understanding of the Q-community tended more and more to focus on the post-Easter exalted Jesus. What Jesus of Nazareth had said became dissolved in what the post-Easter Jesus said through his prophets. If these two categories of material were ever distinguished, they had ceased to be by the time of the redaction of the Q-materials. (Boring, 1982: 182)

Tödt's formulation rests on the assumption that Q already presupposes the pattern of death followed by divine vindication expressed in the archaic formula preserved in Acts 2:22–24 (Tödt, 1965: 251). Richard A. Edwards expresses a similar view when commenting on Q's interpretation of the enigmatic sign of Jonah. For Q, the saying "stresses the continuity of the Son of Man with Jesus, but it is also a statement about the significance of Jesus as the preacher who is now at the right hand of God" (Edwards, 1971: 85). Following Norman Perrin (1968), Boring assumes that Q's identification of Jesus with the coming Son of Man presupposes a pesher exegesis of Dan 7:13–14 by means of Ps 110:1 and argues that this identification can be traced back to Christian prophets, that is, to precisely those persons who were engaged in the active transmission of Q (Boring, 1982: 244–45).

The hermeneutical key to Q's understanding of the resurrection, then, is said to lie in either Acts 2:22–24 or Psalm 110:1. However, if Q's interpretation of persecution and vindication is thoroughly *corporate*, it seems incongruous to balance this with a post-mortem exaltation of an individual, quite apart from the exegetical inconvenience created by the total lack of any use of Psalm 110 in Q. Q seems curiously indifferent to both Jesus' death and a divine rescue of Jesus from death. It is only in Mark 14:62 that the crucial text from Psalm 110:1 is employed in articulating Jesus' post-mortem exaltation unless, of course, one assumes from the outset that the very use of the title Son of Man contains implicitly a reference to Psalm 110.[11]

At this point it may be helpful to comment briefly on the genre of Q and the particular hermeneutic(s) proper to that genre. This is an important issue in this context given the dialectical relationship between genre and content: the form and character of the traditions which constitute a document contribute to an understanding of its literary genre, but at the same time, the genre conception of its compiler (and audience) determines both the principles of selection of the materials and how those materials are to be construed.

I have argued elsewhere that the composition of Q may be understood in three phases, beginning as a collection of six analogously structured instructional units: (1) Q 6:20b–49; (2) 9:57–62; 10:2–11, 16; (3) 11:2–4, 9–13; (4) 12:2–7, 11–12; (5) 12:22b–31, 33–34; and (6) 13:24; 14:26–27; 17:33; 14:34–35. This formative stratum then underwent a secondary expansion through the addition of polemical materials directed against the impenitence of "this generation." These include both interpolations into the instructional units (e.g., Q 6:23c; 10:13–15, 21–24; 12:8–9, 10; 13:26–30, 34–35; 14:16–24) and the insertion of several blocks of prophetic and apocalyptic sayings, mostly formulated as chriae: (1) Q 3:7–9, 16–17; (2) Q 7:1–10, 18–35; 16:16; (3) Q 11:14–26, 29–36, 39–52; (4) 12:39–40, 42–46, 49, 51–59; and (5) 17:23–24, 26–30, 34–35, 37b. Finally, the temptation story (Q 4:1-13) was placed between John's prediction of the coming one (Q 3:16-17) and the inaugural sermon of Jesus (Q 6:20b-49). This final addition had the effect of moving Q more clearly in the direction of a biographical presentation of Jesus' words (Kloppenborg, 1986b; 1987).

The formative stratum of Q corresponds closely in genre to the instruction, a well-defined Near Eastern genre of didactic literature (Kloppenborg, 1987: 263-89). Like the instruction, this stratum of Q is characterized by admonitions with motive clauses gathered into thematically coherent clusters, often prefaced with a programmatic wisdom pronouncement and concluded aphoristically. The secondary expansion of this collection by the addition of chriae which pit Jesus and John against an impenitent Israel did not remove Q from the orbit of wisdom collections as a whole, but it did propel Q beyond the generic boundaries of the instruction. At this stage, Q is at home with a wide range of hellenistic chriae collections and gnomologia. Neither the chriae collection nor the gnomologium was so narrowly defined as the instruction (which is normally dominated by monostichic or binary imperatives). Moreover, the genre of the chriae collection permitted considerable latitude in the content and form of its constituent sayings. Chriae could be simple (attributed) declarations (ἀποφαντικός) on a given subject, either prompted or unprompted, or responses (ἀποκριτικός) of the sage to a question or inquiry (see Theon's discussion in Hock and O'Neil, 1986: 84-85). Chriae were occasionally organized on the basis of a common theme or catchword but more often were gathered without any obvious thematic connection.[12]

According to the "theology" of the instructional genre, the goal of instruction was to inculcate in the pupil the basic values of sagacity, considered judgment and the ability to perceive the divinely created order hidden within the everyday. The acquisition of wisdom was depicted metaphorically as the pursuit of the heavenly Sophia, if one happened to be a Jewish sage, or the assimilation of an ethos which enabled the sage to "speak Maʿat, do Maʿat," if one happened to be Egyptian. In both cases, the source of wisdom is not human ingenuity but resides in a primordial aspect of the divine, either Sophia who is with God at creation, or Maʿat, an associate of Reʿ. Typically, the instruction does not represent the particular wisdom sentences and admonitions as the creations of the sage. Instead, the sage reflects upon received wisdom, penetrating its opacity and formulating counsel and advice on the basis of his or her discoveries. Sir 39:1-9 sets forth programmatically the task of the sage:

(1) On the other hand he who devotes himself to the study of the law of the Most High will seek out the wisdom of all the ancients, and will be concerned with prophecies;
(2) he will preserve the discourse of notable men and penetrate the subtleties of parables;
(3) he will seek out the hidden meanings of proverbs and be at home with the obscurities of parables....
(6) If the great Lord is willing, he will be filled with the spirit of understanding; he will pour forth words of wisdom and give thanks to the Lord in prayer.
(7) He will direct his counsel and knowledge aright, and meditate on his secrets.
(8) He will reveal instruction in his teaching, and will glory in the law of the Lord's covenant.
(9) Many will praise his understanding, and it will never be blotted out; his memory will not disappear, and his name will live through all generations. (Sir 39:1-3, 6-9)

Thus the content of the sage's instruction is doubly guaranteed. As the repetition and interpretation of the "discourse of notable men" it conveys what has been tried and proven by those whose sagacity and character merited them continued respect. And the teacher's wisdom is guaranteed by the transcendental source of wisdom, Sophia or Maʿat.

Some chriae collections also provide instances of the association of the speaker of the wise sayings with a divine source. This motif is present in *m. ʾAbot* 1.1–18, which contains aphorisms and admonitions ascribed to named sages, each standing in an unbroken chain of tradents of the Torah which begins with the giving of the Law on Sinai. The value of each saying is thus guaranteed not only by its association with a sage of repute, but even more importantly, with a specific line of sages through whom the authorized interpretation of the Torah has been conveyed.

With Cynic chriae collections, however, the appeal to a transcendental guarantor is relatively rare, notwithstanding Epictetus' description of the Cynic as a messenger of the gods (*Diss.* 3.22.23, 46–47, 56–57, 82, etc.), a description which may owe more to Epictetus' Stoicism than it does to Cynicism. Nonetheless, the attachment of the witty or wise saying to a teacher of repute functions to undergird and legitimate its authority. And it is precisely as sayings of "men of repute" that these chriae acquire special value for the inculcation of virtue, however virtue was defined.

Although direct evidence concerning the actual use of chriae within Cynic circles is scarce, we may presume that such stories were memorized, expanded and adapted in the interests of instilling Cynic virtues.

That is at least how Theon of Alexandria understood the chriae to work in the context of a school of rhetoric:

καὶ μὴν ἡ διὰ τῆς χρείας γυμνασία οὐ μόνον τινὰ δύναμιν λόγων ἐργάζεται, ἀλλὰ καὶ χρηστόν τι ἦθος ἐγγυμναζομένων ἡμῶν τοῖς τῶν σοφῶν ἀποφθέγμασιν. (Theon *Progymnasmata* 1; Spengel, 1853–56: 2. 60)
Indeed practicing with chriae not only produces a certain capacity with words, but also good character, if we practice with the pronouncements of the sages.

While Theon evidently preferred moralizing and edifying chriae to the sharply anti-social Cynic chriae of Diogenes of Sinope,[13] one of his major sources of chriae, he did apparently maintain the traditional importance placed upon *mimesis* ("imitation") in the inculcation of virtue. If the pupil "practices" with the chriae of "approved persons" (δεδοκιμασμένοι, Spengel, 1853–56: 2. 103) the results will be beneficial.[14]

Legitimation of wisdom sayings, whether they were transmitted in the instruction genre, or in gnomologia or chriae-collections, was a requirement common to virtually all sapiential collections. A variety of strategies was available to deal with the problem: attachment of the sayings to a sage of repute, association of the sage with a transcendent figure or the addition of heroic testing or ordeal stories, especially if the sage was otherwise unknown. If Q began as an instruction and subsequently redaction moved it closer to hellenistic chriae collections, we might well ask, Must Q presume anything of the nature of the resurrection of Jesus in order to undergird its counsels? Neither instructions nor chriae collections appealed to anything of the sort, but contented themselves with an appeal to the reputation of the sage or to transcendental authority.

Q, in fact, uses a combination of the typical strategies of legitimation. Q's sayings are attributed to known teachers, Jesus and John, and they find their ultimate warrant in Sophia whose children Jesus and John are (Q 7:35) and who is responsible for the sending of the prophets (11:49). In the final editing of Q a testing story was added to guarantee further the character of the speaker and to legitimate his sayings.

As in both instructions and chriae collections, *mimesis* also plays a central role in Q sayings. Q 6:35–36 offers the model of divine mercy for imitation and Q 9:57–58 holds out the itinerant lifestyle of the Son of Man as a model for would-be followers. The latter saying might just as easily have been found in a collection of Cynic chriae. But Q's Jesus is not represented simply as the transmitter of wisdom, or a good model for imitation, or even a kind of sage *par excellence* whose wisdom is unparalleled among his peers.

In the dynamics of the instruction the sage acts as the guarantor and perhaps even embodiment of the wise sayings. His or her sagacity and behavior provide a model for imitation and the introduction and conclusion of the instruction frequently contain stereotyped admonitions to heed the sage's words (see Kloppenborg, 1987: 266–72, 276–82). But the sage is never regarded as the exclusive mediator of wisdom. Q, however, associates the acquisition of saving knowledge specifically with attachment to Jesus and his words. Thus Q speaks of "being worthy of me" (Matt 10:37–38) or "being my disciple" (Luke 14:26–27), of calling upon Jesus as κύριε ("Lord," Q 6:46) and of hearing "my words" (Q 6:47). The conclusion of Q's mission instruction positions the ostensible speaker of the words between God and the disciples:

ὁ ἀκούων ὑμῶν ἐμοῦ ἀκούει,
καὶ ὁ ἀθετῶν ὑμᾶς ἐμὲ ἀθετεῖ·
ὁ δὲ ἐμὲ ἀθετῶν ἀθετεῖ τὸν ἀποστείλαντά με.
The one who listens to you listens to me,
and the one who rejects you rejects me;
the one who rejects me rejects him who sent me. (Q 10:16)[15]

The use of the emphatic form of the first person pronoun (ἐμοῦ in Luke, ἐμέ in Matthew) and the a/b/b¹/a construction of each of the first two clauses, which places those pronouns at the centre of attention, make it clear that Jesus is not dispensable in the chain between the preachers of the kingdom (10:9) and God, the ultimate commissioning authority (10:2), but is rather an essential element in that chain. Steck rightly observes that Q 10:16 in effect puts Jesus in the position of Sophia sending the prophets to Israel (Steck, 1967: 286 n. 9). At this formative stage of Q, we are still very far from articulate Christology; but a significant step has been taken beyond the typicalities of the instructional genre.

In the second stratum of Q, this trajectory becomes much clearer. Q 12:8–9 implies a unique mediation of salvation by Jesus by coordinating confession of Jesus with confession by the Son of Man. Q 6:22 declares blessed those who suffer ἕνεκα τοῦ υἱοῦ τοῦ ἀνθρώπου ("for the sake of the Son of Man") and Q 11:29–32 implies that Jesus' preaching is greater than even Jonah's preaching or Solomon's wisdom. The most unambiguous assertion of exclusive mediation of salvific knowledge occurs in Q 10:21–22. This thanksgiving borrows the sapiential motifs of the intimate relation of Sophia and God and of Sophia's exclusive mediation of heavenly secrets and applies them to the Father-Son relationship. Q 10:21–22 makes Jesus functionally equivalent to Sophia.

Sayings such as those mentioned above indicate that it is not just Jesus' *wisdom* that is important, but the fact that it is *Jesus'* wisdom. The question to be asked at this point is, How is the soteriological intensification of Jesus' words to be understood and justified in the context of a sapiential genre?

In his 1981 presidential address to the Society of Biblical Literature, James M. Robinson noted the indifference of the genre sayings collection to the placement of Easter and the hermeneutical shift which Easter occasioned. "In fact it is characteristic of such early sayings collections that they contain no thematic discussion of the turning point of death and resurrection about which the subsequent hermeneutical debate revolved, even though in a sense they straddle that turning point" (Robinson, 1982: 22). Both Q and the *Gospel of Thomas* juxtapose with remarkable indifference sayings which derive from the earthly Jesus and obviously post-resurrectional words. Our inclination to read Q as a collection of pre-Easter sayings of Jesus derives from our knowledge of the later evangelists' placement of Q. It may be doubted whether Q itself intended such a reading. The same may be said of the *Gospel of Thomas*. The "living Jesus" of the incipit is neither the pre-Easter nor the post-Easter Jesus notwithstanding the penchant of later Gnostics to compose post-resurrection dialogues.

The so-called Johannine thunderbolt, Q 10:21–22, illustrates Q's indifference to Easter, at least insofar as it is visualized as a narratable event. The assertion "All things have been delivered to me by my Father" (10:22a) falls in the middle of Q. But this scarcely implies that Easter falls in the middle of Q nor does it mean that "the 'Easter' authorization has been transferred back into the public ministry" (Robinson, 1982: 23). Matthew could place this saying where he does (Matt 11:25–27) because he already projects the *exousia* ["authority"] of the risen Jesus (Matt 28:18) back into his pre-Easter ministry (see Bornkamm, 1971: 208). Luke's redactional association of Jesus with the Spirit at the beginning of this pericope (10:21a: "In that same hour he rejoiced in the Holy Spirit and said...") performs a parallel function for Luke: the pre-Easter Jesus enjoys *exousia* by virtue of his possession of the Spirit, which will be conferred upon all his followers at Easter. But for Q, these options are not open.

Citing Q 12:10, "And every one who speaks a word against the Son of Man will be forgiven; but he who blasphemes the Holy Spirit will not be forgiven," Robinson observes that Q seems to give priority to the Spirit after Easter. He then reformulates Bultmann's famous dictum that Jesus has risen in the kerygma (Bultmann, 1964: 42):

> ...Jesus rose, as the revalidation of his word, into the Holy Spirit. Thus, rather than narrating a resurrection story, Q demonstrates its reality by presenting Jesus' sayings in their revalidated state as the guidance of the

Holy Spirit. Easter is then not a point in time in Q, but rather permeates Q
as the reality of Jesus' word being valid now. (Robinson, 1982: 24)

I have already observed that in neither the formative stratum nor the secondary redaction of Q is authorization of Jesus' sayings connected with vindication after death. Nor is Q interested in Jesus' death as such. Indeed, this is probably an outcome of the sapiential nature of Q's genre. Virtually all wisdom collections trace themselves back to dead sages, but the death of the sage is rarely, if ever, an issue in the genre. Nor do wisdom collections visualize the exaltation of the dead sage, although they may hold out the general expectation that those who live in accord with the instruction will succeed in this life or be vindicated in the next. It is not the death of the sage or his subsequent vindication that interests sapiential genres, but the sage's living presence in his or her words. Hence it is a bit misleading even to evoke the notion of "resurrection" in respect to Q, at least insofar as the term implies a narratible event having to do with the overcoming of an individual's death. The notion of resurrection is absent from Q not because Q already presupposes the resurrection and exaltation of Jesus to the right hand of God as a narratible event, but because this metaphor is fundamentally inappropriate to the genre and theology of Q. What other primitive Christian theologies achieve by means of an appeal to the vindication of Jesus after the cross, Q accomplishes by quite another means.

The metaphor of resurrection—both that of Jesus and that of his followers—is, of course, an apocalyptic metaphor deriving ultimately from Daniel 12 and Isaiah 26. The impact of apocalypticism upon the literature of primitive Christianity is profound but not, I think, ubiquitous. Especially in Q there is a peculiar reserve towards apocalypticism and despite the appearance of several well-known apocalyptic *topoi*, Q does not share the pessimism and dualism characteristic of apocalyptic. The expectation that Jesus' followers will "sit on twelve thrones judging the tribes of Israel" (Q 22:28–30) need not presuppose the Danielic notion of resurrection followed by judgment, but more likely conforms to the expectation of a post-mortem judgment of the wicked in the divine court, such as is found in Wis 5:1–5 or Wis 3:8 ("[the righteous dead] will govern nations and rule over peoples"), or to the general affirmation that "the one who obeys [Sophia] will judge the nations" (Sir 4:15).

Rather than invoking the apocalyptic metaphor of resurrection, Q understands the authorization of Jesus' soteriologically intensified words by implying a functional identification of Jesus and Sophia. Thus the speaker of the wise words is *never* without legitimation for his sayings although it is always legitimation *coram Deo* and not necessarily *coram hominibus*—in the human forum. No special moment of vindication is required. If one wishes to speak of Easter at all, one must say that what the Markan and post-Markan Easter traditions localize and particularize by narration, Q assumes to have always been a characteristic of Jesus' words as the words of Sophia. Sophia's envoy is always justified, and conversely, Sophia is justified in the activities of her children, though this vindication is not manifest empirically in history.

In 1972 Rudolf Pesch put forth the bold hypothesis that the origins of the Easter faith were not to be found in either the empty tomb stories or the reports of Jesus' appearances (1 Cor 15:5–7). The former are legendary and apologetic developments which presuppose a corporeal view of resurrection and the latter should be understood as formulaic assertions of the legitimacy of the witness(es) named in the formula (e.g., Cephas, the twelve, James, etc.). "The assertion that 'he appeared' [ὤφθη] is every bit as much a theological assertion as is the statement 'raised on the third day.' Hence it cannot be equated with 'and was buried' [1 Cor 15:4] on the level of historical verifiability" (Pesch, 1973: 215).

Having discounted the so-called Easter events as the point of origin of the Easter faith, Pesch looks for its origin in the pre-Easter period. He argues, first, that neither the Baptist's death nor those of the prophets constituted insuperable obstacles requiring some spectacular negation or vindication. The death of the Baptist did not apparently prevent some from supposing that he lived on in Jesus (Mark 6:14, 16) and others from promulgating lofty opinions which the fourth evangelist felt compelled to combat. Second, Pesch maintained that it is hardly imaginable that Jesus did not foresee at least the possibility of his own violent death and prepare his disciples in some way for that eventuality. Finally, the work of Klaus Berger (1976) indicates that the notion of the resurrection of a prophet was already available as an interpretive category and that it is likely that this notion would have been current in the circles of John and Jesus (Pesch, 1973: 223–24). Thus it is quite conceivable that the pre-Easter "faith" of the disciples survived the events of Good Friday and led to the Easter proclamation:

> The proclamation of the resurrection of Jesus is then an expression of acknowledgment of the eschatological significance of Jesus, his mission and authority, and his divine legitimation in view of his death. (Pesch, 1973: 226)

I do not wish to engage Pesch's thesis here or to comment on its cogency as an historical explanation of the Easter faith.[16] He has, however, described a scenario which is similar to what I have conjectured for the Q community living already at some remove from "Easter."

In the first place, the death of Jesus was evidently not considered to be an insuperable obstacle, requiring a special moment of divine vindication. The genre of the Sayings Gospel normally displays no special interest in post-mortem vindications of the sage. Jesus' death and the deaths of those associated with God's activity are, moreover, quite intelligible given the deuteronomistic understanding of the fate of the prophets and given a corporate (though not narrative) deployment of motifs associated with the vindication of the just in the genre of the wisdom tale. In both the deuteronomistic tradition and the wisdom-tale, the sage's or prophet's mission ends in failure, at least by any empirical or historical standards, and Sophia's envoys cannot expect a dramatic vindication of their work in history. But the sage or prophet is always justified before God, just as God is vindicated in the sage. The genre of Sayings Gospel here exploits the polarities of the manifest and the hidden, apparent injustice and divine approbation, failure *coram hominibus* and vindication *coram Deo*.

Second, even though Q displays a "soteriological intensification" that exceeds the typicalities of sapiential and chriae collections, there is no reason, nor is there any warrant, to presuppose that the Sayings Gospel would ground this intensification in an appeal to the "resurrection" of Jesus. On the contrary, the soteriological intensification of Jesus' sayings and the authority that accrued to them are not grounded in an event at the end of his life, but instead arise out of the character of his words as words of, and ultimately guaranteed by, Sophia.

The "Easter faith" of Q represents every bit as much a transformation of the pre-Easter Jesus-tradition as do other streams of primitive theologizing. But for Q the *locus* of transformation is the sayings tradition itself. "Easter," if one can still use that term in respect to Q, is not a narratible, temporal event, but a hermeneutical one. In this sense we may say, paraphrasing Bultmann, that for the Sayings Gospel "Jesus arose in his words."

NOTES

[1] Q texts are cited by their Lukan versification. This does not imply, however, that Lukan wording is necessarily that of Q.

[2] The specific nature of Q's itinerancy has been questioned by Leif Vaage (1987: 358–401), who concludes that Cynics afford the closest analogy, and that attempts to distinguish the behavior of the Q group from that of Cynics are misplaced and apologetic.

3 Similarly, when this saying recurs in 1 Tim 5:18 and *Did.* 13.1–2 it is directed not to the wandering missionaries themselves, but to supporting communities.

4 Vaage (1986: 7; 1987: 431–92) has drawn attention to the impressive parallels between Q 12:31 and hellenistic exhortations to a simple, detached life made by Dio Chrysostom (10.15–16) and Seneca (*De beneficiis* 7.10.6).

5 Crossan, 1987; 1988. Crossan argues that rather than presenting the death of Jesus as an exclusive, personal and individual passion, the "Cross Gospel" treats both the death and resurrection of Jesus as "inclusive, communal, and collective for both Jesus and the holy ones of Israel" (1987: 20). See also the contribution of Dewey in this volume.

6 The key elements of the generic pattern are italicized.

7 The participle ψευδόμενοι is not even textually secure in Matthew: it is omitted in D it sy[S] and by Tertullian.

8 See Kloppenborg, 1986a: 38–44 for a discussion of this point and for a reconstruction of Q 6:22–23.

9 Sato (1984: 447–48) makes an analogous argument, assuming that Q conforms to the genre of the prophetic book: "Q, which was formulated consciously in analogy to a prophetic book, therefore probably did not include a passion narrative because it intended to be a prophetic book."

10 The narrative world embraces "the sum of propositions a narrative implies or expresses about its actors and their actions in space and time" (Petersen, 1978: 40). Plotted time, on the other hand, has to do with the selection and arrangements of incidents into a plot sequence.

11 Perrin's hypothesis that Mark 14:62 is the result of a Christian pesher exegesis of Dan 7:13–14 and Ps 110:1 (and Psalm 8) is convincing. However, the conclusion that this represents one of the initial stages of the Christian Son of Man title encounters the objection that Q, which is usually dated somewhat prior to Mark, contains no such reference to Psalm 110 even though some verbal similarities exist between Psalm 8 and Q 9:58. The latter is, of course, is the only Son of Man saying present in the *Gospel of Thomas* (saying 86). We urgently need a re-examination of the Son of Man problem from the standpoint of the results of recent redaction-critical work on Q. For an insightful exposition of the Son of Man problem and tradition history, see Walker, 1983.

12 For a convenient treatment of chriae, see the collection of texts, translations and introductions in Hock and O'Neil, 1986.

13 Mack (1989: 41–42, 45–51) notes the moralizing and edifying tendencies in Theon's presentation of chriae, and suggests that while it was perhaps the Cynic chriae which first caught the attention of teachers of rhetoric, Theon "may stand toward the end of [the Cynic chria's] history of usefulness in the progymnasmata tradition" (1989: 51).

14 For this section I am indebted at many points to Mack's discussion of the function and application of chriae in hellenistic schools (Mack, 1989).

[15] For reconstructions of Q 10:16, see Schulz, 1972: 457–58; Polag, 1979: 46–47.

[16] Pesch's thesis is discussed by Schelkle, Kasper, Stuhlmacher and Hengel in *TQ* 153 (1973).

WORKS CONSULTED

Berger, Klaus
    1976   *Die Auferstehung des Propheten und die Erhöhung des Menschensohn: Traditionsgeschichtliche Untersuchungen zur Deutung des Geschickes Jesu in frühchristlichen Texten.* SUNT 13. Göttingen: Vandenhoeck & Ruprecht.

Boring, M. Eugene
    1982   *Sayings of the Risen Jesus: Christian Prophecy in the Synoptic Tradition.* SNTSMS 46. Cambridge: Cambridge University Press.

Bornkamm, Günther
    1971   "The Risen Lord and the Earthly Jesus: Matthew 28.16–20." Pp. 203–29 in *The Future of Our Religious Past: Essays in Honour of Rudolf Bultmann.* Ed. James M. Robinson. New York/Evanston/San Francisco: Harper & Row.

Bultmann, Rudolf
    1964   "The Primitive Christian Kerygma and the Historical Jesus." Pp. 15–42 in *The Historical Jesus and the Kerygmatic Christ: Essays on the New Quest of the Historical Jesus.* Ed. Carl E. Braaten and R. A. Harrisville. New York/Nashville: Abingdon.

Crossan, John Dominic
    1987   "The Cross that Spoke: The Earliest Narrative of the Passion and Resurrection." *Forum* 3/2: 3–22.
    1988   *The Cross that Spoke: The Origins of the Passion Narrative.* San Francisco: Harper & Row.

Dautzenberg, Gerhard
    1979   "Der Wandel der Reich-Gottes-Verkündigung in der urchristlichen Mission." Pp. 11–32 in *Zur Geschichte des Urchristentums.* Ed. Gerhard Dautzenberg, Helmut Merklein and Karlheinz Müller. Quaestiones Disputatae 87. Freiburg: Herder & Herder.

Delobel, Joël, ed.
1982 *Logia: Les Paroles de Jésus—The Sayings of Jesus: Mémorial Joseph Coppens*. BETL 59. Leuven: Peeters and Leuven University Press.

Dibelius, Martin
1935 *From Tradition to Gospel*. Trans. Bertram Lee Woolf. New York: Charles Scribner's Sons.

Donahue, John R.
1976 "Introduction: From Passion Traditions to Passion Narrative." Pp. 1–20 in *The Passion in Mark: Studies on Mark 14–16*. Ed. Werner H. Kelber. Philadephia: Fortress.

Edwards, Richard A.
1971 *The Sign of Jonah in the Theology of the Evangelists and Q*. SBT 2/18. London: SCM.

Hock, Ronald F., and Edward N. O'Neil, eds. and trans.
1986 "The Chreia Discussion of Aelius Theon of Alexandria." Pp. 61–112 in *The Chreia in Ancient Rhetoric*. Vol. 1: *The Progymnasmata*. Ed. Ronald F. Hock and Edward N. O'Neil. SBLTT 27. Graeco-Roman Religion Series 9. Atlanta: Scholars.

Hoffmann, Paul
1970 "Jesusverkündigung in der Logienquelle." Pp. 50–70 in *Jesus in den Evangelien*. SBS 45. Stuttgart: KBW.
1971 "Lk 10, 5–11 in der Instruktionsrede der Logienquelle." Pp. 37–51 in *EKKNT Vorarbeiten Heft 3*. Neukirchen-Vluyn: Neukirchener Verlag; Einseideln: Benzinger Verlag.
1975 *Studien zur Theologie der Logienquelle*. NTAbh NS 8. 2d ed. Münster: Aschendorff.

Jacobson, Arland D.
1978 "Wisdom Christology in Q." Ph.D. diss., Claremont Graduate School.
1982a "The Literary Unity of Q." *JBL* 101: 365–89.
1982b "The Literary Unity of Q: Lc 10, 2–16 and Parallels as a Test Case." Pp. 419–23 in Delobel, 1982.

Käsemann, Ernst
1969 "On the Subject of Primitive Christian Apocalyptic." Pp. 108–37 in *New Testament Questions of Today*. Trans. W. J. Montague. London: SCM.

Kee, Howard Clark
1975 "The Function of Scriptural Quotations and Allusions in Mark 11–16." Pp. 165–88 in *Jesus und Paulus: Festschrift für Werner Georg Kümmel*. Ed. E. Earle Ellis and Erich Grässer. Göttingen: Vandenhoeck & Ruprecht.

Kelber, Werner
1976a *The Passion in Mark: Studies on Mark 14–16*. Ed. Werner H. Kelber. Philadelphia: Fortress.
1976b "Conclusion: From Passion Narrative to Gospel." Pp. 153–80 in Kelber, 1976a.
1983 *The Oral and the Written Gospel: The Hermeneutics of Speaking and Writing in the Synoptic Tradition, Mark, Paul, and Q*. Philadelphia: Fortress.

Kloppenborg, John S.
1986a "Blessing and Marginality: The 'Persecution Beatitude' in Q, Thomas & Early Christianity." *Forum* 2/3: 36–56.
1986b "The Formation of Q and Antique Instructional Genres." *JBL* 105: 443–62.
1987 *The Formation of Q: Trajectories in Ancient Wisdom Collections*. Studies in Antiquity and Christianity. Philadelphia: Fortress.

Kümmel, Werner Georg
1975 *Introduction to the New Testament*. Rev. ed. Trans. H. C. Kee. New York/Nashville: Abingdon.

Lindars, Barnabas
1961 *New Testament Apologetic: The Doctrinal Significance of the Old Testament Quotations*. London: SCM.

Mack, Burton L.
1989 "Elaboration of the Chreia in the Hellenistic School." Pp. 31–67 in *Patterns of Persuasion in the Gospels*. Ed. Burton L. Mack and Vernon K. Robbins. Foundations and Facets. Sonoma, CA: Polebridge.

Manson, T. W.
1949 *The Sayings of Jesus*. London: SCM.

Nickelsburg, George W. E., Jr.
1972 *Resurrection, Immortality, and Eternal Life in Intertestamental Judaism*. HTS 26. Cambridge: Harvard University Press.

1980 "The Genre and Function of the Markan Passion Narrative." *HTR* 73: 153–84.

Perrin, Norman
1968 "The Son of Man in the Synoptic Tradition." *BR* 13: 3–25. Repr. with a postscript as pp. 57–83 in *A Modern Pilgrimage in New Testament Christology*. Philadelphia: Fortress, 1974.

Pesch, Rudolf
1973 "Zur Entstehung des Glaubens an die Auferstehung Jesu: Ein Vorschlag zur Diskussion." *TQ* 153: 201–28. (Based on a 1972 lecture at Tübingen).

Petersen, Norman R.
1978 *Literary Criticism for New Testament Critics*. Guides to Biblical Scholarship. Philadelphia: Fortress.

Polag, Athanasius
1979 *Fragmenta Q: Textheft zur Logienquelle*. Neukirchen-Vluyn: Neukirchener Verlag.

Robinson, James M.
1982 "Jesus: From Easter to Valentinus (or to the Apostles' Creed)." *JBL* 101: 5–37.

Sato, Migaku
1984 "Q und Prophetie: Studien zur Gattungs- und Traditionsgeschichte der Quelle Q." Inauguraldissertation, Evangelisch-Theologische Fakultät, Bern. Forthcoming as *Q und Prophetie: Studien zur Gattungs- und Traditionsgeschichte der Quelle Q* (WUNT 2/29; Tübingen: Mohr-Siebeck, 1987).

Schürmann, Heinz
1982 "Das Zeugnis der Redenquelle für die Basileia-Verkündigung Jesu." Pp. 121–200 in Delobel, 1982.

Schulz, Siegfried
1972 *Q: Die Spruchquelle der Evangelisten*. Zurich: Theologischer Verlag.

Spengel, Leonard, ed.
1853-56 *Rhetores Graeci*. 3 vols. Leipzig: Teubner.

Steck, Odil Hannes
1967 *Israel und das gewaltsame Geschick der Propheten: Untersuchungen zur Überlieferung des deuteronomistischen*

Geschichtsbildes im Alten Testament, Spätjudentum und Urchristentum. WMANT 23. Neukirchen-Vluyn: Neukirchener Verlag.

Streeter, B. H.
1924   *The Four Gospels.* London: Macmillan & Co.

Tödt, Heinz Eduard
1965   *Der Menschensohn in der synoptischen Überlieferung.* Diss. Heidelberg, 1956; Gütersloh: Gerd Mohn, 1959; 1963²; ET: *The Son of Man in the Synoptic Tradition.* Trans. Dorothea M. Barton. London: SCM, 1965.

Vaage, Leif
1986   "The Kingdom of God in Q." Paper presented at the Fall Meeting of the Jesus Seminar, Notre Dame, IN, 4–7 October 1986. Forthcoming in *Forum.* (Cited in typescript).
1987   "Q: The Ethos and Ethics of an Itinerant Intelligence." Ph.D. diss., Claremont Graduate School.

Vielhauer, Philipp
1975   *Geschichte der urchristlichen Literatur: Einleitung in das Neue Testament, die Apokryphen und die Apostolischen Väter.* De Gruyter Lehrbuch. Berlin and New York: De Gruyter.

Walker, William O.
1983   "The Son of Man Question and the Synoptic Problem." Pp. 261–301 in *New Synoptic Studies: The Cambridge Gospel Conference and Beyond.* Ed. William R. Farmer. Macon: Mercer University Press.

Wilckens, Ulrich
1967   "Tradition de Jésus et kérygme du Christ: Le double histoire de la tradition au sein du christianisme primitif." *RHPR* 47: 1–20.
1968   "The Tradition-history of the Resurrection of Jesus." Pp. 51–76 in *The Significance of the Message of the Resurrection for Faith in Jesus Christ.* Ed. C. F. D. Moule. SBT 2/8. London: SCM.

Zeller, Dieter
1977   *Die weisheitlichen Mahnsprüche bei den Synoptikern.* FB 17. Würzburg: Echter Verlag.

1982 "Redaktionsprozesse und weckselnder 'Sitz im Leben' beim Q-Material." Pp. 395–409 in Delobel, 1982.

"TIME TO MURDER AND CREATE":
VISIONS AND REVISIONS IN THE *GOSPEL OF PETER*

Arthur J. Dewey
Xavier University

ABSTRACT

This paper presents a critical counterpoint to Crossan's recent contributions concerning the compositional development, genre, and theology of *Gos. Pet.* Through rigorous analysis of the various redactional issues, and in conjunction with Nickelsburg's observations regarding the component elements of the stories of persecution and vindication of the righteous, it is argued that the primary compositional layer of *Gos. Pet.* discloses a fragmentary story of the suffering righteous one. This version may well have been a creative response to earlier ideological and political speculations over the fate of Jesus. A secondary layer can also be detected with its own formal characteristics (that of an epiphany story) and redactional elements. A third layer (narrative fragments and redactional ties) further "fills out" the narrative scheme as well as suggests a more specific social definition. The final layer of *Gos. Pet.* appears to have been composed some time after the fall of Jerusalem. A group, identified with Simon Peter and alienated from its Jewish matrix, has once again revised and redirected this "oft-told tale."

0. Introduction

Quite recently the intriguing insights of John Dominic Crossan have shaken many from their exegetical slumber (Crossan, 1985; 1987; 1988). He has taken seriously the challenge delivered by Helmut Koester to begin to write a literary history of all the available gospel materials (Koester, 1983: 62). In particular he has advanced an argument regarding the compositional development, genre, and theology of the fragment entitled the *Gospel of Peter* (*Gos. Pet.*). Since his argument has been presented adequately elsewhere there is no need to rehearse it in detail here. The task of this paper is fundamentally "revisionist." In my opinion there are certain formal, redactional, and generic issues still in question. The answers to these questions may well suggest an alternative construction to the history of the development of the *Gos. Pet.* Indeed, a reassessment of the contents and genre of the passion narrative in *Gos. Pet.* will be crucial to this alternative construction.

1. Redactional Observations

1.1 The Crossan Hypothesis

Basically the hypothesis of Crossan attempts to move beyond the critical impasse set up soon after the discovery of *Gos. Pet.* The works of Adolf Harnack (1893) and Theodor Zahn (1893) have framed the subsequent discussion: is *Gos. Pet.* dependent upon or independent of the four canonical gospels? Crossan has tailored the question further to that of the relationship between the various passion-resurrection accounts (1987: 4). His proposal sails carefully between the Scylla of independence and the Charybdis of dependence. Calling it a "third option," Crossan suggests that the present text of *Gos. Pet.* is both independent of and dependent upon the four canonical gospels. He sees within the text three successive layers which can each be divided into three units.

The first layer, or the "Cross Gospel," has according to Crossan its own textual integrity, generic identity, and theological dignity (1987: 5–6). It is prior to the four canonical gospels and was used by all of them. The following represents the earliest layer (1988: 16):

(1a) Crucifixion and Deposition in 1.1–2 and 2.5b–6.22.
(1b) Tomb and Guards in 7.25 and 8.28–9.34.
(1c) Resurrection and Confession in 9.35–10.42 and 11.45–49.

A second layer can be detected according to Crossan. The following units were taken by the final redactor from the four canonical gospels and inserted into the earlier material (20):

(2a) Joseph and Burial in 6.23–24.
(2b) Women and Youth in 12.50–13.57.
(2c) Disciples and Apparition in 14.60.

It is the final layer which Crossan describes as "crucial," for he sees in this material "the clear fingerprints of the final author and the major textual argument for the complicated three-layer composition" (1987: 5). Each of the following units prepares the reader for what comes later, thereby clearing up any difficulties in making the insertion of later material into the earlier text (1988: 21):

(3a) Joseph in 2.3–5a
    to prepare for (2a) Joseph and Burial in 6.23–24.
(3b) Disciples in 7.26–27 and 14.58–59

to prepare for (2c) Disciples and Apparition in 14.60.
(3c) Youth in 11.43–44
to prepare for (2b) Women and Youth in 12.50–13.57.

First of all, it must be observed that Crossan's work represents a major redactional advance. He has read the text closely and sensitively and has introduced a new vantage point concerning the possible compositional levels of *Gos. Pet.* Moreover, he has brought the literary insight of intertextuality to bear upon the long-standing dilemma regarding the relationship of *Gos. Pet.* to the canonical gospels. It must further be noted that he does not merely observe literary inconsistencies without recognizing the need to place them within the larger issue of the compositional history of the gospel.

1.2 Methodological Considerations

Crossan's provocative insight into the compositional development of *Gos. Pet.* has come about through his recognition of what he sees as three crucial redactional "fingerprints." The strength of such observations needs to be tested more rigorously through a closer redactional inspection of the entire document. It is my contention that a more thoroughgoing analysis of *Gos. Pet.* will raise serious questions as to the redactional and compositional conclusions of Crossan.

There is, however, a prior need to spell out the very criteria upon which one makes such literary discernments. Precisely because *Gos. Pet.* has had so little serious critical attention, an analysis of the entire text demands a clarification of the methodology used to open up the compositional layers of this material. The method which I shall use for this analysis is quite in line with similar studies. First, the apparent compositional aporiae can be recognized by interruptions, shifts, contradictions, or jumps in grammar, train of thought, motif, characterization, audience, tradition, or theology. Second, during the assessment of such compositional aporiae, independent formal units can be determined. They can be teased out according to their formal structure, contents, theme, and possible social situation. Third, with a growing sense of the various aporiae and independent formal units, one can begin to determine more clearly additions and secondary expansions to the earlier material. Fourth, the various elements under investigation will be compared with relevant overlapping and parallel material. Thus, for example, a direct comparison with *P. Oxy.* 2949 may be indicated in the case of overlapping material, while a comparison of *Gos. Pet.* with analogous compositional developments in the gospel traditions (such as the Gospel of John) might well be of immense assistance. Fifth, upon a determination of the various units in the text, one must then discern the various levels of compositional development and by what principles of composition they have been combined.

1.3 Redactional Analysis

Gos. Pet. 2.3 interrupts what we now possess as a fragmented beginning:

> 1.1 ...of the Jews no one washed his hands, neither Herod nor any one of his judges. Since they were unwilling to wash, Pilate stood up.
> 1.2 Then Herod the king ordered the Lord to be taken away, saying to them, "What I commanded you to do to him, do (it)."
> 2.3 *Now Joseph stood there, the friend of Pilate and the Lord, and when he realized that they were about to crucify him, he went to Pilate and asked for the body of the Lord for burial.*
> 2.4 And Pilate sent to Herod and asked for his body.

Not only is Joseph introduced as a new character in the narrative (Ἱστήκει δὲ ἐκεῖ Ἰωσήφ) but also the concern for burial before the death of Jesus is quite different from the Synoptic versions. Crossan has rightly suggested that 6.23–24 are anticipated by this interpolation of Joseph material (1985: 133):

> 6.23 Now the Jews rejoiced and gave his body to Joseph so that he might bury it, since he had seen how much good he had done.
> 6.24 He took the Lord, and washed (him) and wound (him) in linen and brought (him) to his own tomb called "Garden of Joseph."

However, certain other points need be made. First, Pilate and Herod no longer seem to be in the same place. The narrative of 2.3–4 would definitely suggest different locations for Joseph and Pilate ("and Pilate sent to Herod") and for Herod. Yet, there is no hint of this in 1.2. Second, the concern for the burial of the body of the Lord becomes a matter of legal observance in 2.5b:

> ...since the sabbath is drawing near. For it is written in the Law, "The sun shall not set upon one who has been killed."

Indeed, we find in 2.5b the only self-conscious use of scripture in Gos. Pet. (This recurs in 5.15b,c, and is implied in 6.22, 23a.) These observations become even more curious when we bring P. Oxy. 2949 into play. From this quite fragmentary material we can see some very interesting similarities with Gos. Pet. 2.3–5 (Browne, 1972: 15–16):

Frg. (1)

1		]τ[
2		abraded
3		]ν..[
4		abraded
5		]οφιλοσπ[.]ιλα[.]ου.[
		]ὁ φίλος Π[ε]ιλά[τ]ου .[
	cf. Gos. Pet. 2.3	ὁ φίλος Πειλάτου καὶ τοῦ κυρίου
6		].ισοτιεκελευσεν[
		].ις ὅτι ἐκέλευσεν [
	cf. Gos. Pet. 2.3	εἰδὼς ὅτι σταυρίσκειν αὐτὸν μέλλουσιν
7		]θωνπροσπειλατο[
		ελ]θὼν πρὸς Πειλᾶτο[ν
	cf. Gos. Pet. 2.3	ἦλθεν πρὸς τὸν Πειλᾶτον
8		]..σωμαεισταφην[
		]τὸ σῶμα εἰς ταφὴν [
	cf. Gos. Pet. 2.3	τὸ σῶμα τοῦ κυρίου πρὸς ταφήν
9		]ηνητησα[
		Ἡρῴδ]ην ᾐτήσα[το
	cf. Gos. Pet. 2.4	πρὸς Ἡῴδην ᾔτησεν
10		]ηναιειπω[
		]ηναι εἰπὼ[ν
	cf. Gos. Pet. 2.5 (?)	ὁ Ἡρῴδης ἔφη
11		]αιτησα.[
		]αιτησα.[
	cf. Gos. Pet. 2.5	τις αὐτὸν ᾐτήκει
12		]αυτον[
		]αὐτὸν[
13		].οτια[
		]. ὅτι α[

Frg. (2)

14		μου[
		μου[
15		πειλ[
		Πειλ[ατ-
16		τισα[
		τις α[ὐτὸν (?)
	cf. Gos. Pet. 3.8	τις αὐτῶν

17	μεν[
	μεν[
18	.[
	.[

It is clear that we do not have the exact same material (Lührmann, 1981). Nor can we say that there is any indication of the scriptural citation found in *Gos. Pet.* 2.5. We can also agree with R. A. Coles (Browne, 1972: 16) that this material does seem to indicate a petition for the body before the execution. What I would conclude from all this at present is that 2.3–4 may well represent not simply a redactional preparation which Crossan rightly suggests but also a fragment of an independent tradition of which *P. Oxy.* 2949 is a variant. Moreover, the Joseph material may well have been originally circulated as a whole (such as found in Mark 15:42–47) but with the differences in the time of the petition for the body and the role of Herod. If that is so, we may well see in *Gos. Pet.* 2.3–4; 6.23–24 a redactional split of previously united material. For the sake of identification we shall call this block of material the "Joseph Fragment."

The Joseph Fragment

2.3 Now Joseph stood there, the friend of Pilate and the Lord, and when he realized that they were about to crucify him, he went to Pilate and asked for the body of the Lord for burial.

2.4 And Pilate sent to Herod and asked for his body.

6.23b ...and gave his body to Joseph so that he might bury it, since he had seen how much good he had done.

6.24 He took the Lord, and washed (him) and wound (him) in linen and brought (him) to his own tomb called "Garden of Joseph."

Furthermore, because of the points just advanced, I would also contend that 2.5a,b represent a further addition to this redactional activity:

And Herod said, "Brother Pilate, even if no one had asked for him, we would have buried him, since the sabbath is drawing near. For it is written in the Law, 'The sun shall not set upon one who has been killed.'"

As we move from 2.5b we can discern a rather curious phenomenon. With the exception of the title "the Lord" (3.6, 8; 4.10; 5.19; 6.21) we have no other instance of proper names or titles until 6.23. The antagonists of the Lord are presented in a fashion quite similar to those anonymous antagonists of the just one in Wisdom of Solomon 2–5.

Second, in 5.15b,c we have a resumption of the concern for the burial according to religious convention (cf. 2.5):

and they were confused and anxious that the sun had set, since he was still alive. <For> it is written for them, "The sun shall not set upon one who has been killed."

If this is from the same hand as 2.5a,b, then we could also remove this as a redactional level.

Third, the various reactions to the death of the Lord must be noted. Besides the seismic shocks (5.20; 6.21), we have "the Jews rejoicing" that the sun had not set in 6.23a, the "Jews, elders and priests" considering the implications of their deed (7.25), the weeping and hiding of Simon Peter and company (7.26), and the report of the "scribes, pharisees and priests" of the repentance of the people (8.28). I would argue that 6.23a ("now the Jews rejoiced") is of the same redactional hand as that found in 2.5a,b, and 5.15b,c. The removal of 6.23a would not interrupt the Joseph legend material. Indeed, the original subject who "gave" the body to Joseph may well have been either Herod or Pilate. (Does *P. Oxy.* 2949 line 10 cited above have any bearing on this? Cf. Matt 27:58b.) Moreover, the presence of 6.22 ("then the sun shone and it was found to be the ninth hour") may well be simply there for the reaction of 6.23a, in light of what was said in 5.15a ("it was midday and darkness covered all Judea"). While Jürgen Denker (1975: 70) has quite rightly argued for a prophetic background for 5.15a (cf. Amos 8:9–10), 6.22, however, moves beyond this to a more historicized description. I would connect 6.23b–24 with 2.3–4 and separate this out as a later redactional level.

Fourth, 7.25 certainly needs consideration:

> 7.25 Then the Jews and the elders and the priests knew what evil they had done to themselves, and began to beat their breasts and say, "Woe for our sins, for the judgment and the end of Jerusalem has come near."

This seems to contradict the reaction of 6.23a, while at the same time being quite different from the other reaction indicated in 8.28a, 29, 30:

> 8.28 When the scribes and the pharisees and the priests gathered together with one another, having heard that all the people were murmuring and beating their breasts, saying, "If by his death these very great signs have happened, see how just he was,"
> 8.29 they became frightened...and went to Pilate, entreating him and saying,
> 8.30 "Give us soldiers so that <we> may guard his tomb for three (days), lest his disciples come and steal him and the people assume that he is risen from the dead and do us harm."

Moreover, the explicit mentioning of the end of Jerusalem may well give us a basis for the dating of this material. But more of this later. At this point I would suggest that this reaction is not only different but also suggests another redactional level. 7.26–27 also interrupt the narrative with the introduction of the first person singular and plural (cf. 14.59–60). This is the first time we have had any indication of the disciples of the Lord:

> 7.26 But I with my friends wept, and quivering with fear in our hearts, we hid ourselves; for we were sought by them as criminals and as ones wishing to burn down the temple.
> 7.27 In addition to all these things, we fasted and sat mourning and weeping night and day until the sabbath.

We should also note that 7.26b may well be linked to the previous verse. The suspicion of "wishing to burn down the temple" would place it within the same range as 7.25.

Fifth, with 6.22–7.27 removed on redactional grounds, 8.28 becomes the reaction to the events surrounding the crucifixion. I would argue that 8.28b is the more original reaction:

> all the people were murmuring and beating their breasts, saying, "If by his death these very great signs have happened, see how just he was,"

with 8.28a being a redactional tie:

> When the scribes and the pharisees and the priests gathered together with one another, having heard that....

Notice that "the people" repent at seeing the "great signs" which had been given in 5.15a, 18, 20; 6.21. Further, the term "the people" mentioned at the end of the passion events also comes at the beginning of the passion material (2.5c: "and he handed him over to the people...").

2. The Question of Genre

2.1 The Generic Components of the Persecution Story

In light of these observations it is now important to concentrate on the material still intact. I contend that what we find in *Gos. Pet.* 2.5c–5.15a; 5.16–6.21; 8.28b is an early passion narrative which recounts the death and exaltation of the Lord through the employment of the genre of the story of the just one. While I agree with Crossan (1987: 12) that the observations of George W. E. Nickelsburg, Jr., are most appropriate for *Gos. Pet.*, I would argue that a level, earlier than the first level presented by Crossan, can be detected. The best way of seeing this is to use what Nickelsburg has determined as the generic components of the Stories of Persecution and Vindication. This will allow us to do two things. First, we shall be able to discern a basic pattern within the material under consideration. Second, and equally significant, we can go on to see how and why the various secondary elements have been inserted into what we now call *Gos. Pet.* The following breakdown of the material under discussion is made according to Nickelsburg's narrative elements or components, most of which describe "actions," while a few of them present "emotions." The components perform particular functions within the flow and logic of the story (Nickelsburg, 1980: 153–84).

CONDEMNATION: Here the protagonist is formally condemned to death:

> And he handed him over to the people on the day before the unleavened bread, their feast. (2.5c)

ORDEAL: The protagonist's imminent destruction becomes a test of his claims or validity. This component includes some expression by the antagonists such as, "Let us (or: we will) see...":

> Taking the Lord, they pushed him; and running (along), they said, *"Let's drag the son of God along,* since we have power over him." (3.6)

INVESTITURE, ACCLAMATION: In the usual format the *investiture* comes upon the *vindication* and *exaltation* of the protagonist. The character is appropriately invested with royal robes. The new status of the protagonist is then acclaimed. Here, however, we have in ironic fashion an "enthronement." The *acclamation* may also be an indirect indication of the *accusation*, which we do not have in this fragment:

> And they threw a purple robe around him and sat him upon the judgment seat and said, "Judge justly, king of Israel." And one of them brought a crown of thorns and set it on the head of the Lord. (3.7, 8)

ORDEAL: The testing continues. What we have here is quite reminiscent of the Servant Songs of Isaiah and the revision in the Wisdom of Solomon. The testing of a "son of God" is paramount:

> And others standing about spit in his eyes, and some slapped his face, others poked him with a reed, and some scourged him as they said, "With such honor let us honor the son of God." And they brought two criminals and crucified the Lord in their midst. (3.9; 4.10a)

REACTION: Reactions, both positive and negative, in this genre occur at different points and in different fashions. Here the reaction of the Lord suggests the trust and obedience of the just sufferer:

> But he himself remained silent, as if in no pain. (4.10b)

ACCLAMATION: In contrast to the usual format, an ironic angle is present in the superscription. We may have another intimation of the *accusation*:

> And when they set up the cross, they wrote on (it), "This is the king of Israel." (4.11)

REACTION: Here we see the varied reactions to the fate of the just one:

> And setting his clothing in front of him they divided it among themselves, and they cast lots for them. A certain one of those criminals reproached them and said, "We're suffering so for the evil that we've done, but this one, who has become a savior of humanity, what wrong has he done to you?" And becoming angry at him, they ordered that his legs not be broken so that he might die in agony. (4.12–14)

PUNISHMENT: The corollary of the vindication of the righteous one is the punishment and destruction of the antagonists. Just as the investiture is anticipated here so also is the reaction of nature (cf. Wis 5:17, 20):

> It was midday and darkness covered all Judea; and they were confused. (5.15a)

ORDEAL: This may well be the coup de grace (could the drink be understood as poisonous?):

> And one of them said, "Give him bitters with vinegar to drink." And mixing it, they gave it to him to drink. (5.16)

PUNISHMENT: Further indications of the punishment towards the antagonists are made. These also are anticipations (cf. Wis 4:20):

> And they fulfilled all things and brought to completion the sins on their head. Now many went about with lamps, thinking that it was night, (and) took their rest. (5.17, 18)

PRAYER: Within this genre the righteous one will express his innocence, frustration, or trust in prayer. Here the cry of abandonment can be seen as a prayer for deliverance:

> And the Lord cried out, saying, "My power, (my) power, you have abandoned me." (5.19a)

RESCUE: Usually the protagonist is delivered at the very brink of death. Only in Wis 3:2–4 and 2 Maccabees 7 are there "post mortem" *rescues*. Here the *rescue* is combined with an *exaltation*, which in most cases occurs in a court setting:

> When he said (this), he was taken up. (5.19b)

VINDICATION: In this component the protagonist is shown to have been right or innocent. The vindication, as is the case here, may be demonstrated by the turn of events:

> And at the same time, the veil of the temple of Jerusalem was torn in two. And then they pulled the nails from the Lord's hands and set him on the ground. And the entire ground shook and there was great fear. (5.20–6.21)

REACTION/ACCLAMATION: The antagonists' wonder and astonishment over the *rescue* and *vindication* of the protagonist are noted. This surprise is a consequence of the antagonists' assumptions suggested in the *ordeal*. Here the people, upon witnessing the seismic events, declare the Lord to be "just" and repent of their action:

> All the people were murmuring and beating their breasts, saying, "If by his death these very great signs have happened, see how just he was." (8.28b)

What we have, then, is a narrative which manifests many of the generic components of the story of persecution and vindication. In contrast to the prevailing style of this tradition (e.g., 2 Maccabees 7, where specific characters are given for protagonists and antagonists), this story apparently follows more closely the narrative style of the Wisdom of Solomon, where the only one entitled is the "just one," the "son of God." With the use of the title "the Lord" we are only one step removed from a reading of the story of the righteous one as a type.

2.2 Questions and Complications

We also must note that some rather significant components of this genre are missing, such as *provocation, conspiracy,* and *accusation*. One could simply point out that the fragmentary nature of the evidence precludes them. On the other hand, as I have noted above, there may well be some indirect indications regarding the charges leveled against the "just one." In 3.7b and 4.11 we have such a possibility in the title "king of

Israel." Could there have been some prior material which served as a *provocation*, leading to such a charge? Of course, one must further take into consideration that, in the tradition of this genre, such an *accusation* would be from the outset subject to misapprehension and probable irony. In other words, it may not even have been a direct claim to kingship which provoked the action. Such language may better represent the misinterpreted response of the "people."

This last point raises a further question over the term ὁ λαός ("the people"). Why is it that this primary level of narrative has such a collective term? Would this not be an indication of a later tradition? Is this usage simply in line with the style of the antagonists found, for example, in Wisdom of Solomon 2–5? Could there be some clue here for a better understanding of this narrative?

Finally, does the term παρέδωκεν ("he handed over") (2.5c) give us any possibility of seeing a *conspiracy* at work, despite the fact that the earlier material is nonexistent? Who is to be understood as the one who hands the Lord over? In the later version this ambiguity is cleared up. Could there even be some sense of an originally divine or fated "handing over"? In pointing out how the term παραδιδόναι did not refer in Paul (1 Cor 11:23) to betrayal but to a martyr's fate, Burton L. Mack (1988: 299) has argued that Mark took full advantage of the narrative potential of that term to connect cultic meal etiology with the wisdom tale of persecution. In this regard, the character Judas both fills out the tale and furthers the narrative complication of Mark. Could we see in *Gos. Pet.* an earlier attempt of amplifying the notion of a martyr's fate?

Now Nickelsburg has offered an hypothesis of a pre-Markan passion narrative, which already employed the genre of the story of the righteous one (1980: 183). In this hypothetical story there would have been the use of a "Wisdom christology" to explain how the death and exaltation of Jesus spelled the end for the old order, particularly the temple authorities. The threat to destroy and rebuild the temple would be placed upon Jesus' lips. The *provocation* for the subsequent action and vindication would certainly be there. In light of his creative suggestion, one could argue that this primary narrative of *Gos. Pet.* follows according to Nickelsburg's hypothesis. One could even point to 5.20 where the visible vindication would entail the temple.

There are serious problems with this position. First, unlike Mark 15:38, there are more elements of *vindication* here than the tearing of the temple curtain. 6.21 speaks of seismic shocks as well. Second, there is no argument, at this level, against temple authorities; on the contrary, the "people" figure as the antagonists. Third, even if the charge is skewed, the question of the title "king of Israel" cannot be overlooked. The indirect *accusation* may well suggest as a provocative action some deed or claim for kingship.

A possible solution may be found by a close inspection of the taunt of 3.7: "Judge justly, king of Israel." I have argued that this line functions as part of the *ordeal* of the righteous sufferer. However, if we move for a moment to the content of the material, and ask the question of possible traditions lurking in this language, what can be determined? Is there a tradition which contains a just ruler, some provocation or testing, and an emphasis on the "people"? At this point I would suggest that what we see here is rather reminiscent of the tradition surrounding the judges of the people of Israel. Indeed, in Judg 2:6–3:6 we have not only an interesting resume of the cyclic apostasy, enslavement, and deliverance of the people by the judges but also a telling vocabulary. Here the people provoke the Lord into handing them over (παρέδωκεν, 2:14) to their despoilers. It is the Lord who hears their groaning and raises up judges as saviors of the people of Israel (2:18; 3:9). This time is seen as a moment of testing of Israel (2:22).

Yet, the story given in the primary level of *Gos. Pet.* does not exactly square with the earlier tradition. This point may be the most significant for my argument. By this I mean that what the narrative of *Gos. Pet.* is presenting may well be a response to a previous ideological understanding, which might have echoed or played upon such an ancient tradition. Denker has observed (1975: 58–77), as both Crossan (1985: 138–39) and Koester (1980: 127–28) agree, that behind the passion material of *Gos. Pet.* we have some school activity upon a limited number of texts from the prophets and psalms. I would suggest, in addition, that the ideology coming from the ancient Israelite tradition may well have played a decisive part in this literary (and political) picture. The narrative of the suffering righteous one, however, has already transmuted what might have been a previous interpretation of the message and action of Jesus of Nazareth. Here the recent work of Richard A. Horsley may well have a bearing. Horsley has argued rather convincingly the political reality and implications of Jesus' practice and preaching of the kingdom of God (1987: 201–8). The concern for God's rule could have been understood quite well within the "judges" tradition wherein the people of Israel reassert their independence from conquerors or exploiters. However, the problematic moment comes when such a "savior" or proclaimer of this manifestation of God's justice meets his doom. What the narrative of *Gos. Pet.* has done is to face squarely this ultimate test through the application of the genre of the suffering righteous one. From a rather different angle Mack has suggested the possibility of a formation of a "congregation of Israel" wherein what was happening to certain

Galilean elements of the Jesus movements was interpreted from the epic and haggadic readings of the scriptures, not from the model of Israel as a temple state based on cultic law (1988: 224). Could this application of the persecution story have been a turning point in the process of that social formation? Moreover, could this introduction of the wisdom tale have come through Antiochene influence where Jewish piety was "anchored in images drawn from the epic traditions," was not interested in a restoration of the Second Temple pattern, and was reconceptualizing in 4 Maccabees and the Wisdom of Solomon the righteousness of Israel (1988: 108)? Thus, I would not find it improbable, despite Mack's assertion (1988: 268), that there was a pre-Markan narrative which may well have influenced Mark's creative construction. I would agree, however, with Mack that this would not be some historical kernel, substantiating early kerygma. Rather, even before Mark's contribution, the fictional nucleus of a passion narrative had emerged.

This attempt at a creative response to the shock of Jesus' fate may well be recognized in what Nickelsburg has also noted for the Gospel of Mark, namely, anticipated elements within the *ordeal* itself (1980: 174–76). We have seen both positive and negative elements. *Punishment* and *investiture/acclamation* are present in the very midst of disaster. Moreover, the *exaltation* is given solely in the verb "he was taken up" (ἀνελήφθη). *Vindication* comes not in the heavenly realms but through earthly wonders. In effect, the future (or otherworldly) focus found in the Wisdom of Solomon, for example, is brought directly before the eyes of the "people." The reason for such a dramatic departure from the usual format may well be this intent to redefine radically the fate of Jesus and his fractured claims (could the παρέδωκεν of 2.5c carry with it now a theological weight?). In attempting to assess the meaning of Jesus, already couched in the political trappings of a reformist ideology, the writer turns the naiveté of the earlier tradition against itself and presents a critical opportunity for revision by the people themselves (8.28b).

3. The Retelling of the Tale

3.1 The Epiphany Material

It is incumbent upon this writer to fill out the compositional history of *Gos. Pet.* so that the above argument might be seen as fully as possible. The haunting issue of genre is still before us. Is it possible to discern why the other material in *Gos. Pet.* has been added and at what level? Does the contention of a basic story of persecution and vindication enable us to see any possibilities?

In order to come to some determination of these questions we must return to a further critical appraisal of the remaining verses in *Gos. Pet.*

First of all, we must agree with Crossan that the pre-narrative scribal activity is not in evidence once we move away from the passion narrative into the burial account (1985: 180–81). Second, while 8.28–11.49 appear to be a self-contained unit, beginning with the various leaders of the Jews going to Pilate and then returning to him (in both cases urging him to issue a command: 8.30–31; 11.47, 49), there are significant problems with simply maintaining that, with the removal of 11.43–44 as a redactional anticipation, this is a single compositional piece on one historical level. I have already argued for the earlier status of 8.28b. Then there is 10.41–42 which seems to come literally out of the blue! Crossan has rightly argued that 10.44 prepares for 12.50–13.57, with no other reason for its existence at that place in the narrative (1985: 134). Further, 11.46 is quite unexpected from the immediately preceding verse:

> 11.45 When those in the centurion's company saw these things, they rushed by night to Pilate, having left the tomb which they were guarding, and they explained all that they had seen, being greatly disturbed and saying, "Truly, he was a son of God!"
> 11.46 Pilate answered and said, "I am clean of the blood of the son of God; but this was decided by you."
> 11.47 Then they all arrived and were beseeching and urging him to order the centurion and his soldiers to tell no one what they saw.

Pilate is not even speaking to those witnesses but is actually speaking of matters that would make sense to those who will not have arrived until the next verse (11.47)! Pilate's declaration of innocence ties in with 1.1:

> 1.1 …of the Jews no one washed his hands, neither Herod nor any one of his judges. Since they were unwilling to wash, Pilate stood up.

One could also say that the notion of purity/defilement registered in 11.46 continues in 11.48 ("to incur the charge of the greatest sin before God"). I would suggest that the materials that have already been removed from the passion narrative which pertain to the sense of cultic defilement may well be linked with these verses (1.1; 2.5a,b; 6.22–23a).

A more significant matter is the very format of this material. Koester has argued that the basis of this section bears the features of a miraculous epiphany story (1980: 126–30). The above mentioned redactional issues become clarified, I believe, when one discerns the early epiphany story. Following Koester's proposal we can see the following:

| Introduction | 8.28–9.34 |
| Epiphany | 9.35–36 |

Miracle	9.37
Appearance	10.39–40
Reaction of Witnesses	11.45

I would add nuance to Koester's suggestion of the Introductory material by noting that 8.28b would be separate and that 8.28a could have led directly into 8.29b:

> 8.28a When the scribes and the pharisees and the priests had gathered together with one another,...8.29b they went to Pilate, entreating him....

8.29a ("they became frightened") and 8.28b ("having heard that") I would consider as being included during the interpolation of 8.28b. The latter would nicely serve to include the earlier material, while the former would add motive and additional reaction. We should note that Crossan considers 7.25–11.49 to be two distinct narrative units which—minus the particular "preparational" material (7.26–27; 11.43–44)—would be on the earliest historical level. The difficulty I have with Crossan's position is that he does not deal formally with the verses which he patterns into narrative units. If Koester is correct about the epiphany form and if my earlier formal and redactional observations have any merit, then one must reevaluate Crossan's primary narrative units. On the other hand, his redactional points should not be lost. Indeed, it is precisely the considerations of the form of the miraculous epiphany story which would more cogently push for a detection of secondary material within 8.28–11.49.

With this in mind one can argue that 10.38 is a secondary expansion which "tries to involve the centurion and the other witnesses" (Koester, 1980: 128 n. 72):

> Now when these soldiers saw (this) they roused the centurion from sleep and the elders—for they were also there keeping watch.

This actually contradicts the later 11.45 (which is part of the original epiphany story) while it sets up the basis for the sinfulness of those who would cover up the event (11.48):

> "For," they said, "it is better for us to incur the charge of the greatest sin before God than to fall into the hands of the people of the Jews and be stoned."

One can also consider as secondary 10.39a ("while they were explaining what they had seen"), since it follows from 10.38 and provides a redactional link with the original 10.39b:

again they saw leaving the tomb three men, two were supporting the other one and a cross was following them.

10.41–42 would also be distinctly secondary as a surprising intrusion into the material:

> And they heard a voice from the heavens, saying, "Have you preached to those who sleep?" And an answer was heard from the cross, "Yes!"

I think that 10.39c ("and a cross was following them") may well be a redactional insertion preparing for this unusual fragmentary material. 11.43 is both a redactional seam for 10.42 and for what happens in 11.44:

> These men therefore consulted with one another to go and report these things to Pilate.

I agree with Crossan as to its redactional preparation for 12.50–13.57 and would therefore place it on the same level as that material. In regard to 11.45 I would agree with Koester in saying that the description of the report to Pilate interrupts the context and seems designed to exonerate Pilate—a secondary motif (1980: 129 n. 74). We have noted already the problems in 11.46. We should simply point out that this apologetic *pro Pilato* continues in 11.46–48. 11.49 ends this secondary material:

> Pilate ordered the centurion and the soldiers to say nothing.

Thus, one can distill the following as the miraculous epiphany story:

Introduction
When the scribes and the pharisees and the priests had gathered together with one another, they went to Pilate, entreating him and saying, "Give us soldiers so that <we> may guard his tomb for three (days), lest his disciples come and steal him and the people assume that he is risen from the dead and do us harm." Now Pilate gave them Petronius the centurion with soldiers to guard the tomb. And with them went elders and scribes to the tomb. And all who were there with the centurion and the soldiers rolled a large stone and placed it against the entrance to the tomb, and they put seven seals on it and, having pitched a tent there, kept watch. Early, as the sabbath dawned, a crowd came from Jerusalem and the surrounding countryside to see the sealed tomb. (8.28a; 8.29b–9.34)

Epiphany
But in the night on which the Lord's day dawned, while the soldiers were guarding, two by two during the watch, there was a great sound in

heaven, and they saw the heavens opened and two men came down from there in great brilliance and approached the tomb. (9.35–36)

Miracle
Now that stone which had been pushed against the entrance began to roll by itself and moved away to one side; and the tomb was opened and both youths entered. (9.37)

Appearance
Again they saw leaving the tomb three men, two were supporting the other one and a cross was following them, the heads of the two stretched to heaven, while that of the one whom they led by the hand surpassed the heavens. (10.39b–40)

Reaction of Witnesses
When those in the centurion's company saw these things, they rushed by night to Pilate, having left the tomb which they were guarding, and they explained all that they had seen, being greatly disturbed and saying, "Truly, he was a son of God!" (11.45)

Having separated out this probable epiphany story, we must now see how it fits in with the earlier passion narrative. I would point out that with the simple redactional tie-in of 8.28a with 8.28b (and the filling in of 8.29a) we have a major revision of the original story of persecution and vindication. The epiphany material now functions as an intensification of the vindication side of the story. Certainly the *reaction* (11.45c) of the guards is an *acclamation*. One could also argue that the elements of persecution are still echoing throughout this material. A *conspiracy* is present in 8.28–31. Even an *ordeal* could be seen in the setting of the guard, the rolling of the stone, and the sealing of the tomb (8.31b–33). The *rescue* could be viewed in 9.35–37; 10.39b, 40. There are, however, significant differences which would argue for more than a simple repetition of the genre of the righteous sufferer. One can note, for example, that the *accusation* is now found in the charge that the disciples would steal the body to produce a fraud (8.30b). Here we see a good indication that the focus upon the figure of the suffering righteous one is being displaced by later concerns. What one can say is that the original narrative provides a basic skeletal frame for a variety of shifts, changes of direction, and significant transformations. In this instance, the addition of the epiphany narrative both expands and reinforces the claims of the original. At the same time, however, there are very important changes. The miraculous apparition outshines the muted exaltation of the crucified just one. Certain historicizing tendencies have markedly entered the picture. This amalgamation of passion narrative and epiphany story may even have been intended to provide a more balanced narrative, wherein the downbeat of the persecution is matched by the miraculous note of triumph. What might have been almost an apologetic attempt to make sense of the fate of Jesus becomes a powerful story that could well serve both missionary and defensive purposes. Another way of putting it is that the introduction of the epiphany material may well be an indication of social redefinition. As Mack has cogently argued (1988: 223), such material may emerge out of a community's attempt to gain social orientation and identity. There may well be suggested here an attempt to adjust to a more Gentile audience, while simultaneously maintaining Jewish ties.

3.2 *Redactional and Secondary Elements*

It is now appropriate to take into consideration those verses which have been separated out as secondary, either to the original passion narrative or to the epiphany story (for a schematic outline of the various layers of *Gos. Pet.*, see the Appendix below). 1.1 and 11.46 would seem to come from the same hand. 1.2 is linked with 1.1, while 11.47–49 follow upon 11.46 (as argued above). The concern for purity/defilement noted in 11.48 seems consistent with the burial taboo noted in 2.5a,b (and hence with 5.15b; 6.22, 23a). But this material seems to have become linked with the Joseph tradition (2.3–4; 6.23b–24). 10.38–39a prepare for 11.46–49. 10.39c anticipates the enclosed independent fragment of 10.41–42. 11.43 serves as a redactional seam for the previous interpolation.

When we include this secondary material into the narrative level we see that the story now moves decisively to a focus on individual characters, to a more precise drawing of lines between individuals and groups. One can also still see some telltale indications of building upon the skeletal story frame of the original version. Joseph fills out the generic lines of *assistance* in the righteous sufferer tradition (Nickelsburg, 1980: 160). Indeed, the figure of Pilate functions within the component of *protest* in that tradition. There is now an assignment or discrimination of those who are guilty, especially of covering up the *acclamation* of the son of God. Herod is explicitly named as the one who issues the *condemnation*. This order is juxtaposed with the hypocritical concern for burial observances. This last point would reinforce the focus on the drawing of social lines or boundaries. Even the mysterious 10.39c, 41–42 may well touch upon the *vindication* of the just one, who receives an otherworldly reversal of fate. In other words, we have the early generic lines of the story of the persecuted righteous one now filled in by specific characters in a more historicized and socially defined context. While space does not permit it here, it would be worth investigating whether a structural analysis of this material could flesh out these narrative ramifications. One could further say that, with more lines of discrimination drawn, the political reality out of which this revision emerged may well have greatly shifted. Crossan has pointed out that there seems to be a decided shift in his original Cross Gospel. A first stage wherein there is no hint of discord between authorities and people gives way to a second where matters are quite changed (1987: 10). That observation, however, rests upon little redactional rigor. The reason for the apparent shift is that there are two distinct layers of composition, wherein the discord between people and the leaders (intimated already in the redactional material of 8.28b, 29a) is explicitly brought out in this secondary material. Perhaps quite significant to our discussion is the simple phrase "people of the Jews" (11.48). This should be seen in contrast to the term "the people" (8.30) found within the addition of the epiphany narrative. The phrase in 11.48 places the leaders over against their own people. While the Jewish leaders would fall in line with the other symbols of political oppression, Herod and Pilate (linked together in this later material), it is quite possible that this level of material, which presents the only scriptural citation, along with concerns for purity, may well reflect further disagreement within the diaspora synagogue. It is also crucial to see that the term "the Jews" dealt with below would represent a further development in terms of social definition and, most likely, alienation. The story, then, recast with the varied secondary additions, focuses more explicitly upon the political dark side. One wonders whether this would mirror at all the political upheavals emerging before the siege of Jerusalem.

3.3 *The Final Layer*

There are as yet some verses of *Gos. Pet.* still outstanding. We have argued above that 7.25 appears to be linked on the same redactional level as 7.26–27. Accordingly 14.58–60 would be found there also:

> Then the Jews and the elders and the priests knew what evil they had done to themselves, and began to beat their breasts and say, "Woe for our sins, for the judgment and the end of Jerusalem has come near." But I with my friends wept, and quivering with fear in our hearts, we hid ourselves; for we were sought by them as criminals and as ones wishing to burn down the temple. In addition to all these things, we fasted and sat mourning and weeping night and day until the sabbath. (7.25–27)

> Now it was the last day of the unleavened bread and many began to return to their homes since the feast was over. But we, the twelve disciples of the Lord, wept and mourned and each one, grieving on account of what had happened, withdrew to his own home. But I, Simon Peter, and Andrew, my brother, took our fishing nets and went away to the sea. And with us was Levi, the son of Alphaeus, whom the Lord.... (14.58–60)

We can likewise point out that 12.50b, 52a (and 54a?) seem to come from that same redactional level (cf. 7.26–27; 14.58–60):

> who, being fearful on account of the Jews, since they were inflamed with wrath.... (12.50b)

> And they were afraid that the Jews might see them and were saying.... (12.52a)

> For great was the stone, and we fear that someone might see us. (12.54a)

The fear of "the Jews," as well as the "weeping and mourning" of the disciples (male and female), would suggest a definite linkage. Of course, the observation of the first person, singular and plural, has been stressed above. There are further elements which should be indicated. First, we seem to be at a time after the fall of Jerusalem (7.25–26). Second, we now have for the first time a self-conscious indication of a community over against the "Jews." The "us vs. them" mentality, perhaps already gaining impetus in the assignment of guilt to the leaders in the previous version of this tradition, now comes to the fore. Third, the concern for the fate of the Temple (cf. esp. 7.26) enters at this level and may have something to say about what Nickelsburg has speculated as to a pre-Markan tradition featuring such a component (1980: 183). Fourth, we have an empty tomb story (12.50–13.57) which Crossan argues is dependent upon Mark 16:1–8. His argument basically stands upon the contention that it is the author of Mark who is responsible for the creation of the empty tomb narrative (1976: 135–52; 1985: 157–64). While I find this argument fascinating I am not thoroughly convinced. Despite Crossan's argument that Mark 16:7 is so "strange" that it necessitated revision from the slightest (Matt 28:10) to the greatest (John 20:17), I find it difficult to understand why the final redactor of *Gos. Pet.* has removed a verse which would anticipate 14.60. Furthermore, when one removes what appears to be the final level of redaction from the empty tomb story in *Gos. Pet.* (12.50b, 52a, 54a?), one is left with a format strikingly similar to Mark 16:1–8 (minus vs 7). Although Crossan is loathe to multiply solutions, I would suggest that there may well be a pre-Markan and pre-Petrine tradition, utilized by each independently. The question of the dependency of later portions of *Gos. Pet.* upon the canonical gospels is further brought out in regard to 14.58–60 which Crossan argues is dependent upon John 21:7–8. I am not at all convinced about the dependency of 14.58–60 upon John 21. First, only Simon Peter is the same in both accounts; second, we do not have very similar language—no more than is found in Luke 5:1–11, where there is a mention of nets, or Mark 1:16–20. The presumption might well be that 14.58–60 matches John 21 since both are post-resurrection stories.

But, have not there been similar arguments proposed for Luke 5:1–11 (Fuller, 1980: 160–61)?

From these observations one can see that this final layer of material enters into the compositional development of *Gos. Pet.* certainly sometime after the group identified with Simon Peter has become alienated from their Jewish matrix. In addition, the brief remarks about the temple might well suggest that we are in the post 70 C.E. period. We should also note there are echoes—but only distant ones—of the original story format. The addition of the empty tomb story reemphasizes the note of *vindication* somewhat muted by the ending of the third version's negative polemic. The women would certainly present still another *reaction*, while the references to "the Jews" might imply the element of *ordeal* or *conspiracy*. However, too great a focus on these weakening reverberations would obscure the true direction and function of the revised material. The story now works within a strikingly different social and historical situation. The original attempt to come to grips with the fate of Jesus, which, in turn, felt the explosive force of the addition of the epiphany material, and, then, received further political and social correction through the addition of fragmentary material, is once more redirected by means of further additions according to the needs of the community identified around the figure of Simon Peter. Here the lines of inner and outer, of "us" and "Jews," become keenly drawn. Could the Antiochene connection be reasserting itself here? Perhaps it may be better stated that there seems to be a definite alienation from those who would claim social identity either from the ideology of the Second Temple or its revision in the Pharisaic reinterpretation.

3.4 *Gos. Pet. 5.17: Some Historical Correlations*

An illustration of how the compositional history and development of *Gos. Pet.* suggested in this paper may be discerned in regard to the larger historical situation of the first century may be found in the following observations on 5.17:

> And they fulfilled all things and brought to completion the sins on their head.

Barn. 5.11 has already turned the "completion of the total of the sins upon those who persecuted his prophets" into a christological interpretation. The fulfillment motif of biblical texts is quite explicit. In John 19:28–30 we have a complete reworking of the language, historicizing it under the figure of Jesus who completes all. In Matt 23:32 we find "Fill up the measure of your fathers," referring to the Jewish critique against those who persecute the prophets. While Q material is the background for that verse, there is no sense of "measure" indicated in Q (Luke 11:47–48). Finally, in 1 Thess 2:14–16 we find very suggestive language. The anonymous "they" in *Gos. Pet.* 5.17 now are identified as the "Jews" (1 Thess 2:14) who are responsible for the killing of "the Lord" and the prophets. "They" also are persecuting the disciples, are found displeasing to God, and oppose the salvation of the Gentiles. All of this scurrilous activity results in their "filling up the measure of their sins" (1 Thess 2:16a). It is stated that the wrath of God has come upon them at last. I would argue that this interpolation in 1 Thessalonians (Pearson, 1971; cf. Meeks, 1983: 227 n. 117), which may well come shortly following the fall of Jerusalem, bears similarities to the concerns of the final redactional layer of *Gos. Pet.* Unlike the original understanding of 5.17, where the guilty are anonymous types, the material in 1 Thessalonians as well as the final layer of *Gos. Pet.* would see the world divided into opposing camps. Indeed, the "Jews" are no longer just the leaders but all those who are not under the "Jesus" umbrella. The connection of the death of the Lord to that of the prophets is made explicit. In *Gos. Pet.* 5.17 it is implicit and actually tied to the stories of the righteous. Evidently, a tradition such as we find in Q (Luke 11:45–51) has entered into the picture. But there is even more social definition and alienation. It is not simply a Jewish self-critique any longer. It is now a polemic used by separated and ideologically defined parties. *Barn.* 5.11 continues in this development along further established christological lines, while John 19, a product of the alienation from the Jewish matrix, carries this furthest in terms of historicizing the text, while forgetting the prophetic and critical nature of the tradition. Thus, a consideration of a seemingly insignificant verse suggests some definite lines of development and social alienation within the compositional history of *Gos. Pet.*

4. Summation

This paper has suggested that there are some fundamental questions regarding the formal, redactional, and generic elements of *Gos. Pet.* My contention is that a close analysis of the text yields rather significant possibilities, especially if we consider the basic genre of what can be detected as original material. The genre of the persecution and vindication of the just one appears to have been the format in which the earliest content, derived from speculation upon the prophets, psalms, and, possibly, the ancient political ideology of Israel, has been set. While the first layer of material is meager, I would argue that we have enough material to conclude that the story of the vindication of the righteous is both anticipated and acknowledged in the death scene of the Lord. I would further suggest that this narrative was used originally to come to grips with the probable collision of ideological expectation and the political failure of Jesus of Nazareth. I have further argued that there is a second layer, which expanded the story of the righteous one by the addition of a miraculous epiphany story. This expansion may well have come during the early stages of missionary advancement by the Jesus movement. A third layer can be detected where the starkness of the first version and the emotional force of the second become complicated by an emphasis upon particular individuals and by a focus upon the guilt of the leaders of the people. Definite social lines are being drawn. The "people" are now over against those who would oppose the vindication of the story. Finally, the latest layer of *Gos. Pet.* comes, in all likelihood, from after the fall of Jerusalem, when there has been a decided self-definition of the disciples of the Lord over against "the Jews." In light of this argument one can well begin to speculate upon the various implications for the writing of the history of the development of gospel materials. I have intimated that my proposed line of composition may well fit in with what is emerging as the picture of historical development of the many-sided Jesus movements in the first century. One can further point out that not only would *Gos. Pet.* carry some of the earliest gospel material but also we may well have, in its final redaction, a composition chronologically equivalent to Mark. But most significant of all is the possibility that the earliest stage of *Gos. Pet.* holds within it the generic seeds of the subsequent passion narratives. At the earliest stage we do not have sheer historical report; on the contrary, we have an imaginative attempt to discern the Wisdom of God.

APPENDIX

THE LINES OF DEVELOPMENT FOR *GOS. PET.*

ORIGINAL LAYER (story of the vindicated just one)
  2.5c–5.15a; 5.16–6.21; 8.28b

SECONDARY LAYER (epiphany story)
  8.28a; 8.29b–9.37; 10.39b; 10.40; 11.45

TERTIARY LAYER (fragments & redactional elements)
  2.3–4; 6.23b–24 (Joseph frg.); 10.41–42 (Cross frg.); 1.1–2; 2.5a,b; 5.15b; 6.22–23a; 8.29a; 10.38–39a,c; 10.43; 11.46–49

FINAL REDACTIONAL LAYER (*Gospel of Peter*)
  7.25; 7.26–27; 11.44; 12.50–13.57; 14.58–60

WORKS CONSULTED

Beyschlag, Karlmann
   1969   *Die verborgene Überlieferung von Christus.* Siebenstern Taschenbuch 136. Munich/Hamburg: Siebenstern Taschenbuch.

Bouriant, Urbain
   1892   "Fragments du texte grec du livre d'Enoch et de quelques écrits attribués a Saint Pierre." Pp. 137–42 in *Mémoires publiés par les membres de la Mission archéologique française au Caire* 9/1. Paris: Libraire de la Société asiatique.

Brown, Raymond E.
   1987   "The *Gospel of Peter* and Canonical Gospel Priority." *NTS* 33: 321–43.

Browne, G. M., et al.
   1972   *The Oxyrhynchus Papyri.* Vol. 41. London: Egypt Exploration Society.

Cameron, Ron
   1982   *The Other Gospels: Non-Canonical Gospel Texts.* Philadelphia: Westminster.

Crossan, John Dominic
   1976   "Empty Tomb and Absent Lord (Mark 16:1–8)." Pp. 135–52 in *The Passion in Mark: Studies on Mark 14–16.* Ed. Werner H. Kelber. Philadelphia: Fortress.
   1985   *Four Other Gospels: Shadows on the Contours of Canon.* Minneapolis: Winston.
   1987   "The Cross that Spoke: The Earliest Narrative of the Passion and Resurrection." *Forum* 3/2: 3–22.
   1988   *The Cross that Spoke: The Origins of the Passion Narrative.* San Francisco: Harper & Row.

Denker, Jürgen
   1975   *Die theologiegeschichtliche Stellung des Petrusevangeliums: Ein Beitrag zur frühgeschichte des Doketismus.* Europäische Hochschulschriften 23/36. Bern/Frankfurt: Lang.

Dibelius, Martin
1918 "Die alttestamentliche Motive in der Leidensgeschichte des Petrus- und Johannes-Evangeliums." *BZAW* 33: 125–50. Repr. pp. 221–47 in *Botschaft und Geschichte*. Vol. 1. Tübingen: Mohr-Siebeck, 1953.

Fuller, Reginald H.
1980 *The Formation of the Resurrection Narratives*. Philadelphia: Fortress.

Gardner-Smith, P.
1925-26a "The Gospel of Peter." *JTS* 27: 255–71.
1925-26b "The Date of the Gospel of Peter." *JTS* 27: 401–7.

Harnack, Adolf
1893 *Bruchstücke des Evangeliums und der Apocalypse des Petrus*. TU 9. 2d ed. Leipzig: Hinrichs.

Horsley, Richard A.
1987 *Jesus and the Spiral of Violence: Popular Jewish Resistance in Roman Palestine*. San Francisco: Harper & Row.

Johnson, Benjamin A.
1965 "Empty Tomb Tradition in the Gospel of Peter." Th.D. diss., Harvard University.
1985 "The Gospel of Peter: Between Apocalypse and Romance." Pp. 170–74 in *Studia Patristica* 16. TU 129. Berlin: Akademie-Verlag.

Koester, Helmut
1980 "Apocryphal and Canonical Gospels." *HTR* 73: 105–30.
1983 "History and Development of Mark's Gospel (From Mark to *Secret Mark* and 'Canonical' Mark)." Pp. 35–57 in *Colloquy on New Testament Studies: A Time for Reappraisal and Fresh Approaches*. Ed. Bruce Corley. Macon, GA: Mercer University Press. [Pp. 59–85: "Seminar Dialogue with Helmut Koester."]

Lods, A.
1893 "Reproduction en héliogravure du manuscript d'Enoch et des écrits attribués a Saint Pierre." Pp. 219–24, with Plates II–VI, in *Mémoires publiés par les membres de la Mission archéologique française au Caire* 9/3. Paris: Libraire de la Société asiatique.

Lührmann, Dieter
1981 "P Ox 2949: EvPt 3–5 in einer Handschrift des 2./3. Jahrhunderts." *ZNW* 72: 216–26.

Mack, Burton L.
1988 *A Myth of Innocence: Mark and Christian Origins.* Philadelphia: Fortress.

Meeks, Wayne A.
1983 *The First Urban Christians: The Social World of the Apostle Paul.* New Haven/London: Yale University Press.

Nickelsburg, George W. E., Jr.
1972 *Resurrection, Immortality, and Eternal Life in Intertestamental Judaism.* HTS 26. Cambridge: Harvard University Press; London: Oxford University Press.
1980 "The Genre and Function of the Markan Passion Narrative." *HTR* 73: 153–84.

Pearson, Birger A.
1971 "1 Thessalonians 2:13–16: A Deutero-Pauline Interpolation." *HTR* 64: 79–94.

Robinson, James M.
1982 "Jesus: From Easter to Valentinus (or to the Apostles' Creed)." *JBL* 101: 5–37.

Schmidt, Karl Ludwig
1944 *Kanonische und apokryphe Evangelien und Apostelgeschichten.* AThANT 5. Basel: Majer.

Swete, Henry Barclay
1893 Εὐαγγέλιον κατὰ Πέτρον: *The Akhmîm Fragment of the Apocryphal Gospel of St. Peter.* London: Macmillan.

Vaganay, Léon
1930 *L'Evangile de Pierre.* EtBib. 2d ed. Paris: Gabalda.

Zahn, Theodor
1893 *Das Evangelium des Petrus.* Erlangen/Leipzig: Deichert.

THE YOUTH IN THE *SECRET GOSPEL OF MARK*

Marvin W. Meyer
Chapman College

ABSTRACT

Recent studies on the *Secret Gospel of Mark* suggest that the significance of this text may very well be realized through a redaction-critical study of the Secret Gospel. Such a study discloses a subplot involving a νεανίσκος ("youth") in *Secret Mark*, a subplot presented in only a truncated fashion in canonical Mark. The five pericopae that advance the subplot (Mark 10:17–22; *Secret Mark* fragment 1; *Secret Mark* fragment 2; Mark 14:51–52; Mark 16:1–8) serve to communicate *Secret Mark*'s vision of discipleship, which is exemplified in the story of the νεανίσκος. This role of the νεανίσκος in the Markan tradition parallels that of the Beloved Disciple in the Gospel of John.

0. Discovery

In the summer of 1958, as Morton Smith tells the story, there occurred a remarkable manuscript discovery in the Judean desert. Some seventeen years after he had first visited the Greek Orthodox Monastery of Mar Saba during the winter of 1941, Smith returned to the monastery, with the permission of the Patriarch Benedict, in order to study and catalogue the manuscripts in the monastery library (see Smith, 1960). "Then," Smith reports in the popular publication of his findings, "one afternoon near the end of my stay, I found myself in my cell, staring incredulously at a text written in a tiny scrawl I had not even tried to read in the tower when I picked out the book containing it. But now that I came to puzzle it out, it began, 'From the letters of the most holy Clement, the author of the *Stromateis*. To Theodore,' and it went on to praise the recipient for having 'shut up' the Carpocratians" (1973a: 12). This text attributed to Clement of Alexandria was written in cursive Greek on two and a half pages at the back of a printed edition of the letters of Ignatius of Antioch (Isaac Voss, ed., *Epistulae genuinae S. Ignatii Martyris* [Amsterdam: Blaeu, 1646]). Smith quickly photographed the manuscript, "three times for good measure" (1973a: 13); to the present those photographs (cf. Smith, 1973b: 449, 451, 453; 1973a: 38) remain the only published facsimiles of the text. A number of scholars examined the photographs of the manuscript in order to attempt to date the scribal hand. "The consensus,"

Smith concludes, "would date the hand about 1750, plus or minus about fifty years" (1973b: 1).

In 1973, fifteen years after the manuscript discovery itself, the scholarly and popular editions of the text appeared, and almost at once controversy began to swirl around the text. Such controversy has focused upon questions concerning the authenticity, the contents, and the interpretation of the text. As John Dominic Crossan has said briefly and well, "The authenticity of a text can only be established by the consensus of experts who have studied the original document under scientifically appropriate circumstances" (100). In the case of the Mar Saba manuscript, Morton Smith seems to be the only scholar who actually has seen the original text, and his photographs have proved to be the only other verification of the text. This situation has led to the famous intimations of possible forgery (cf. Quesnell) and the refutations by Smith (1976). Some of these intimations have continued to the present day, with the publication of Per Beskow's *Strange Tales about Jesus*, corrected in response to Smith's letter in the *Journal of Biblical Literature* (1984). To be sure, there have been attempts by at least one other scholar to view the original text. Thomas Talley recalls his efforts: "My own attempts to see the manuscript in January of 1980 were frustrated, but as witnesses to its existence I can cite the Archimandrite Meliton of the Jerusalem Greek Patriarchate who, after the publication of Smith's work, found the volume at Mar Saba and removed it to the patriarchal library, and the patriarchal librarian, Father Kallistos, who told me that the manuscript (two folios) has been removed from the printed volume and is being repaired" (45). I concur with Crossan that the further study of the Mar Saba document should include the independent scholarly verification of the text by means of a careful examination of the original manuscript, and an adequate publication of the text in facsimile edition.

1. Contents

The Mar Saba manuscript is written in the form of a fragment of a letter from Clement of Alexandria to a certain recipient named Theodore. The fragmentary state of the letter, Smith speculates, may derive from the following circumstances. (1) John of Damascus worked at Mar Saba from 716 to 749 C.E., and cited three passages (in his *Sacra Parallela*) from a collection of letters of Clement of Alexandria. This fact compares well with the *incipit* of the Mar Saba manuscript: ἐκ τῶν ἐπιστολῶν τοῦ ἁγιωτάτου Κλήμεντος τοῦ Στρωματέως ("From the letters of the most holy Clement, [author] of the *Stromateis*," 1r:1). (2) According to J. Phokylides, in the early eighteenth century a great fire burned through a cave used for the storage of manuscripts, and Smith suggests that the collection of Clement's letters may have perished in that disaster. Presumably, however, a number of loose leaves might have been salvaged from the remains of the books and manuscripts. (3) "The fragmentary state of the present letter," Smith hypothesizes, "is best explained by supposing it a copy of such an isolated leaf. Ehrhard (Kloster 67) remarks on the large amount of copying of older MSS which went on at Mar Saba in the seventeenth and eighteenth centuries. No doubt someone's attention was attracted by the surprising content of this isolated folio. He studied the text, corrected it to the best of his ability, and copied it into the back of the monastery's edition of the letters of Ignatius, since it resembled them in being a letter from an early father, attacking gnostic heretics" (1973b: 289).

The letter of Clement is written to commend and support the recipient for his opposition to the Gnostic Carpocratians. The Carpocratians were libertine Gnostics who allegedly maintained that they were free to do whatever they wished, "sola enim humana opinione negotia mala et bona dicunt" ("for they say that circumstances are evil and good only in human opinion," Irenaeus of Lyons, Adversus haereses 1.25.4). The allegation that a studied libertinism is based upon a distinction between φύσις ("nature") and νόμος or θέσις ("convention" or "opinion") is attested as early as the Greek Sophists, and this theory became an important part of philosophical and theological discussion during antiquity (cf., for example, Gal 4:8 and 1 Cor 8:4–6). Irenaeus goes on to declare that in the Carpocratian writings it is stated that "Jesum...in mysterio discipulis suis et apostolis seorsum locutum" ("Jesus spoke in a mystery to his disciples and apostles privately," 1.25.5), a statement which may be compared with the private communication of τὸ μυστήριον τῆς βασιλείας τοῦ θεοῦ ("the mystery of the kingdom of God") in the Mar Saba manuscript (2r:10). Furthermore, elsewhere in Clement's discussion of the Carpocratians (Stromateis 3.2.11) he employs a passage from Jude (vss 8–16) just as in the Mar Saba letter (1r:3: οὗτοι γάρ οἱ προφητευθέντες ἀστέρες πλανῆται, "for these are the wandering stars that have been prophesied"; cf. Jude 13; and Smith, 1973b: 8).

In its discussion of the Carpocratian Gnostics, the letter of Clement uses typical heresiological terminology. They have gone astray as "wandering stars," οἱ ἀπὸ τῆς στενῆς τῶν ἐντολῶν ὁδοῦ εἰς ἀπέρατον ἄβυσσον πλανώμενοι τῶν σαρκικῶν καὶ ἐνσωμάτων ἁμαρτιῶν ("who wander from the narrow way of the commandments into an infinite abyss of carnal and bodily sins," 1r:3–4). Though they claim to have knowledge τῶν βαθέων τοῦ σατανᾶ ("of the deep things of Satan," 1r:5; cf. Rev 2:24), they are falling into falsehood. Though they claim to be free, δοῦλοι γεγόνασιν ἀνδραποδώδων ἐπιθυμιῶν ("they have become slaves of base desires," 1r:7). They are, in fact, taught by the μιαρῶν δαιμόνων ("foul demons," 1v:2–3), and for this reason the Carpocratians accomplish demonic things.

Among their despicable deeds is their use of the Gospel of Mark. According to the Mar Saba letter, a demonically inspired Carpocrates managed to obtain a copy of the Gospel of Mark—τοῦ μυστικοῦ εὐαγγελίου ("the secret gospel," 1v:6)—from a presbyter in the Alexandrian church. Carpocrates falsified this *Secret Gospel of Mark* in two ways: he interpreted it κατὰ τὴν βλασφημὸν καὶ σαρκικὴν αὐτοῦ δόξαν ("according to his blasphemous and carnal opinion"), and he polluted it by ταῖς ἀχράντοις καὶ ἁγίαις λέξεσιν ἀναμιγνὺς ἀναιδέστατα ψεύσματα ("mixing the most shameless lies with the undefiled and holy words," 1v:7–9).

In order to distinguish what is holy and true from what is false in the literary tradition of Mark, Clement expands upon the versions of Mark with which he is familiar. Clement grounds Mark in the Petrine apostolic tradition (cf. also *Adumbrationes Clementis Alexandrini in epistolas canonicas;* Eusebius of Caesarea, *Historia ecclesiastica* 2.15; 6.14.5–7; 3.39.15 [Papias]; these texts are conveniently assembled in Smith, 1973b: 20–21). In doing so Clement isolates three different written versions of the Gospel of Mark. (1) While Peter was still in Rome, Mark composed an account of τὰς πράξεις τοῦ κυρίου ("the acts of the Lord," 1r:16) for those who were being instructed toward faith and, presumably, baptism. This account constituted a public Gospel of Mark, and in the public version the author presented some of the Lord's deeds, οὐ μέντοι πάσας ἐξαγγέλλων· οὐδὲ μὴν τὰς μυστικὰς ὑποσημαίνων ("though not reporting them all, and not even hinting at the secret ones," 1r:16–17). The public Gospel of Mark seems to be identical, or nearly identical, with the present canonical Gospel of Mark. (2) After the martyrdom of Peter, Mark came to Alexandria, taking with him καὶ τατ αυτοῦ (sic; cf. Smith, 1973b: 28) καὶ τὰ τοῦ Πέτρου ὑπομνήματα ("both his own and Peter's notes," 1r:19–20). From those ὑπομνήματα, Clement states, Mark added more Petrine materials to the public Gospel of Mark in order to produce a Secret Gospel (πνευματικώτερον εὐαγγέλιον εἰς τὴν τῶν τελειουμένων χρῆσιν, "a more spiritual gospel for the use of those being perfected" [or: "initiated"]), an amplified version of Mark that also included τὰ τοῖς προκόπτουσι περὶ τὴν γνῶσιν κατάλληλα ("the things appropriate for those progressing in knowledge," 1r:20–22). Clement specifies only two relatively brief sections added to public Mark to produce *Secret Mark*. It may be the case, then, that *Secret Mark* is only slightly longer than public Mark. When Mark died, Clement continues, he left the Secret Gospel to the care of the church at Alexandria, ὅπου εἰσέτι νῦν ἀσφαλῶς εὖ μάλα τηρεῖται· ἀναγινωσκόμενον πρὸς αὐτοὺς μόνους τοὺς μυουμένους τὰ μεγάλα μυστήρια ("where even now it is very carefully guarded, being read only to those being initiated into the great mysteries," 1v:1-2). Here, and throughout this section of the Mar Saba letter, Clement utilizes language derived from the world of the Greco-Roman mysteries (e.g., τὴν ἱεροφαντικὴν διδασκαλίαν τοῦ κυρίου; λόγιά τινα ὧν ἠπίστατο τὴν ἐξήγησιν μυσταγωγήσειν τοὺς ἀκροατὰς εἰς τὸ ἄδυτον τῆς ἑπτάκις [sic] κεκαλυμμένης ἀληθείας; "the hierophantic teaching of the Lord"; "certain sayings whose interpretation, he knew, would act as a mystagogue to lead the hearers into the inner shrine of the truth hidden seven times," 1r:23-24, 25-26). Such usage is very much in keeping with other passages in Clement of Alexandria, for instance his *Protreptikos pros Hellenas*, in which he refutes the other mysteries in order to show Christianity to be the true, sacred mystery. (3) Clement claims that the Carpocratians used a falsified version of the Secret Gospel that has been amplified and interpreted by means of materials congenial with Carpocratian teachings (cf. γυμνὸς γυμνῷ, "naked person with naked person," 2r:13). Possibly this Carpocratian version was a substantially longer version (cf. τὰ δὲ ἄλλα τὰ πολλὰ ἃ ἔγραψας ψεύσματα καὶ φαίνεται καὶ ἔστιν, "But the many other matters about which you wrote both appear to be and are lies," 2r:17). Clement declares that the Carpocratian Gospel of Mark, unlike the public and secret versions, is not authoritative, since the "holy words" of *Secret Mark* have been polluted and falsified. (4) Besides these three written versions of Mark, Clement asserts that unutterable, esoteric truths constituting "the hierophantic teaching of the Lord" (1r:23-24) were not written down by Mark. Rather, this unwritten material was to remain the secret, oral lore of true Christian γνῶσις ("knowledge").

According to the Mar Saba letter, the *Secret Gospel of Mark* contains two sections not included in the public Gospel of Mark: 1v:23-2r:11, and 2r:14-16. The first section, to be located immediately after Mark 10:34, recounts the story of the raising of the νεανίσκος ("youth") of Bethany. At the request of the sister of the νεανίσκος, Jesus raised the youth from the tomb. The youth, who loved Jesus, is then taught "the mystery of the kingdom of God." The second section, to be located within Mark 10:46, describes Jesus refusing to accept three women, including the sister and the mother of the νεανίσκος.

For obvious reasons, scholarly research on the Mar Saba manuscript has concentrated on these two fragmentary but fascinating sections, and the perplexing question of the interpretation of the *Secret Gospel of Mark*. To some of the most recent research on these two sections we now turn.

2. Research

While a full discussion of the scholarly literature on the *Secret Gospel of Mark* cannot be attempted here, four contributions deserve brief comment. These four contributions give serious attention to the Secret Gospel, and suggest creative approaches to the text. The four studies are: (1) Morton Smith, "Clement of Alexandria and Secret Mark: The Score at the End of the First Decade" (1982); (2) Helmut Koester, "History and Development of Mark's Gospel (From Mark to *Secret Mark* and 'Canonical' Mark)" (1983); (3) Hans-Martin Schenke, "The Mystery of the Gospel of Mark" (1984); and (4) John Dominic Crossan, "The Secret Gospel of Mark," in his book *Four Other Gospels* (1985).

2.1. As the subtitle of Smith's review article indicates, his study is an assessment of ten years of comments on the *Secret Gospel of Mark*. Smith bases his review on some 150 publications, and judges that these publications are representative of scholarly opinion on the Secret Gospel. Smith begins his reflections by addressing himself to the question of the authenticity of the letter of Clement and the fragments contained within the letter, and concludes that most scholars now are willing to attribute the letter itself to Clement of Alexandria. Of the scholars Smith lists in his bibliography, the vote is as follows: "twenty-five have agreed in attributing the letter to Clement, six have suspended judgment or have not discussed the question, and only four have denied the attribution" (1982: 450). Regarding the authenticity of the fragments of the Secret Gospel, Smith concludes that "Clement's attribution of the gospel to 'Mark' is universally rejected," and lists three basic positions evident among scholars: some suggest that the Secret Gospel fragments represent a second-century "apocryphal" gospel, others consider the fragments to be "a pastiche composed from the canonical gospels," and still others propose that the Secret Gospel is "an expansion of Mark which imitated Markan style, but used earlier material" (457). Smith also adds that a number of scholars "seemed inclined" to accept at least some of the points suggested by Smith himself in his outline of the literary history of the Markan materials.

When Smith turns briefly to his interpretation of *Secret Mark* as providing evidence for the historical Jesus as a practitioner of secret initiation and an advocate of a libertine and magical life style, he notes, "Of course nobody accepted the proposed explanation," though some scholars did leave open the possibility of secret ceremonies in the movement around Jesus, and magical concerns in the early church. One of the chief sources of disagreement, Smith states, was from scholars who are "the adherents of current exegetic cliques (form criticism, redaction criticism, etc.) who were outraged that I had not given their literature of mutually contradictory conjectures the attention they thought it deserved" (455). Naturally, Smith's evaluation of the "current exegetic cliques" is deliberately polemical, and reflective of Smith's own exegetical approach. Yet, in spite of these vehement words, with their rejection of form-critical and redaction-critical scholarship, Smith's statement still points us toward a most fruitful way of approaching the *Secret Gospel of Mark*. Instead of using the fragments to formulate conjectures about the historical Jesus, after the manner of Smith, we may rather interpret the fragments within the redactional history of the Markan tradition.

2.2.   Such an interest in the stages of redaction in the Markan trajectory occupies the attention of Helmut Koester in his article on Secret and canonical Mark (cf. also his Yale Shaffer Lectures). Koester ventures to list several proposed stages of redaction as Mark went through several editions. The first stage (1a), says Koester, is the original Gospel of Mark, which was based on a collection of miracle stories and a passion narrative, both with Johannine affinities. A second stage (1b) is an enlarged edition of the original Gospel of Mark, written to include the miracle stories of Mark 6:45–8:26. The next stage (2) is the Gospel of Matthew, a thoroughly revised edition based, in large part, on the enlarged edition of the original Gospel of Mark that constitutes the second redactional stage (1b). A further stage (3) is the Gospel of Luke, another dramatically new edition which is based, in part, on the original Gospel of Mark (1a), but which employs other materials as well. The next stage (4a), Koester continues, is the *Secret Gospel of Mark*, which incorporates the account of, and subsequent reference to, the νεανίσκος who is raised from the dead and initiated into the Jesus movement. A related stage (4b) is the Carpocratian edition of the Secret Gospel. The next stage of redaction in the Markan tradition (5a) is the canonical Gospel of Mark, with the Secret Gospel's two reports about the νεανίσκος excised from the text. Finally, Koester concludes, the several endings (the shorter ending, the longer ending, and the Freer Logion) added in many later manuscripts after Mark 16:8 illustrate the last redactional stage (5b), and "demonstrate that the history of 'canonical Mark' was still continuing" (1983: 57).

   The intricacies of this ingenious theory of Helmut Koester need not detain us here. Doubtless the details will receive ample attention in the scholarly debates on Mark. For our purposes it is his statement about the relationship between Secret and canonical Mark that is of paramount concern. For "the conclusion," he writes, "is unavoidable: Canonical Mark is derived from *Secret Mark*" (56). Koester thus accepts Clement's suggestion of a close link between canonical (or public) Mark and *Secret*

Mark, but disagrees with Clement's theory of transmission. Koester supports his contention, first of all, with various pieces of evidence meant to illustrate the close parallels between peculiar features of canonical Mark and the Secret Gospel. For example, Mark 4:11 is unique among the synoptics (contrast Matt 13:11 // Luke 8:10) in using the singular form μυστήριον ("mystery") in its reference to the μυστήριον of the kingdom of God; the Secret Gospel (2r:10) also describes Jesus teaching the νεανίσκος the μυστήριον of the kingdom of God (cf. again the citation from Irenaeus, *Adversus haereses* 1.25.5, on the Carpocratians). Likewise, Mark 10:21 is unique among the synoptics (contrast Matt 19:21 // Luke 18:22) in describing the love of Jesus for the rich interlocutor; both fragments of the Secret Gospel also describe the love between Jesus and the νεανίσκος. One final example of Koester's evidence: Mark 14:51–52, the famous pericope about the youth who flees naked at the time of Jesus' arrest, is unique among the synoptics and has proved to be an interpretive nightmare for a very long time; now the Secret Gospel also presents a youth dressed in similar fashion and learning from Jesus about the kingdom of God.

After Koester thus establishes the intimate relationship between leading characteristics of *Secret Mark* and some unusual traits of canonical Mark, and judges that they reflect the same secondary redaction, he can move to his conclusion on the priority of the *Secret Gospel of Mark*. "The basic difference between the two," he offers, "seems to be that the redactor of canonical Mark eliminated the story of the raising of the youth and the reference to this story in Mk 10:46" (56). The rationale for eliminating this story, Koester observes, is clear enough: it was deemed unacceptable for public use in the church, as Clement himself implies. It certainly seems appropriate to assume, along with Koester (and against Clement), that the story of the raising of the youth was eliminated from canonical Mark subsequent to the compilation of *Secret Mark*, particularly since many of the peculiar traits that apparently derive from the Secret Markan redaction linger on the pages of canonical Mark. Further, the Markan account simply reads in an easier and more natural manner when the special materials of the Secret Gospel are allowed to function within the story-line. Canonical Mark is more abrupt, more opaque at key points, as we should anticipate in a document from which important passages have been removed. Precisely how the text of the Secret Gospel allows for a sensible and reasonable reading of the Markan text will be the focus of the next part of this paper.

2.3.   The third study under discussion, the 1984 article of Hans-Martin Schenke (originally delivered as a paper during his 1982 tour of the United States), bases itself very sympathetically upon the prior work of Smith and Koester. Schenke opens his study with a discussion of problems in the Gospel of Mark, including the question of the conclusion of the gospel, the nature of the Markan account of Jesus' baptism, and the enigma of Mark 14:51–52. In this discussion two statements of Schenke hint at his eventual conclusions: first, he suggests that there may be a "possible affinity between the text of Mark and Gnostic interpretation" (1984: 67); and second, he admits, "I was already more favorably predisposed to Smith's discovery than were a great many of my colleagues" (69). Following a substantial review of scholarly comments and criticisms of Smith's work on the Secret Gospel, Schenke turns to Koester approvingly, and acknowledges that he intends to raise additional questions derived from Koester's argument. Schenke's further questions lead him to a provocative proposal, namely that the Carpocratian Gospel of Mark may be taken as the prior form of Mark, from which emerge, consecutively, the "purified and shortened" *Secret Gospel of Mark* and canonical Gospel of Mark (76). Much more convincing, in my opinion, is his observation, so reminiscent of the study by Robin Scroggs and Kent Groff, that the νεανίσκος of the canonical and Secret Gospels of Mark functions as a "prototype and a symbol of all those who are to be initiated into the higher discipleship of Jesus" (77–78). The balance of the present paper will enter into the discussion of *Secret Mark* by focusing upon this νεανίσκος as a paradigm of discipleship in Mark.

2.4. The final study to be mentioned is that of Crossan. Crossan analyzes four extracanonical texts, including the *Secret Gospel of Mark*, and shows the light these texts may shed upon the traditions about Jesus and the foundations of Christianity. Crossan employs a "working hypothesis" that is, in part, similar to that of Koester: "I consider that canonical Mark is a very deliberate revision of *Secret Mark*" (108). Yet his rejection of Koester's "earlier Proto-Mark gospel which was first used in different versions by Luke and Matthew" (119; cf. Koester's stage 1a) leaves him without an adequate explanation for the absence of certain redactional traits of *Secret Mark* (dispersed throughout canonical Mark) in the texts of Matthew and Luke (cf. Cameron, 1987: 559). Crossan rightly recognizes, with Koester, parallels between canonical and *Secret Mark*, but copes with these parallels by means of a rather idiosyncratic theory. Crossan posits that canonical Mark, with anti-Carpocratian intentions, eliminated units of the Secret Gospel in this manner: "It is now impossible to tell the full scope of that revision but two features seem certain. First, canonical Mark eliminated both *SGM* [*Secret Mark*] 2 and 5 [i.e., the quotations peculiar to *Secret Mark*] as discrete literary units. Second, canonical Mark scattered the dismembered elements of these units throughout his gospel" (108; cf. 119–20). This dismembering and scattering, according to Crossan, account for features of Mark in such passages as 10:17-22 (the story of the rich inquirer), 14:51-52 (the pericope about the naked youth in flight), and 16:1-8 (the νεανίσκος and the women at the tomb).

To sum up on these four recent studies of the *Secret Gospel of Mark*: (1) The studies summarized suggest that a number of scholars seem willing to give the Mar Saba text and the *Secret Gospel of Mark* considerable attention, and to assume thereby the authenticity of the letter of Clement as an ancient text. This assumption is also reflected in the decision to include the Mar Saba text in the second edition of Otto Stählin's *Clemens Alexandrinus* (1980). (2) Few scholars (and none in the studies discussed here) have been convinced by Smith's reconstruction of a libertine Christian tradition grounded in secret teachings of the historical Jesus. Rather, several scholars (e.g., Koester; Schenke; Crossan) encourage us to evaluate the place of the Secret Gospel within early stages of redaction in the Markan tradition. On the other hand, as we have seen, there is still substantial disagreement about specific redactional issues and reconstructions among these scholars. (3) The studies by Koester, Schenke, and Crossan are unanimous in advocating the priority of the text of *Secret Mark* to that of canonical Mark, although they disagree about other matters of transmission within the Markan literary tradition.

3. Interpretation

My thesis in the balance of the present study builds self-consciously upon the conclusions just drawn. I assume the authenticity of the Mar Saba letter as a copy of an ancient text, and I suggest an interpretation that seeks to understand the text of *Secret Mark* within the Markan redactional tradition. Here we shall undertake a reading of the *Secret Gospel of Mark* that attempts to place the two fragments from Mar Saba within the broader context of the entire Secret Gospel. Such an attempt must remain somewhat tentative, on account of uncertainties about the text tradition and textual peculiarities represented by Clement's citations of public and *Secret Mark*, and the relationship of that text tradition to known Markan texts. Further, the precise contours of *Secret Mark* are not known, though the comments of Clement lead us to conclude that *Secret Mark* closely resembled public (or canonical) Mark, except for the inclusion of the two fragments Clement cites. In the surviving portion of his letter Clement himself indicates nothing whatsoever to contradict such a conclusion, and he appears to be turning away from the discussion of peculiarities of *Secret Mark* in the final surviving lines (2r:17-18).

I propose that a reading of the *Secret Gospel of Mark* exposes a subplot involving the νεανίσκος in the text of *Secret Mark*, a subplot that is presented in only an imperfect and truncated fashion in canonical Mark. This story of the νεανίσκος, I submit, communicates *Secret Mark's* vision of the life and challenge of discipleship, as that is exemplified in the career of the νεανίσκος. This subplot may be elucidated first by means of a word study of the key term νεανίσκος, and then through an exegesis of five pericopae from *Secret Mark*, each of which deals with a νεανίσκος, and each of which is linked to the other pericopae by means of a series of literary connections.

The term νεανίσκος is a widely attested Greek word used to denote a young person or at times a servant. The range in age assumed to be fitting for a νεανίσκος generally includes the twenties and sometimes also the thirties. According to the description of the stages in one's life in Diogenes Laertius, one remains a child (παῖς) for twenty years, then a youth (νεηνίσκος) for twenty more years, a mature person (νεηνίης) for another twenty years, and an older person (γέρων) for a final twenty years (8.10). According to Philo of Alexandria, Hippocrates said that there are seven stages of human life, and the fourth is that of the νεανίσκος: one is νεανίσκος δ' ἄχρις αὐξήσιος ὅλου τοῦ σώματος, ἐς τὰ τετράκις ἑπτά— from τὰ τρὶς ἑπτά ("a youth until the growth of the whole body, up to four times seven [years]"—from "three times seven," *De opificio mundi* 105). In the New Testament and other early Christian literature, too, there are instances of such a general usage of the word νεανίσκος and related terms. In Luke 7:14, where the dead son of the widow of Nain is raised by Jesus in a pericope (7:11–17) without specific parallel in the synoptics, the youth is addressed as a νεανίσκος. (There are a few parallels between this story and the raising of the νεανίσκος in *Secret Mark*: a νεανίσκος has died, leaving his mother in mourning; upon arriving, Jesus touches the coffin and addresses the young man with the command ἐγέρθητι ["arise," 7:14], καὶ ἀνεκάθισεν ὁ νεκρὸς καὶ ἤρξατο λαλεῖν ["and the dead man sat up and began to speak," 7:15]. These parallels may be coincidental, and of no particular importance for our discussion here. Conversely, a case might be made to relate the Lukan pericope more closely to the account in *Secret Mark*. See Smith, 1973b: 109.) In the Acts of the Apostles the word νεανίσκος is employed several times: in Acts 2:17 the author uses the poetic parallelism of Joel 2:28 (3:1) to evaluate the Pentecost experience of the νεανίσκοι and the πρεσβύτεροι ("elders"); in Acts 5:10 οἱ νεανίσκοι of the congregation remove the corpse of Sapphira from the presence of Peter (οἱ νεώτεροι ["the young men"] had accomplished the same task, in 5:6, with Ananias); in Acts 20:12 the most reliable texts recount the story of Paul's raising the παῖς ("child") Eutychus, but Codex Bezae (D) refers to him as a νεανίσκος; and in Acts 23:16–22 Paul's nephew is called, in successive statements, a νεανίας ("young man") and a νεανίσκος. Again, 1 John 2:13–14, in the context of the author's affectionate references to his believing readers as τεκνία ("little children") and παιδία ("children"), explains why he is writing to the νεανίσκοι: ὅτι ἰσχυροί ἐστε καὶ ὁ λόγος τοῦ θεοῦ ἐν ὑμῖν μένει καὶ νενικήκατε τὸν πονηρόν ("because you are strong, and the word of God remains in you, and you have vanquished the evil one"). Lastly, it may be noted that νεανίσκοι also appear on the pages of the *Visions* and *Similitudes* of Hermas, and the *Gospel of Peter*: in the former they usually function as visionary or angelic beings; in the latter they play roles within the passion narrative (*Gos. Pet.* 9.37 refers to two young men from heaven, in a manner reminiscent of Luke 24:4—cf. also Matt 28:2–4; *Gos. Pet.* 13.55 refers to a single νεανίσκος in the otherwise empty tomb, in a manner much like Mark 16:5).

Such references in early Christian literature probably demonstrate only a rather general use of the term νεανίσκος. Scroggs and Groff suggest, "The word *neaniskos* is just possibly a quasi-technical term denoting the class of initiates," but they immediately add, "the evidence is extremely tenuous" (542). Several other passages in the Markan tradition, however, may focus more clearly and specifically upon the νεανίσκος as a paradigmatic disciple, and thus may employ the term νεανίσκος in a more technical sense. Since these passages are all interrelated, in my interpretation, as vignettes which together narrate a significant story about discipleship, I shall offer a brief analysis of five important pericopae which serve to advance the plot of this little story. These passages all are found in the second half of the Gospel of Mark, in Mark 10:13–16:8, and include, of course, the fragments of *Secret Mark*.

3.1.   Mark 10:17–22 narrates the story of the so-called rich young ruler. Mark describes this candidate for discipleship only as a rich man (ἔχων κτήματα πολλά, "having many possessions," 10:22) who claimed to have kept the commandments ἐκ νεότητος ("from youth," 10:20). Luke adds that he was a ruler (τις...ἄρχων, "a certain ruler," 18:18) who was very rich (ἦν γὰρ πλούσιος σφόδρα, "for he was very rich," 18:23); Luke's wording is nearly identical to that of *Secret Mark*, which says of the νεανίσκος, ἦν γὰρ πλούσιος ("for he was rich," 2r:6). (Mark also uses πλούσιος, "rich," in 10:17 according to several texts, chiefly A, K, and W.) Matthew twice calls the candidate a νεανίσκος (19:20, 22). In his use of this term Matthew arguably may preserve some of the original wording of the pericope: only here, in a synoptic pericope with clear links to the story of the νεανίσκος in *Secret Mark*, does Matthew employ the term. Furthermore, according to Mark 10:21, Jesus ἐμβλέψας αὐτῷ ἠγάπησεν αὐτόν ("looking upon him, loved him"). This reference to the love of Jesus for the youth is made here alone among the synoptics, although both of the Secret Gospel fragments (2r:4; 2r:15) employ the same theme of love between Jesus and the νεανίσκος; the first fragment reproduces Mark 10:21 word for word, but attributes the love to the νεανίσκος. (The issue of Lazarus and the Beloved Disciple in the Gospel of John will be addressed below.) The candidate of Mark 10:17–22, however, is scandalized by the cost of discipleship, and he turns away in sadness, unwilling to follow Jesus. This scene in the career of the νεανίσκος ends in vs 22, with the departure of the youth, but the discussion in the following verses of the Gospel of Mark (10:23–31) continues to consider the difficulties, and vicissitudes, of the life of the disciple: it is hard to enter the kingdom of God, and the cost is high.

The account of the rich youth in Mark 10:17–22 follows a related pericope about discipleship, namely the pronouncement story describing the disciples rebuking (ἐπετίμησαν αὐτοῖς, "they rebuked them") but Jesus blessing the παιδία ("children," Mark 10:13–16). This familiar scene is common in the world of the Middle East: the children come to see the teacher who is in the village. Yet it is clear from vss 14 and (especially) 15 that in its present form the pericope is not concerned merely with children: the kingdom of God, Mark writes, belongs to such people as the children (so vs 14); and Jesus is made to go on to observe, ἀμὴν λέγω ὑμῖν, ὃς ἂν μὴ δέξηται τὴν βασιλείαν τοῦ θεοῦ ὡς παιδίον, οὐ μὴ εἰσέλθῃ εἰς αὐτήν ("Truly I say to you, whoever does not receive the kingdom of God like a child shall not enter it," vs 15). In other words, in a manner typical of much of early Christian literature, the children are presented as typifying discipleship and the life of discipleship. Such becomes even clearer in vs 24, where Jesus is made to turn to his disciples themselves and address them as children: τέκνα, πῶς δύσκολόν ἐστιν εἰς τὴν βασιλείαν τοῦ θεοῦ εἰσελθεῖν ("Children, how difficult it is to enter the kingdom of God"). Although we may not be able to conclude that the author necessarily means to refer to baptism in vss 13–16, certainly the broader context of the pericope raises the issue of baptism (cf. vss 38–40), namely baptism as sacramental participation in the suffering of Jesus on the part of his disciples.

3.2.   The first fragment of the *Secret Gospel of Mark* (1v:23–2r:11), to be placed after Mark 10:34, presents the miracle story of the raising of a νεανίσκος. The parallels noted between the description of the νεανίσκος in this fragment and in Mark 10:17–22 suggest that this youth in *Secret Mark* is the same νεανίσκος as the rich man who refused to follow Jesus in Mark 10:17–22: in turning from Jesus, it may then be implied, he has turned from life and embraced death. As has been widely discussed in the scholarly literature, the scene described in this fragment is similar to the miracle story of the raising of Lazarus in John 11. A woman in Bethany, in mourning over the death of her brother, approaches Jesus and asks his help. The disciples rebuke her (ἐπετίμησαν αὐτῇ, "they rebuked her," 1v:25; cf. Mark 10:13), but Jesus goes to the tomb and raises the νεανίσκος from the dead. It is then that the νεανίσκος looks upon Jesus and loves him (2r:4): this verbatim parallel to Mark 10:21 suggests that only after being brought from death to life does the youth return the love with which Jesus loves him in Mark 10:21. Jesus and the νεανίσκος return to the young man's house, and it is added (2r:6), in a clear reference to Mark 10:22 (cf. also the wording of Luke 18:23), that the νεανίσκος is πλούσιος ("rich"). The final lines of this fragment of *Secret Mark* depict Jesus initiating the νεανίσκος, now dressed in what several scholars have interpreted to be the ritual garb of early Christian baptism (linen clothing over the naked body; see Morton Smith, 1973b; Jonathan Z. Smith; Scroggs and Groff; Crossan), and teaching him the mystery of the kingdom of God. In these lines the language of *Secret Mark* (2r:8) is precisely the same as Mark 14:51: in both cases the νεανίσκος is described περιβεβλημένος σινδόνα ἐπὶ γυμνοῦ ("wearing a linen cloth on his naked body").

The key to understanding the significance of the word σινδών ("linen") in the *Secret Gospel of Mark* and Mark 14:51 may be found in the only other instance of the usage of this term in the Gospel of Mark: Mark 15:46, where Joseph of Arimathea is said to have wrapped the corpse of Jesus in a σινδών, a linen shroud. In the Markan tradition a σινδών may represent two items of clothing: the linen garment of initiation of the νεανίσκος, and the linen burial shroud of Jesus. Yet the interplay between the two uses of the term, and the link between baptism and suffering in the Gospel of Mark, lead us to conclude that the σινδών of the νεανίσκος is quite the same as Jesus' shroud: the νεανίσκος participates in baptism as an experience of sharing in the suffering and death of Christ, and wears ritual clothing appropriate for such an experience.

The reference to six days (καὶ μεθ' ἡμέρας ἕξ, "and after six days," Jesus gives instruction to the νεανίσκος, 2r:6–7) in the first fragment of *Secret Mark* has provoked a considerable amount of scholarly speculation. This specific reference might be taken to be merely a temporal connective with a designated interval of time (cf. Smith, 1973b: 115); the fact that the immediate context in Mark refers to the resurrection μετὰ τρεῖς ἡμέρας ("after three days," 10:34) might also be significant in this regard. Yet a similar Markan reference to a six-day interval of time in 9:2 has prompted additional interpretations of the passage in *Secret Mark*. "After six days" might be interpreted as communicating an interval of a week; Luke's apparent revision of Mark 9:2 to read ὡσεὶ ἡμέραι ὀκτώ ("about eight days," 9:28) might indicate as much. Six days could also be understood as symbolizing an appropriate time of preparation and purification before an experience of meeting the divine (e.g., Exod 24:16). According to *Gos. Thom.* 4, "The person old in days will not hesitate to ask a little child of seven days (ⲟⲩⲕⲟⲩⲉⲓ ⲛ̄ϣⲏⲣⲉ ϣⲏⲙ ⲉϥ︤ⲛ︥ ⲥⲁϣϥ̄ ⲛ̄ⲍⲟⲟⲩ) about the place of life, and this person will live" (Nag Hammadi Codex II 33,5–9). Here the reference to "a little child of seven days" may derive from the Jewish practice of circumcising Jewish boys on the eighth day (cf. Gen 17:12; Phil 3:5). In the *Gospel of Thomas* the child who communicates knowledge is so innocent that he has not yet been circumcised. (In Hippolytus, *Refutatio omnium haeresium* 5.7.20, it is said that a Gospel according to Thomas refers to children of seven *years*.) Schenke appeals to the well-known theory that the story of the transfiguration originally was a narrative of a post-resurrection appearance of Christ, and connects these two instances of "after six days" in Mark to suggest that both proclaim the resurrection: "Once one imagines the transfiguration functioning as an appearance and glorification of Jesus at the end of Mark, then the correspondence emerges clearly: the phrase 'after six days' connects resurrection and metamorphosis in both cases. The resurrection and initiation of the ideal disciple represent the resurrection and deification of Jesus" (1984: 80). Talley, on the other hand, posits an interpretation based upon the Coptic liturgical calendar: "A peculiar aspect of the Coptic tradition is that it identifies the baptismal day, the sixth day of the sixth week, with a tradition which asserted that that was the day on which Jesus baptized his disciples" (44). Hence, Talley concludes, "we can see a pattern which is compellingly suggestive of a course reading of Mark beginning on January 6: the Baptism of Jesus on that day, the beginning of the imitation of Jesus' fast on the following day with the continued reading of the gospel during the weeks of the fast so as to arrive at chapter 10 by the sixth week, the reading of the secret gospel inserted into chapter 10 in close conjunction with the conferral of baptism in that sixth week, and the celebration of the entry into Jerusalem with chapter 11 of Mark on the following Sunday" (45–46).

3.3.   The third pericope concerned with the νεανίσκος in Mark is the scene found in the second fragment of *Secret Mark* (2r:14–16), which Clement states the Secret Gospel includes in Mark 10:46. *Secret Mark* 10:46 thus may be reconstructed to read approximately as follows: "And he comes to Jericho. And the sister of the youth whom Jesus loved and his mother and Salome were there, and Jesus did not receive them (fem.). And as he was leaving Jericho with his disciples and a large crowd, Bartimaeus son of Timaeus, a blind beggar, was sitting by the side of the road." This reference to the νεανίσκος and the women allows for a fuller and more felicitous reading of Mark 10:46, without the brusqueness of the canonical rendering: καὶ ἔρχονται εἰς Ἰεριχώ. καὶ ἐκπορευομένου αὐτοῦ ἀπὸ Ἰεριχώ... ("And they come to Jericho. And as he was leaving Jericho..."). Here canonical Mark gives the impression that the discussion of what transpired in Jericho has been omitted: according to the canonical text, nothing happened in Jericho! Clement's suggestion of the singular ἔρχεται ("he comes") differs from the plural ἔρχονται ("they come") in canonical Mark, the only such instance of disagreement between canonical Mark and citations from public Mark in the Mar Saba letter. (Notice should be taken that Luke 18:35 provides a paraphrase of the singular ἔρχεται of *Secret Mark* [ἐγένετο δὲ ἐν τῷ ἐγγίζειν αὐτὸν εἰς Ἰεριχώ..., "And it happened that as he approached Jericho..."], and that B* omits the clause in Mark 10:46 altogether.) The singular ἔρχεται reads more naturally with the following καὶ ἐκπορευομένου αὐτοῦ ("And as he was leaving"), also in the singular. The mention of Salome in the *Secret Mark* fragment is particularly striking, since in the New Testament writings Salome is mentioned by name only in the Gospel of Mark (15:40; 16:1); she plays a much more prominent role in Gnostic and extracanonical sources (see Smith, 1973b: 190–91).

Secret Mark 10:46 reiterates the love of Jesus for the νεανίσκος (cf. Mark 10:21; also *Secret Mark* 2r:4), and adds a detail significant for our further observations of the interaction between the νεανίσκος and the disciples or women: while Jesus loves the νεανίσκος, he does not accept the women. The description of the νεανίσκος as one ὃν ἠγάπα αὐτὸν ὁ Ἰησοῦς ("whom Jesus loved") calls to mind at once the Beloved Disciple in John. The contrary statement that Jesus did not "receive" or "accept" the women has prompted Morton Smith to suggest that the original text here has been censored. Smith's careful examination of the vocabulary, phraseology, and grammar of the Secret Gospel fragments leads him to conclude that in general these fragments are characteristically and preponderantly Markan (1973b: 123–35); but the use of ἀπεδέξατο ("he received") is an exception. "In the NT, ἀποδέχομαι is found only in Lk.-Acts," Smith observes (1973b: 121), and Clement uses the verb frequently too. Smith posits that the story as transmitted by Clement "has no apparently significant content. There is no miracle, no saying, nothing but Jesus' refusal to receive, on one occasion, three women." What was censored, Smith concludes, was in all likelihood "a conversation with Salome" (122; compare *Gos. Thom.* 61). Crossan concurs with Smith's interpretation (109). Yet it must be acknowledged that the root verb δέχεσθαι ("to receive") is used several times in the Gospel of Mark, and often in a sense not unlike that of the ἀπεδέξατο of *Secret Mark* (e.g., Mark 6:11; 9:37; 10:15). Further, there may in fact be "significant content" to the pericope as transmitted by Clement. That content will be clarified by the actions of the women in Mark 16:1–8.

3.4. Mark 14:51–52 portrays a νεανίσκος who is dressed in σινδών ("linen") and is seized at the time of the arrest of Jesus. (The reference to οἱ νεανίσκοι in some late texts of Mark seems designed to resolve the enigma of the single νεανίσκος; this attempt at textual clarification need not concern us here.) Just as all the other disciples forsook Jesus and fled, so also the νεανίσκος runs away, leaving his σινδών behind and escaping naked. On account of the obvious verbal links between this passage and the fragments of the *Secret Gospel of Mark* (νεανίσκος...περιβεβλημένος σινδόνα ἐπὶ γυμνοῦ..., "a youth...wearing a linen cloth on his naked body..."), I interpret the youth of Mark 14:51–52 to be the same paradigmatic disciple as the νεανίσκος in *Secret Mark*. Once dressed in the ritual garment of initiation, he has abandoned his baptismal robes and fled.

Many commentators have attempted interpretations of this elusive passage, but few of the interpretations are satisfying. Many have suggested that the νεανίσκος was an historical disciple, perhaps an unnamed eyewitness or even Mark inserting himself into the plot of the gospel (e.g., Lagrange; Taylor). Others have sought to derive this reference to the νεανίσκος from Gen 39:12—Joseph fleeing, *sans* cloak, from Potiphar's wife—or Amos 2:16—the brave fleeing naked on that Day (e.g., Montefiore; Waetjen); Vincent Taylor rightly dismisses such efforts as "desperate in the extreme" (561). Other scholars are probably closer to a correct interpretation in proposing that the figure of the νεανίσκος represents Christ or the Christian: the νεανίσκος prefigures Christ, especially the risen Christ (e.g., Knox; Vanhoye), dramatizes the flight of the disciples (Fleddermann), or symbolizes the Christian initiate who becomes like Christ (e.g., Scroggs and Groff; Schenke, 1984).

In an Addendum to their article, Scroggs and Groff discuss these two verses in relation to the Secret Gospel material that had just been published, but their discussion is problematic. They suggest that the first Secret Gospel fragment could portray "pre-baptismal catechesis, necessarily preceding the actual baptism, which is itself not alluded to until 14:51–52." In Mark 14:51–52, then, "the believer is symbolically baptized," and dies with Christ as he leaves his linen garment behind, only to appear dressed in white baptismal clothing in Mark 16:5 (548). Morton Smith responds to this suggestion by noting sharply, "This interpretation neglects only the main facts: this young man deserted Christ and saved himself" (1982: 457). I agree with Smith. Scroggs and Groff rightly recognize the baptismal significance of the Markan passages under discussion, but seem to locate the baptism itself in the wrong pericope! In

14:51–52 the point of the passage is not the baptizing of the νεανίσκος but rather the forsaking of baptismal loyalties: the paradigmatic disciple is scandalized by the suffering of Jesus no less than the other disciples, and even abandons his sacramental clothes symbolizing his participation in Jesus' passion and death. The viability of discipleship itself seems in doubt as the tension builds in Mark 14.

3.5.   The final pericope in the story of the νεανίσκος as disciple is Mark 16:1–8. The developing tension concerning discipleship, as observed in the Markan passion narrative, is partly resolved (but only partly resolved) in the scene at Jesus' tomb. The women, including Salome, go to the tomb to anoint the body, but what they see there amazes them. Inside the tomb they see the νεανίσκος himself, wearing clothing once again, now περιβεβλημένον στολὴν λευκήν ("wearing a white robe," 16:5). On the basis of this description of the νεανίσκος I interpret this youth in Mark 16 to be the prototypal disciple whose story we have been tracing (against Fleddermann: 418). There is no compelling reason to consider him an angel; here in Mark the scene is quite different from that in both Matt 28:1–10, where an apocalyptic angel is explicitly mentioned and described, and Luke 24:1–11, where two angelic men (24:4: ἄνδρες δύο, "two men"; 24:23: ὀπτασίαν ἀγγέλων, "a vision of angels") in dazzling clothes inspire fear and awe.

Furthermore, the white robe of the youth must be similar to the ritual σινδών he has previously worn and subsequently abandoned. The only substantial difference may be the glory or purity attached to the white robe of chapter 16, which the νεανίσκος wears as he identifies with the dying and rising Christ within the tomb. Scroggs and Groff also understand the στολὴ λευκή ("white robe") of Mark 16:5 to be "the traditional garment put on the person just emerging from the baptismal waters. It symbolizes the new existence of the believer, in effect, his resurrection" (543). Thus the νεανίσκος is portrayed in the same way as the faithful of the book of Revelation: they are περιβεβλημένους στολὰς λευκάς ("wearing white robes," 7:9, etc.). These white robes reserved for glorified Christians recall the garb of initiates into some of the mystery religions of antiquity: in the mysteries of Isis, those of the Orphics, the Andanian mysteries, and the like, the faithful were commonly dressed in white linen. Since such a use of white linen may be of Egyptian origin, the mystery-cult language and the Alexandrian setting in the Mar Saba letter of Clement become all the more interesting.

The νεανίσκος of Mark 16 has reaffirmed his baptismal loyalties, and proceeds to explain to the visiting women how they and the other disciples may see Christ in Galilee. Yet the women are overcome by fear: they flee away, and say nothing about these remarkable matters. With such a description, I suggest, the Gospel of Mark comes to a close. A full discussion of the conclusion of the Gospel of Mark cannot be undertaken here; I simply suggest that Mark originally ended at 16:8, in spite of the creative and imaginative efforts of scholars to demonstrate that an appearance story (perhaps the transfiguration narrative, Mark 9:2–8) may be taken as the original post-resurrection ending of Mark. According to the Gospel of Mark, previously the twelve (or the eleven) had fled from the arrest of Jesus, and Peter had denied Jesus. Now the women too flee from the tomb in fear; only the youth is left to proclaim the crucified and risen Christ. It is no wonder that, as we have seen earlier, the second fragment of the Secret Gospel has Jesus refusing to accept the women who are with the νεανίσκος. They, after all, unlike the νεανίσκος at the end of Mark, do not endure in the life of discipleship.

Lately the interpretation of the role of the women disciples in the Gospel of Mark by Elisabeth Schüssler Fiorenza and Elizabeth Struthers Malbon has presented a different assessment of their role in Mark 16. Fiorenza suggests that "the women disciples flee not from the angel and the resurrection news but from the tomb," and eventually bring the resurrection message "to special designated persons," namely the disciples and Peter, while maintaining silence only to the public. Hence, she concludes, "Despite the extraordinary fear for their lives the women disciples stood with Jesus in his suffering, sought to honor him in his death, and now become the proclaimers of his resurrection" (322). Such an interpretation, attractive as it is, seems to overlook the finality of Mark 16:8 (οὐδενὶ οὐδὲν εἶπαν, "they said nothing to any one"; it does not seem to me that the similar clause in Mark 1:44 mitigates this finality), and minimizes the force of the women disciples' act of flight (ἔφυγον, "they fled," also used to describe the flight of the male disciples in 14:50 and that of the νεανίσκος in 14:52). Still it should be noted, with Fiorenza, that the women disciples are present at the crucifixion, as they look on from afar (Mark 15:40–41): "Though the twelve have forsaken Jesus, betrayed and denied him, the women disciples, by contrast, are found under the cross, risking their own lives and safety" (320). The significance of these women disciples at the cross must not be ignored, nor should the roles of such followers as Bartimaeus (Mark 10:52), Simon of Cyrene (15:21), the centurion (15:39), and Joseph of Arimathea (15:43–46). Yet it is also likely that the flight of the women in Mark 16:8 should be seen as the culminating stage in the progressive defection of the disciples. After Judas (Mark 14:43–45), the rest of the male disciples (14:50), the νεανίσκος (14:52), and Peter (14:66–72) all fail to follow Jesus, the women, too, finally flee in fear (cf. Munro: 239–40).

With the abrupt ending of Mark the attention turns to the implied reader, for only he or she can resolve the remaining tensions in the gospel (Petersen). All the closest followers of Jesus have fled in the face of the cross and the resurrection, but the νεανίσκος has faced the difficulties and challenges of discipleship, and in the end has identified with Christ in death and resurrection. Throughout the Markan subplot about the νεανίσκος we may notice that the νεανίσκος and the disciples commonly are set over against each other for comparison or contrast. Thus the wealthy young man of Mark 10:17–22 turns away from following Jesus, but the disciples counter by insisting, through Peter, that they have left all and followed Jesus (10:28). Again, the wealthy νεανίσκος of the fragments of *Secret Mark* is baptized by Jesus, just as the disciples are to be baptized into the suffering of Jesus (10:38–39); the text of *Secret Mark* goes on to observe that the νεανίσκος is loved by Jesus and returns the love, while the women are not a part of this network of love. Once again, the νεανίσκος of Mark 14:51–52 flees from Jesus, as the other disciples also have done. But in chapter 16 the νεανίσκος alone, in the face of the defection of the other disciples, can challenge the reader of Mark. Will the reader flee from Mark's theology of the cross and resurrection, like the twelve and even the women? Or will the reader see himself or herself in the νεανίσκος, and also take up the costly life of discipleship? With such a challenge the Gospel of Mark abruptly, but fittingly, comes to a conclusion.

4. *Implications*

If this thesis concerning the subplot about the νεανίσκος is convincing, then some of the implications for further Markan research are noteworthy. Several questions might be addressed in subsequent discussion. For instance, what is the origin and development of the subplot itself? Did it emerge from an aretalogical source as the miracle story of the raising of a dead youth (understood as the νεανίσκος in *Secret Mark* and Lazarus in John 11), only to be expanded and modified into the subplot on discipleship in the *Secret Gospel of Mark*? Was the subplot once an independent story in the tradition, or did it develop as a series of vignettes projected intermittently into the gospel account? And finally, what does this subplot, intricately woven as it is into the fabric of *Secret Mark*, do to clarify, confuse, or complicate the knotty questions of the niceties of redactional development in the Markan trajectory?

The study of the *Secret Gospel of Mark* may also advance the discussion of the relationship between the Markan and Johannine traditions, and the role of the Beloved Disciple in the Gospel of John. The miracle story of the raising of the νεανίσκος in *Secret Mark* is remarkably similar to the story of Lazarus in John 11, except that the Secret Gospel account has features suggesting that it is more primitive than the Johannine account, and that the Johannine account is dependent, directly or indirectly, upon the Secret Gospel account (so Smith; Koester; Crossan; Bruce begs to disagree). The Markan story of the νεανίσκος in the Mar Saba manuscript lacks the details we expect in a more developed tradition (personal names, descriptions of features of the miracle, etc.), and shows no evidence of specifically Johannine traits (vocabulary, delay of the miracle, aretalogical self-predication). The presentation of the νεανίσκος in Mark also bears striking resemblance to the Beloved Disciple in John, as Schenke has noted (1984: 77). The youth ὃν ἠγάπα αὐτὸν ὁ Ἰησοῦς ("whom Jesus loved," 2r:15) resembles the disciple ὃν ἠγάπα ὁ Ἰησοῦς in the Gospel of John (13:23–26; 19:26–27; 20:2–10; 21:7, 20–23, 24; cf. also ὁ μαθητὴς ὁ ἄλλος, "the other disciple"/ἄλλος μαθητής, "another disciple" in 18:15–16; 20:2–10). The Johannine Beloved Disciple has been widely discussed in the scholarly literature, and has been identified, variously, as John the son of Zebedee, John Mark, Lazarus (cf. John 11:3, 5, 11, 36), or (since the discovery of the Nag Hammadi codices) as Judas Thomas (cf. *Gospel of Thomas*, *Book of Thomas*), Mary Magdalene (cf. *Gospel of Philip*, *Gospel of Mary*), or even James the brother of the Lord (cf. *Apocryphon of James*; Schenke, 1986). Finally, Raymond E. Brown rightly observes, "There is little doubt that in Johannine thought the Beloved Disciple can symbolize the Christian" (1966–70: 924). This symbolic understanding of the Beloved Disciple, together with the parallels between the raising of the νεανίσκος and the story of Lazarus, brings us especially close to the interpretation presented here of the νεανίσκος as a paradigm for discipleship in canonical and *Secret Mark*.

WORKS CONSULTED

Beskow, Per
    1983   *Strange Tales about Jesus: A Survey of Unfamiliar Gospels*. Philadelphia: Fortress.

Brown, Raymond E.
    1966-70 *The Gospel According to John*. Anchor Bible 29–29A. Garden City, NY: Doubleday.
    1974   "The Relation of 'The Secret Gospel of Mark' to the Fourth Gospel." *CBQ* 36: 466–85.

Bruce, F. F.
1974 *The 'Secret' Gospel of Mark*. Ethel M. Wood Lecture. London: Athlone.

Cameron, Ron
1982 (ed.) *The Other Gospels: Non-Canonical Gospel Texts*. Philadelphia: Westminster.
1987 Review of Crossan, 1985 in *JBL* 106: 558–60.

Crossan, John Dominic
1985 *Four Other Gospels: Shadows on the Contours of Canon*. Minneapolis: Winston.

Fiorenza, Elisabeth Schüssler
1983 *In Memory of Her: A Feminist Theological Reconstruction of Christian Origins*. New York: Crossroad.

Fleddermann, Harry
1979 "The Flight of a Naked Young Man (Mark 14:51–52)." *CBQ* 41: 412–18.

Fuller, Reginald H.
1976 *Longer Mark: Forgery, Interpolation, or Old Tradition?* Center for Hermeneutical Studies in Hellenistic and Modern Culture, Colloquy 18. Ed. Wilhelm H. Wuellner. Berkeley: Center for Hermeneutical Studies.

Gourgues, Michel
1981 "À propos du symbolisme christologique et baptismal de Marc 16.5." *NTS* 27: 672–78.

Kermode, Frank
1979 *The Genesis of Secrecy: On the Interpretation of Narrative*. Cambridge: Harvard University Press.

Knox, John
1951 "A Note on Mark 14:51–52." Pp. 27–30 in *The Joy of Study: Papers on New Testament and Related Subjects Presented to Honor Frederick Clifton Grant*. Ed. Sherman E. Johnson. New York: Macmillan.

Koester, Helmut
1980 "Tradition and History of the Early Christian Gospel Literature." Shaffer Lectures, Yale University. (Cited in typescript).

1982	*History and Literature of Early Christianity.* Vol. 2 of *Introduction to the New Testament.* Philadelphia: Fortress.
1983	"History and Development of Mark's Gospel (From Mark to Secret Mark and 'Canonical' Mark)." Pp. 35–57 in *Colloquy on New Testament Studies: A Time for Reappraisal and Fresh Approaches.* Ed. Bruce Corley. Macon, GA: Mercer University Press.
1984	"Überlieferung und Geschichte der frühchristlichen Evangelienliteratur." Pp. 1463–1542 in *ANRW* 2.25.2. Ed. Hildegard Temporini and Wolfgang Haase. Berlin/New York: De Gruyter.

Lagrange, Marie-Joseph
1929   *Évangile selon Saint Marc.* EtBib. Paris: Gabalda.

Malbon, Elizabeth Struthers
1983   "Fallible Followers: Women and Men in the Gospel of Mark." *Semeia* 28: 29–48.

Meyer, Marvin W.
1983   "The νεανίσκος in Canonical and Secret Mark." Paper presented at the One Hundred Nineteenth Annual Meeting of the Society of Biblical Literature, Dallas, TX, 19–22 December 1983, and forthcoming in *The Second Century.*

Montefiore, C. G.
1927   *The Synoptic Gospels.* 2 vols. London: Macmillan.

Munro, Winsome
1982   "Women Disciples in Mark?" *CBQ* 44: 225–41.

Neirynck, Frans
1979   "La fuite du jeune homme en Mc 14,51–52." *EThL* 55: 43–66.

Petersen, Norman R.
1980   "When is the End not the End? Literary Reflections on the Ending of Mark's Narrative." *Int* 34: 151–66.

Quesnell, Quentin
1975   "The Mar Saba Clementine: A Question of Evidence." *CBQ* 37: 48–67.
1976   "A Reply to Morton Smith." *CBQ* 38: 200–203.

Schenke, Hans-Martin
  1984   "The Mystery of the Gospel of Mark." *The Second Century* 4: 65–82.
  1986   "The Function and Background of the Beloved Disciple in the Gospel of John." Pp. 111–25 in *Nag Hammadi, Gnosticism, and Early Christianity*. Ed. Charles W. Hedrick and Robert Hodgson, Jr. Peabody, MA: Hendrickson.

Scroggs, Robin, and Kent I. Groff
  1973   "Baptism in Mark: Dying and Rising with Christ." *JBL* 92: 531–48.

Smith, Jonathan Z.
  1966   "The Garments of Shame." *HR* 5: 217–38.

Smith, Morton
  1960   "Monasteries and Their Manuscripts." *Archaeology* 13: 172–77.
  1973a *The Secret Gospel: The Discovery and Interpretation of the Secret Gospel According to Mark*. New York: Harper & Row.
  1973b *Clement of Alexandria and a Secret Gospel of Mark*. Cambridge: Harvard University Press.
  1976   "On the Authenticity of the Mar Saba Letter of Clement." *CBQ* 38: 196–99.
  1982   "Clement of Alexandria and Secret Mark: The Score at the End of the First Decade." *HTR* 75: 449–61.
  1984   "Regarding *Secret Mark*: A Response by Morton Smith to the Account by Per Beskow." *JBL* 103: 624.

Stählin, Otto, ed.
  1980   *Clemens Alexandrinus 4/1: Register*. 2d ed. Ursula Treu. GCS. Berlin: Akademie-Verlag.

Talley, Thomas
  1982   "Liturgical Time in the Ancient Church: The State of Research." *Studia Liturgica* 14: 34–51.

Tannehill, Robert C.
  1977   "The Disciples in Mark: The Function of a Narrative Role." *JR* 57: 386–405.

Taylor, Vincent
  1966   *The Gospel According to St. Mark*. London: Macmillan.

Vanhoye, Albert
   1971   "La fuite du jeune homme nu (Mc 14,51–52)." *Bib* 52: 401–6.

Waetjen, Herman
   1965   "The Ending of Mark and the Gospel's Shift in Eschatology."
             Annual of the Swedish Theological Institute 4: 114–31.

Thoughts on Two Extracanonical Gospels

John Dominic Crossan
DePaul University

My response is restricted to the articles by Arthur J. Dewey and Marvin W. Meyer which propose alternative redactional analyses for the *Gospel of Peter* and the *Secret Gospel of Mark* than those suggested in my own work. Such very necessary debates should not obscure the fact that we are in fundamental agreement on the importance of these two extracanonical writings for the very genesis of the intracanonical gospels. I also emphasize that I consider our oppositions to be delicate balances of plausibilities. What is most important, in any case, is to have several clear and even bold hypotheses which can then be tested by others both internally and externally.

Vindicated Innocence in the Gospel of Peter and in Mark

Arthur Dewey and I agree on certain major conclusions concerning the *Gospel of Peter* and these are vital enough to be underlined initially lest later disagreements muffle their impact. The last sentences of his Summation conclude, "But most significant of all is the possibility that the earliest stage of *Gos. Pet.* holds within it the generic seeds of the subsequent passion narratives. At the earliest stage we do not have sheer historical report; on the contrary, we have an imaginative attempt to discern the Wisdom of God." If those results were academically accepted and publicly explained, they would do much to remedy the last chapters of the gospels which, when taken literally and historically, serve both to libel Judaism and to trivialize Christianity.

I focus the discussion on one major point where a decision one way or another will affect everything else and where it might be possible to come to some consensus. We are in agreement that the original layer of the *Gospel of Peter* is generically controlled and developed through the traditional Jewish story of the vindicated just one. We are also in agreement that George W. E. Nickelsburg, Jr.'s analysis of that tradition is fundamental for understanding its use in the *Gospel of Peter*. But we disagree quite basically on the content of that original layer, as summarized in Table 1:

Table 1

Narrative Units	Layers (Crossan)	Layers (Dewey)
Passion	= I [1.1–2 & 2.5b–6.22]	= I [2.5c–5.15a; 5.16–6.21; 8.28b]
Guarded Tomb	= I [7.25 & 8.28–9.34]	= II [8.28a; 8.29b–9.34]
Resurrection	= I [9.35–10.42 & 11.45–49]	= II [9.35–37; 10.39b–40; 11.45]

For me, those three narrative units of Passion, Guarded Tomb, and Resurrection form a single compositional layer controlled by the traditional narrative of vindicated innocence and they constitute the original layer of the *Gospel of Peter* (= I). For Dewey only the Passion unit is in that position (= I) while the Guarded Tomb and Resurrection units form a secondary layer (= II) containing an epiphany story. The question under debate is thus quite specific: if one grants the controlling model of the vindicated innocence story, which of those complexes is the more likely original layer based upon it?

Two Modes of Vindicated Innocence.

There is a very basic distinction to be made within the theme of the vindicated innocent one between a vindication *before death here on earth* and a vindication *after death in heaven*. It is that former scenario that appears in Genesis 37–50, Ahikar, Esther, Daniel 3 and 6, Susanna, and 3 Maccabees. It is precisely those writings that give us not only a theme but a plot, not only a claim but a narrative sequence. And in that sequence the vindicated ones are restored in the presence of those very enemies who sought their deaths. I emphasize that point: in this mode, the vindication takes place visibly here on visible earth. In the latter scenario, for example, in 2 Maccabees 7 and Wisdom 2–5, the innocent ones are actually put to death and vindication is asserted in promise and threat for the hereafter. Put bluntly: in Daniel 3 and 6 we have miracles, in 2 Maccabees 7 we have martyrs. For the sake of brevity, I term those twin modes, miracle vindication and martyr vindication.

Three points must be made about those modes. First, we only have a complete story with normal narrative closure in the case of miracle vindication. Since martyr vindication presumes some otherworldly consummation, we do not really have any *narrative* about vindicated innocence but only the theme transfigured by belief in an afterlife and asserted in the face of death. Second, Nickelsburg's examples of miracle vindication outnumber his martyr examples by seven to two and that reminds us that the former were historically the earlier cases. The latter were only possible with belief in an afterlife. I do not, of course, mean that every miracle vindication must be earlier than every martyr vindication but simply that, in terms of the subgeneric development, the former mode antedated that latter one. Third, and presuming that subgeneric sequence, one might well wonder if the martyr vindication was not deliberately intended as a theological corrective to the miracle vindication. Vindication by miracle, for example, might be a very useful paradigm against social discrimination but it could take vindication by martyr (or Maccabee) to handle lethal persecution.

That modal or subgeneric distinction is noted in Nickelsburg's initial study (1972: 170) but is not used in his later application of it to Mark's passion narrative (1980: 158–59). But Mark's passion account, while clearly a narrative of vindicated innocence, emphatically does not follow the miracle but the martyr paradigm. Thus, for example, when Nickelsburg is applying the twenty-one generic components of the Persecution and Vindication genre to Mark's passion, it works quite well for the Persecution section but here is all there is for the Vindication part:

##15–17.	*Rescue, Vindication, Exaltation:*	Mark 14:62
#18.	*Investiture:*	Mark 15:17
#19.	*Acclamation:*	Mark 15:18, 26, 39
#20.	*Reactions:*	none
#21.	*Punishment:*	none

My point is not that Nickelsburg is wrong. He is quite correct in his analysis, but with a martyr as distinct from a miracle vindication that is the best either Mark or he can do. Martyr vindication is open only to the eyes of faith and is present only as assertion and declaration, as threat and promise. For Mark, in fact, the *Acclamation* of the centurion arises not from how Jesus miraculously avoided death but from how, repeated from 15:37 into 15:39, "he breathed his last."

Modes of Vindication in Mark and the Gospel of Peter.

Dewey applies Nickelsburg's genre of Persecution and Vindication to the *Gospel of Peter*. So do I, although I have worked more with a five-fold generic structure rather than with a twenty-one element generic matrix (1988: 297–334). That, however, is not our disagreement. It is that Dewey applies Nickelsburg's genre of Persecution and Vindication or Vindicated Innocence only to the Passion unit of the *Gospel of Peter* while I apply it to the three units of Passion, Guarded Tomb, and Resurrection.

Dewey explains the Vindication section on his hypothesis by noting that "*Vindication* comes not in the heavenly realms but through earthly wonders." Thus, for example, he finds the generic elements of *Prayer, Rescue, Vindication,* and *Reaction/Acclamation* in the following four units respectively:

> [5.19a] And the Lord called out and cried, "My power, O power, thou hast forsaken me!"
> [5.19b] And having said this he was taken up.
> [5.20–6.21] And at the same hour the veil of the temple in Jerusalem was rent in two. And then the Jews drew the nails from the hands of the Lord and laid him on the earth. And the whole earth shook and there came a great fear.
> [8.28b] ...all the people were murmuring and beating their breasts, saying, "If at his death these exceeding great signs have come to pass, behold how righteous he was!"

That is not an impossible position nor even an implausible one. Indeed, if there was any documentary evidence that such a unit had ever existed as a separate writing, one would have to accept such a reading of its ending. But I still think my own reading is a more plausible or even a much more plausible one.

The core of our divergence lies in different modellings of Nickelsburg's generic basis. Figure 1 summarizes the way Nickelsburg himself and then Dewey following him envisage that model:

Figure 1

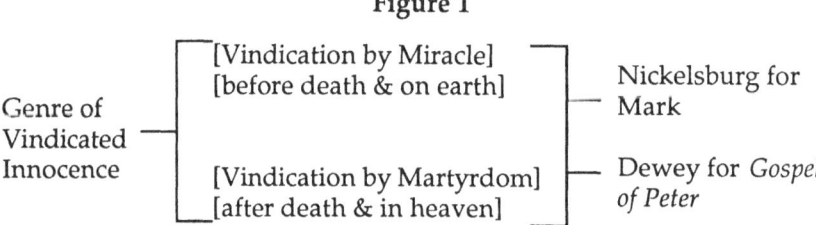

In other words, there is no emphatic distinction made between those twin modes or subgeneric transformations (hence the square brackets on them) and so neither is that distinction of great importance for an application to either Mark or the *Gospel of Peter*. Put another way, Nickelsburg's correct reading of Mark as, in my words, vindication by martyrdom, is much too influential in Dewey's reading of the *Gospel of Peter*, which is not vindication by martyrdom but by miracle. Figure 2 summarizes the way I see the appropriate modelling of Nickelsburg's generic proposal:

Figure 2

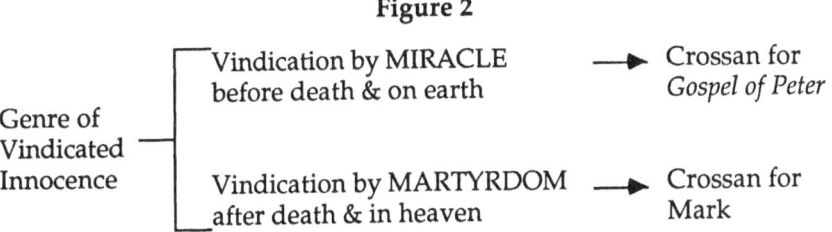

In other words, I make an emphatic distinction between those modes or subgenres (hence capitals instead of brackets) and I argue that miracle vindication determines the structure and content of the *Gospel of Peter* while, to the deliberate converse, martyr vindication determines the passion in Mark. I make no argument about chronological priority based on the far older existence of the miracle over the martyr vindication. Once the latter arrived, both modes remained coexistent. For example, both 3 Maccabees with its miracle vindication and Wisdom (2-5) with its martyr vindication have been plausibly dated to the time and danger of Caligula in 38-41 C.E. (Collins: 106, 182). I do, however, note that martyr vindication, in, for example, Wisdom 2-5, may be precisely a corrective to miracle vindication for and by those whose imagination or experience does not find the latter particularly persuasive.

My own hypothesis, then, is that not just the Passion unit but all of the Passion, Guarded Tomb, and Resurrection units in the *Gospel of Peter* form the original stratum. First, it has narrative integrity. The Jewish authorities and the Jewish people begin in agreement against Jesus. But the miracles attendant upon his death change the people's minds. Hence the Jewish authorities themselves along with Roman guards watch over the tomb. And hence again they are there to see the Resurrection with, of course, divergent reactions. Second, it has generic integrity, but in miracle rather than martyr mode of vindication. The enemies of Jesus are forced to witness his vindication and he is acclaimed by the imperial power. Indeed, the closest model is Daniel 6. Third, it has theological integrity. This is very important for my argument but it is hardly mentioned by Dewey. I consider that the corporate nature of the vindicated innocence genre and the corporate resonances in the passion section demand some corresponding corporate vision in the resurrection section and that, of course, is exactly what the following and speaking cross is all about. We are dealing, in summary, with *corporate* passion and *corporate* resurrection and the attempt to *narrate* them together against the background of the *miracle* mode of the genre of vindicated innocence. That is what the *Cross Gospel* in *Gos. Pet.* 1.1-2; 2.5b-6.22;

7.25; 8.28–10.42; 11.45–49 set out to do and it did it brilliantly. That was what Mark's passion and resurrection account set out to undo on the model of the martyr mode of vindication, and it undid it with equal brilliance.

One final point. Although I still find my own interpretation more plausible than Dewey's, his article has made me think more about what would have been there before my own postulated original layer. There were two basic materials but since I have no reason to presume their conjunction let alone their narrative structuring I would never call them an original stratum or layer. They are the materials out of which the original and narrative layer was created in the *Cross Gospel*. First, there were the manifold units of the prophetic passion, for example,

(1) the authorities at the trial in *Gos. Pet.* 1.1 from Ps 2:1,
(2) the abuse and torture in *Gos. Pet.* 3.9 from Isa 50:6–7 and Zech 12:10,
(3) the death among thieves in *Gos. Pet.* 4.10a from Isa 53:12,
(4) the silence in *Gos. Pet.* 4.10b from Isa 50:7 and 53:7,
(5) the garments and lots in *Gos. Pet.* 4.12 from Ps 22:18,
(6) the darkness at noon in *Gos. Pet.* 5.15 from Amos 8:9,
(7) the gall and vinegar drink in *Gos. Pet.* 5.16 from Ps 69:21,
(8) the death-cry in *Gos. Pet.* 5.19 from Ps 22:1.

Those texts are, of course, explicitly applied to Jesus in other intrabiblical and extrabiblical early Christian texts, and they are very well known. What is now extremely difficult if not impossible for us to do is to hear those individual resonances *not as sequentially discrete moments within a passion narrative but as simultaneously total references to a passion event*. But before anyone even conceived of a passion narrative, say, for instance, the garments and lots from Ps 22:18 could refer to the whole passion as absolutely bereft situation.

Second, there was the epiphanic resurrection account. Dewey considered this a secondary layer in the *Gospel of Peter*. If anything, and with no intention of being unduly perverse, I would presume its absolute primacy. We have, for example, three other independent versions of this basic account in the *Martyrdom and Ascension of Isaiah* 3.13b–18 (*OTP* 2. 160), the Codex Bobiensis just before Mark 16:4 (Metzger: 121–22), and, possibly, the Greek but not the Ethiopic version of *Apocalypse of Peter* 5–6 & 12–13 (*NTA* 2. 680–81). Those independent accounts of what I term the "escorted resurrection" in which the Lord is accompanied heavenwards by two transcendent beings (Crossan, 1988: 337–62) indicate that the core of the resurrection account in the *Gospel of Peter*, but not, of course, anything about the following or talking cross, existed before and continued apart from its use in that document. Once again, I emphasize that the pre-existence of that unit about the escorted resurrection should not be termed an original layer but rather available materials for the *Cross Gospel*. The contribution of that document was to create, as far as we know for the first time, a passion-resurrection *narrative* by uniting the disparate references of the prophetic passion into a sequential story, by leading from that into the story of the guarded tomb, and by finishing with the escorted resurrection tradition including, now, the accompanying and talking cross. All, of course, based on the corporate and inclusive model of the genre of innocence vindicated here on earth and before one's enemies. And if not exactly before death, then, at least, with a very special death whose primary function was to allow the Son of God to infiltrate hell and liberate those who sleep.

Corporate Emphasis and Wisdom Theology.

The last words in Dewey's article are "the Wisdom of God." That reminds us that the story of vindicated innocence or the genre of persecution and vindication comes out of the wisdom tradition. So, of course, does the earlier stratum in Q as proposed by John S. Kloppenborg (1987). Further, in his article for this volume he has noted the corporate and inclusive rather than individual and exclusive manner in which Jesus is united with the rejected representatives of Wisdom in Q and also united with the suffering just ones of Israel in my reconstructed *Cross Gospel*. That means that those two quite separate and independent strands of tradition, the *Sayings Gospel* within Q and the Passion-Resurrection Gospel (*Cross Gospel*) within the *Gospel of Peter*, share alike a common basis in wisdom theology and a common corporate vision of Jesus and Israel's past. That will require further discussion for Christian origins.

The Young Man in Secret Mark and Canonical Mark

Once again, Marvin Meyer and I agree on one very basic fact in discussing the *Secret Gospel of Mark* and the canonical gospel of Mark, namely, that canonical Mark is a revised version of *Secret Mark* rather than the reverse. The debate, therefore, has a common basis and concerns the best explanation for the extent and intention of that "revision."

Meyer notes that "the comments of Clement lead us to conclude that *Secret Mark* closely resembled public (or canonical) Mark, except for the inclusion of the two fragments Clement cites. In the surviving portion of his letter Clement himself indicates nothing whatsoever to contradict such a conclusion." In other words, the "revision" by canonical Mark consisted simply in eliminating two small sections from *Secret Mark*. In thinking of canonical Mark, then, we are hardly dealing with an author, even a redactor, or even an editor. It is almost like a publisher's corrected edition. It required at best some blue slashes through a manuscript. For all practical purposes, *Secret Mark* is canonical Mark. Thus, for instance, when I claimed that (canonical) Mark had created the story of the empty tomb, I simply meant that (secret) Mark did so. Since we never really knew who Mark was in any case, what difference if we now call him secret Mark instead of canonical Mark? This is an attractively simple solution, more attractive and more simple than my own "idiosyncratic" suggestion. Is it, however, more plausible?

Meyer postulates a subplot concerning a νεανίσκος or "youth" which has the following five elements (note abbreviations):

(Y1) The Youth refuses to follow Jesus: Mark 10:17–22
(Y2) The Youth is raised from the dead: *Secret Mark* 1
(Y3) The Youth's family at Jericho: *Secret Mark* 2
(Y4) The Youth flees naked from Gethsemane: Mark 14:51–52
(Y5) The Youth in the empty tomb: Mark 16:1–8

He proposes that all five units of that subplot were present in *Secret Mark* but that canonical Mark reduced it to three units. Please note that, from a documentary point of view, we are certain only that Y2 and Y3 are in *Secret Mark* and Y1, Y4, and Y5 are in canonical Mark. We can only hypothesize that all five units ever existed together anywhere. But it is at least a very interesting hypothesis. I have, however, two difficulties with it, so that, once again, I find my own explanation more plausible.

Secret Mark and the Youth Subplot.

The first problem is whether Y1 was ever originally linked to Y2 in *Secret Mark*. The difficulty is that, in Y1, the word "youth" is not present anywhere in Mark 10:17–22 or Luke 18:18–23 but only in Matt 19:16–22. The key verses are compared in Table 2:

Table 2

Matt 19:16, 20, 22	Mark 10:17, 20	Luke 18:18, 21
one (εἷς) came up to him...	a man (εἷς) ran up...	a ruler (ἄρχων) asked...
The young man (νεανίσκος) said to him, "All these I have observed; what do I still lack?"	And he said to him, "Teacher, all these I have observed from my youth (ἐκ νεότητός μου)."	And he said, "All these I have observed from my youth (ἐκ νεότητος)."
When the young man (νεανίσκος) heard this...	At that saying his countenance fell...	But when he heard this...

That requires some explanation on any hypothesis. And the difficulty is not so much the absence of the term "youth" in Mark (and Luke) as its presence in Matthew. I focus only on Mark in this section and return to consider Matthew and Luke in the section on editions and redactions.

Y1 and the Proposed Youth Subplot.

Is Y1 linked to Y2(–5) in a five-unit subplot? My own earlier explanation was that Y1 in *Secret Mark* was about a rich man who refused to follow Jesus but was not at all about a rich youth, a νεανίσκος (see Crossan, 1985: 113–15). These were my two arguments, in briefest summary. First, in Y2 the youth is introduced as follows: "And they come into Bethany. And a certain woman whose brother had died was there (καὶ ἦν ἐκεῖ μία γυνὴ ἧς ὁ ἀδελφὸς αὐτῆς ἀπέθανεν)." I do not find in that verse opening Y2 any hint that the reader should presume narrative continuity with Y1. Second, Clement wrote a commentary on Mark 10:17–31 entitled *The Rich Man's Salvation* (Butterworth: 270–367) to reassure wealthy Christians that they could be both saved and solvent. If he knew a story concerning a rich young man who first refused to follow Jesus because of his riches but was later saved "from death" and baptized by Jesus, it is hard to imagine him not using it for his homily. And if such a linked story was part of secret baptismal instruction and so unusable in a public homily, then the rich Christians of Alexandria would have already known it and hardly have needed that homily. In summary, a linked subplot connection between Y1 and Y2 has serious problems of plausibility.

Y2 and the Proposed Youth Subplot.

The second major problem is the whole idea of a (1) paradigmatic youth subplot involving (2) all of Y1–Y5 in *Secret Mark*. What exactly is the theological message of the proposed subplot? This question presses since Meyer suggests that the five linked units of the subplot "serve to communicate *Secret Mark*'s vision of discipleship, which is exemplified in the story of the νεανίσκος. This role of the νεανίσκος in the Markan tradition parallels that of the Beloved Disciple in the Gospel of John." Again, I offer two arguments in rebuttal.

First, that paradigmatic message, about which Meyer is not at all clear, would seem to be that one can refuse Jesus (Y1), be saved "from death" and baptized by Jesus (Y2), betray one's baptismal promises (Y4), and still proclaim the resurrection (Y5), although one's family may not do so well (Y3 & Y5). I hope that is not too unfair a summary. The early church certainly debated whether defection under persecution warranted a second chance and it certainly decided that it did. But it tended to exalt as a model not the defector who returned but the martyr who died. Mark 4:17–18 warned that persecution and wealth were the two major causes of default in discipleship. I find it therefore less than plausible that he would exalt as a model of discipleship one who had doubly defaulted, for wealth (Y1) and persecution (Y4), and yet later serenely proclaimed the resurrection without any further explanation (Y5).

Second, I consider that Y2–Y3 is indeed a paradigmatic youth-plot although the elements of Y2 are more certain than those of Y3 (necessity of abandoning one's family?). Those being actually baptized at Alexandria heard this read to them as their own story. They experienced the mystery of the kingdom as they were taken backwards through Genesis 1–3 in a ritual negation of death's victory over them. They were raised "from the dead" by the power of Jesus, they abandoned their garments of shame, and, naked but unashamed like Adam and Eve before their sin, they descended into the waters of creation to rejoin the Light and the Spirit on the first day of the world.

That is very heady stuff and it makes any modern interpretation of baptism as bath, and nakedness as not-getting-your-clothes-wet, an awful theological trivialization. But in *Secret Mark* it is also clear that the paradigmatic relationship of youth and Jesus in this ritual is one of *mutual* love. *Secret Mark* has both the youth loving Jesus in Y2, "the youth, looking upon him, loved him (νεανίσκος ἐμβλέψας αὐτῷ ἠγάπησεν αὐτόν)," and Jesus loving the youth in Y3, "the youth whom Jesus loved (τοῦ νεανίσκου ὃν ἠγάπα αὐτὸν ὁ Ἰησοῦς)." There was, of course, always the internal danger of eroticism and/or the external accusation of eroticism potentially inherent in the nakedness of the baptizant but such nakedness was absolutely dictated by the symbolism. Abandoning it would have been as symbolically difficult as abandoning eucharistic wine because of the dangers of alcoholism. That mutuality in love became in the libertine (gnostic?) version a mutuality in nakedness ("naked man with naked man"). Baptismal symbolism, of course, did not demand a naked baptizer but only a naked baptizant. I presume, by the way, that the Carpocratians inherited rather than invented that interpretation. The erotic reading would have been there as soon as there was naked baptism and a libertine Christianity interested in it. By the middle of the first century?

Short, then, of abandoning naked baptism with the extraordinary symbolic loss which that entailed (and would eventually entail), what could be done to counter the libertine interpretation? Look, for instance, at what happens to this story (Y2) in the Johannine tradition. John has nothing about Lazarus loving Jesus but only the converse, and with a different verb for love, in 11:3, "Lord, he whom you love (ὃν φιλεῖς) is ill," and 11:36, "See how he loved him (ἐφίλει αὐτόν)." And in between those two statements is one which diminishes any hint of exclusivity in that love, in 11:5, "Now Jesus loved (ἠγάπα) Martha and her sister and Lazarus." Once again, with the paradigmatic disciple, there is no mention of him loving Jesus but only of Jesus loving him, now, however, with the verb ἀγαπάω, as in both *Secret Mark* and canonical Mark: see John 13:23; 19:26; 21:7, 20. John performs three major surgeries on that even-by-then dangerous story. He breaks the two-way into a strictly one-way love. He distinguishes between the unnamed paradigmatic disciple whom Jesus loves and the named Lazarus raised from the dead. And Lazarus although still loved is now within a safe and corporate family love and noted in the order "Martha and her sister and Lazarus." In its own way, the Johannine tradition dismembered the story into safer components just as surely as did the Markan tradition.

Canonical Mark and the Youth Subplot.

I have already outlined my own understanding of how canonical Mark sanitized the youth story. He dismembered Y2–Y3 on the level of its words and phrases and he distributed them elsewhere throughout the gospel. That meant that any resurgence of the Y2–Y3 story could easily be dismissed as a pastiche from canonical Mark (1985: 111–19). The difference between Meyer and myself on what *Secret Mark* contained and what canonical Mark did to it is outlined in Figure 3:

Figure 3

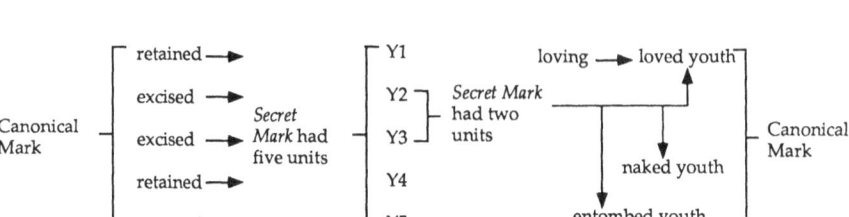

My own reconstruction of canonical Mark's exercise in damage control does not really make him much of an author or even a redactor. He is more like a censor carefully covering his tracks. I presume that his dismemberment and redistribution of Y2–Y3 effected only changes in Y1 and Y5 but not the creation of those units. I think, however, that he created Y4 as a totally new unit.

Markan Editions or Synoptic Redactions.

One final and fairly major point. Both Marvin Meyer in the present article, and Ron Cameron reviewing my book *Four Other Gospels*, have faulted me for not accepting Helmut Koester's suggestion of various editions of Mark with different ones used by Matthew (with Mark 6:45–8:26 added), and Luke (with Mark 6:45–8:26 not yet added), and with both of them using editions without any of the youth subplot. I have one general reason and very many specific reasons for not doing so.

The general reason is that I fear a proposal of undocumented editions is beyond control, beyond proof or disproof, and therefore beyond interest. I prefer to see, for example, if, presuming a planned Luke-Acts writing, Lukan redaction may not be a better explanation of the lack of parallels to Mark 6:45–8:26. I prefer, in other words, to work with synoptic redactions and only to postulate Markan editions if and when those explanations are no longer credible. I have simply not reached that point as yet.

The specific reasons will have to be exemplified by a few cases. First, take the case of Y1 in Mark 10:17–22 = Matt 19:16–22 = Luke 18:18–23. How exactly, presuming the Two Source theory of synoptic relations, does the hypothesis of Markan editions help us with the problem seen earlier that the youth is mentioned only in Matthew but not in Mark or Luke? Since Matt 19:20, 22 have νεανίσκος, we would have to presume he is using the *Secret Mark* edition. But Luke 18:21 follows Mark 10:20 in having only "from my youth" and no mention of νεανίσκος. Since "from my youth" would be considered as canonical Mark's deliberate rephrasing and eliminating of the νεανίσκος theme, Luke would have to be reading the canonical Mark edition. Then, on the other hand but still in Y1, Mark 10:21 has "Jesus looking upon him loved him (ἐμβλέψας αὐτῷ ἠγάπησεν αὐτόν)." I take this to be canonical Mark's deliberate rephrasing and relocation of the resurrected youth loving Jesus in Y2, "the youth, looking upon him, loved him (νεανίσκος ἐμβλέψας αὐτῷ ἠγάπησεν αὐτόν)." But neither Matt 19:21 nor Luke 18:22 has any trace of that sentence. How is that explained? Is neither of them following the canonical Mark edition? Are both of them following the *Secret Mark* edition? And how, then, within this same unit of Y1 and within the hypothesis of different editions does one explain the synoptic phenomena of both those cases?

I presume and accept the coincidence that both Matthew and Luke, independently of one another, were unsatisfied with Mark's gospel. I expect, therefore, that wherever we get closest to Mark's syntax or theology, each may be expected to change or omit sections. I find it absolutely acceptable and even predictable that they would both look at Mark 10:21 where Jesus loves the young man, would wonder what on earth it meant in that context, and both decide to excise it. And I find no hypothesis of editions necessary to explain later the absence of Mark 14:51–52. They both looked at it and like every reader since they wondered what on earth Mark was up to. Except that they did not have to explain it, they could and did excise it.

If Matthew and Luke only acted like that in cases involving the νεανίσκος, it might be plausible that they knew editions without that subplot. But such omissions are but part of the much wider phenomenon of the *negative* minor agreements of Matthew and Luke against Mark, of those cases, in other words, where they both *omit* materials found in their common Markan source. And that happens especially where the units are close to peculiarly (canonical) Markan concerns among which is the dismemberment and redistribution of the Y2–Y3 νεανίσκος units, a phenomenon which created difficulties for the synoptics and every other reader after them.

WORKS CONSULTED

NTA =
Hennecke, Edgar, and Wilhelm Schneemelcher, eds.
    1963-65 *New Testament Apocrypha*. 2 vols. Trans. R. McL. Wilson. London: Lutterworth.

OTP =
Charlesworth, James H., ed.
  1983-85   *The Old Testament Pseudepigrapha.* 2 vols. Garden City, NY: Doubleday.

Butterworth, George William
  1919   *Clement of Alexandria: The Exhortation to the Greeks; The Rich Man's Salvation; To the Newly Baptized.* LCL. Cambridge: Harvard University Press.

Cameron, Ron
  1987   Review of *Four Other Gospels* in *JBL* 106: 558–60.

Collins, John J.
  1983   *Between Athens and Jerusalem: Jewish Identity in the Hellenistic Diaspora.* New York: Crossroad.

Crossan, John Dominic
  1985   *Four Other Gospels: Shadows on the Contours of Canon.* Minneapolis: Winston.
  1988   *The Cross that Spoke: The Origins of the Passion Narrative.* San Francisco: Harper & Row.

Kloppenborg, John S.
  1987   *The Formation of Q: Trajectories in Ancient Wisdom Collections.* Studies in Antiquity and Christianity. Philadelphia: Fortress.

Metzger, Bruce M.
  1971   *A Textual Commentary on the Greek New Testament.* A Companion Volume to the United Bible Societies' *Greek New Testament* (third edition). New York: United Bible Societies.

Nickelsburg, George W. E., Jr.
  1972   *Resurrection, Immortality, and Eternal Life in Intertestamental Judaism.* HTS 26. Cambridge: Harvard University Press.
  1980   "The Genre and Function of the Markan Passion Narrative." *HTR* 73: 153–84.

ALL THE EXTRA JESUSES: CHRISTIAN ORIGINS IN THE LIGHT OF THE EXTRA-CANONICAL GOSPELS

Burton L. Mack
School of Theology at Claremont

0. Extra, Extra, Read all about it

Jonathan Z. Smith once said that "All you need for a founder figure is a name and a place." The implication was that the rest of the picture gets filled in by an exercise of the imagination that historians of religion would call mythmaking. The essays in this issue of *Semeia* identify five moments of mythmaking in early Christian history. These moments are taken from four extra-canonical gospels, three of which (Q, the *Gospel of Peter*, and the *Secret Gospel of Mark*) have been located by recent scholarship at early junctures in the histories of the Jesus movements.

New Testament scholars should no longer be surprised that a focus upon such extra-canonical moments adds yet another set of images to the expanding gallery of the portraits of Jesus that are coming into view. Extra-canonical texts result in extra-canonical Jesuses. The wider lens now being used to search for Christian origins brings myths and movements into view that were erased in that process of selective "memory" we call canonization. This means that the scholarship represented in this set of essays is very important indeed. It is important, that is, if what we want to learn about is the experimental nature of the first chapters of Christian history, what we want to understand are the processes of social formation and mythmaking, and what we want eventually to assess is the reason some experiments survived and others did not.

1. Excavating Extraneous History

The prevailing picture of Christian origins does need to be revised. It is based on (a) an apocalyptic Jesus, (b) the indispensable resurrection, and (c) a first-church of the appearances in Jerusalem as the single center for the two great missions, the first to the Jews and the second to the Gentiles. All New Testament scholars are aware of textual material and historical data that cannot easily be reconciled with this picture. Some scholars are also aware that the literary and historical bases for the traditional reconstruction are very, very shaky. The picture itself has not yet budged, however, and will not budge until alternative explanations for the (sometimes very curious) data available are taken up for forthright discussion and evaluation. This volume of *Semeia* does just that. It not only contains a set of studies that strike to the heart of several privileged assumptions, it also puts considerable pressure on those assumptions and nudges in the direction of a rather radical revision of the status quo. It does that, for the most part, by excavating history traditionally held to be extraneous.

It is not clear that the essays in this volume were planned with the purpose of revising the canonical (essentially Lukan) picture in mind. Three of the studies, those by Julian Hills, Arthur J. Dewey and Marvin W. Meyer, do not require a radical revision of the dramatic theory of Christian origins, dealing as they do with various narrative versions of those origins. Nevertheless, each author treats the gospel account in hand as a particular product of some specific moment of human imagination, not as (and here comes my thin description of the prevailing scholarly approach) the automatic transmission and hermeneutical application of an energizing memory core stemming from the original witnesses to the only authentic, once-for-all performance there was of the crucial Christian theatre. That means that the studies by Meyer, Dewey, and Hills fall easily on the side of a no-nonsense approach to the history of early Christian mythmaking and religion.

Only two moments of mythmaking, those presented by Ron Cameron and John S. Kloppenborg, are set forth as essentially irreconcilable with the prevailing picture. These studies will therefore deserve special attention. It is nevertheless the case that all of the studies in this volume bear directly upon the critical task of historical reconstruction and the way in which that history may eventually force a revision of the prevailing view. The issue raised here is the relationship of the prevailing view of Christian origins, accepted by most of the scholarly guild as history, to the myths of Christian origins that the gospel accounts provide.

All of these authors take social history seriously. None is troubled by the fact that the new historiography results in the identification of many moments, diverse views, and plural social formations as the large scape opens up for viewing. Each takes up the text in hand as a documentation of worthy human endeavor and treats it with genuine human interest. Each attempts to identify a discrete discourse that may be specific to a particular tradition, group, or community. And there are signs, especially in the essays by Cameron, Kloppenborg, and Hills, that the rhetoric of their texts is clearly seen, and that the rhetoric was taken as an invitation to analyze the rhetorical situation within which the text was composed and intended to be heard. In brief, one encounters here with great relief a maturing scholarship that regards the question of early Christianity as a challenge for historians and for historians of religion. This scholarship is no longer determined by the constraints of the New Testament as canon or by the age-old desire for a relevant theological hermeneutic. We therefore stand to learn a great deal.

Since John Dominic Crossan has focused his discussion mainly upon the contributions from Dewey and Meyer, I should like to address myself particularly to the essays by Cameron, Kloppenborg, and Hills. I find them extremely interesting as a set of studies and judge each of them individually to make a significant advance in an important area or method of investigation.

2. *Myths Made of (Extra Curricular) Meshalim*

One feature that the studies by Hills, Cameron, and Kloppenborg have in common is the choice of a text or topic that explores the relation of sayings material in the Jesus traditions to narrative events lying at the heart of the plot shared by the synoptic gospels. This single feature alone is sufficient to mark these studies for special notice. That is because the scholarly reconstruction of Christian origins has always been frustrated by the apparent lack of pre-Markan connections among three disparate traditions—(a) the sayings material of the Jesus traditions; (b) the kerygmatic formulations of the Hellenistic communities reflected in the letters of Paul; and (c) the passion narratives. Only recently have scholarly theses appeared that seriously attempt to account for the mutual relations among these three disparate types of material in any comprehensive historical reconstruction. James M. Robinson's presidential address to the Society of Biblical Literature in 1981, "Jesus: From Easter to Valentinus," was one such attempt. The 1988 study of Christian origins by Burton L. Mack, *A Myth of Innocence*, is another. This volume of *Semeia* studies can now be added to the short list.

Cameron's study directly addresses the question of wisdom and apocalyptic in the sayings material attributed to Jesus in Q. His account does not square with the prevailing scholarly wisdom about the priority of apocalyptic preachments either for Jesus or for John. Kloppenborg's essay explores the curiosity that the Sayings Gospel Q does not appeal to the crucifixion and resurrection of Jesus. His finding, that these events were of no significance for the Q movement, runs counter to the customary assumption that, despite the lack of reference, the people of Q must have participated in the "post-Easter" persuasion of kerygmatic Christianity. Hills focuses on the very interesting use of conventional wisdom to argue for a certain view of the resurrection in the *Epistula Apostolorum*, an obvious case of mythmaking by means of the attribution of sayings to Jesus. Each study deserves an extra-special accolade.

2.1   Hills' study strikes me as an invitation to gather round a new kind of *Osterfeuer*. There are four proverbs that appear in the post-Easter instructions about the reality of the resurrection in the *Epistula Apostolorum*, and Hills plucks them with a slightly syncopated beat. What he is able to demonstrate, moreover, lines out nothing less than an incandescing riff. (I wanted to say "incendiary" to mix the metaphors of music and matches, but incendiary has only a destructive connotation and one would be left uncertain, as with the paintings of Anselm Kiefer, about the constructive nuances that I certainly want to convey.) That is because these proverbs, though attributed to Jesus, could not possibly make their intended point unless they meant what they meant when used in the contemporary world of common cultural convention. In the case of the one proverb that has a parallel in the synoptic tradition, and that therefore might at first be thought to gain its punch primarily as a logion of/from Jesus, Hills shows that its force is derived solely from its common extra-trajectory connotation, not from its earlier use or meaning in the Jesus traditions. Thus the light these proverbs shed on the traditional notion of the resurrection was clearly shining in from outside the inner circle.

There are several important things to notice about this demonstration. One is that the need to imagine Jesus using common proverbs does not appear to have caused any existential consternation on the part of the authors of these texts. The process of attributing sayings to Jesus must have been, instead, a common occurrence accomplished quite easily. A second is that it was precisely the conventional logic attached to these proverbs that made them attractive. This means that the process of attribution took place in the context of reflective activity. A third point is that the proverbs were used as supporting arguments in a sustained argumentation. Hills gets high marks indeed for seeing that these proverbs performed an essentially rhetorical function in the argumentation and that they carried a logical import that was absolutely necessary to that argumentation.

A fourth point of significance is that the attribution of these proverbs to Jesus resulted in a profile of characterization that even hardened scholars should find amazing upon reflection. Not only was Jesus cast as the one to experience the resurrection under discussion, and to pronounce upon its reality as an authority whose word was beyond question, he was also now the one who went on to argue for a certain view of its (physical) reality. He did so by using these proverbs to appeal to conventional forms of reasoning. This overloading of authority upon the single figure of Jesus is not new to the Jesus traditions. The procedure is, in fact, fully in keeping with the way in which various functions of authority were invested in the founder figure in all early Jesus traditions, as for instance in Q, the pronouncement stories, and the *Gospel of Thomas*, to name only three. But New Testament scholars have not always been willing to notice this phenomenon or to investigate the procedures used in the attribution of new sayings to Jesus. That makes Hills' demonstration extremely important, for it leaves no room for a remystification of the post-Easter inspiration variety, and it dispels this mist right at the center of a "post-Easter" meditation, reflection, and argumentation. What Hills has identified is a moment of early Christian mythmaking. His study provides a model for investigating other moments of attribution in the early Jesus traditions as mythmaking as well.

2.2 Kloppenborg's essay works the other way around. What about sayings in the Q tradition where Jesus' death and resurrection are never mentioned? Scholars know, of course, that Q does not refer to the resurrection of Jesus, much less to a kerygmatic significance for his death. But that has not kept the scholarly guild from assuming that a kerygmatic Christianity must be presupposed. That being the case, Kloppenborg's essay is bold indeed because that assumption is exactly what he puts to the test. The essay is, in fact, historic. It simply must be read and debated by all New Testament scholars now. There is no sense in forging ahead with the old paradigm as our presupposition and guide if Kloppenborg is right. Even if he is not thought to be right by some, the burden of proof has suddenly shifted or, to use another metaphor, the worm has turned. That is because the essay is a model of caution and thoroughness. No stone is left unlifted. The traditional view is given every chance to find some trace somewhere in the Q material. None is found and Kloppenborg draws the only conclusion left to him (and I would say, to us), namely, that Q represents a Jesus movement that did not need, know, or cultivate a "Christology" based upon Jesus' death (much less resurrection).

The point should now be allowed to sink in, way in. If that was true for the tradents of Q, what about the pronouncement stories, the miracle stories, the *Gospel of Thomas*, and other written residue from early Jesus traditions? Were there no other ways of cultivating memory traditions, imagining founder figures, and thus investing Jesus with superior forms of authority apart from a resurrection mythologoumenon? One sees that the implications for revising Christian origins are abundant. Kloppenborg sees this and presses the question to the very edge of the texts and language at hand. We should all go along and have a look at the strange terrain beyond the borders. But then, and this is meant as a friendly chiding, one wonders why the language of "Easter faith" should not finally be given up completely. Kloppenborg lets the reader know that this language does not fit his findings, but he continues to use it nonetheless. It does mark the curious characterization of Jesus in Q as an analogue in contrast to the Easter question with which Kloppenborg began. But it does not enlighten the newly espied figure where an extravagant attribution of authority to Jesus was accomplished without reference to a resurrection. That process of attribution, and the resulting characterization, need to be given other names in order to distinguish them clearly from "Easter faith" models currently confusing our discourse.

2.3   Cameron's study is aimed at an enigma that has resisted the newer historiography of the Jesus traditions. The problem has to do with John the Baptist. If John was an apocalyptic preacher, so the argument has been running, and Paul was an apocalyptic theologian, how can we not imagine Jesus also as an apocalyptic proclaimer of the kingdom of God? Q studies since Kloppenborg have been getting used to the idea that John the Baptist does not figure in the earliest layer of the tradition, but that does not solve the problem. A host of questions awaits the inquisitive: Who was John, and what did Jesus and/or the Jesus people have to do with him? The questions are very important, for the earliest history of the Jesus movements reflected in Q and the Gospel of Mark cannot be reconstructed unless they can be answered. Cameron dares to confront this challenge.

The essay is a masterstroke. The John and Jesus section in Q is taken up by design. It is not only the earliest textual evidence we have for John, it is also the critical text for working out the shift in discourse and ideology that took place between the first and the second layers of Q, and, especially because of its position at the beginning of the resulting document, it has been thought to hold some clues for the organization of the whole. It has, unfortunately, been a knotty text to unravel. Cameron marches right in and unties the laces. As they slide apart, it is clear that this pericope was put together on purpose, and that the purpose was mythmaking at a certain juncture in Q's social history. That juncture had to do with rationalizing rejection and justifying the use of the language of judgment, the very situation thought by other scholars to have been addressed by the apocalyptic discourse that emerged in the second layer of Q. So both the question of wisdom and apocalyptic in the teachings of Jesus, and the problem of Jesus' relation to John and the prophets, are solved in principle by Cameron's analysis. They are solved in the sense that one can see them being created right before one's eyes in the construction of this pericope. Cameron not only shows how the pericope came to be, but why. That is because he does not rest content until the rhetorical logic of the several steps of the process has been completely disclosed.

The demonstration is packed with brilliant exegetical observations at every turn of detail. Here it will have to be sufficient to mention the major conclusions of significance. Fundamental to the entire operation is the identification of a chreia (anecdote) at the core of the pericope. Cameron pursues the logic of this chreia at a stage prior to its elaboration. The elaboration is then analyzed and the shifts in focus (from Jesus to John, then to "this generation," and finally to the tradents of Q as the "children of wisdom") are charted. As it turns out, neither John nor Jesus was remembered as an apocalyptic preacher until the tradents of Q "entertained," to use Cameron's word, an apocalyptic imagination. They did this in order to make sense of a difficult situation, and one can imagine how that would have worked. The most amazing part of the study, however, is the demonstration that this apocalyptic imagination was only "entertained." It cannot be read as constitutive even for the tradents of Q who used its language in order to flesh out certain contours of their emerging myth of origins. Cameron's picture is startling in its difference from the traditional view of Q. It is also unnerving just because it finally makes so much simple sense.

3. L'excès de l'extraordinaire

Suppose, now, that these accounts of mythmaking were given their due. Suppose we New Testament scholars were to learn from them how to go about reading all of the moments when early Christians reimagined Jesus, canonical and extra-canonical alike. What then? Then the assumption of a singular extraordinary moment at the beginning would certainly have to be called into question. To question that assumption, moreover, would indicate a huge shift in scholarly paradigm. The important things to understand would no longer be the supposed originary events, but other reasons for the various social formations that emerged, for the many portraits of Jesus produced by early Christians, and why some experiments survived and others did not. Thus it is that the studies in this volume are important. Their demonstrations force the issue of the prevailing scholarly paradigm. And they point the way toward phrasing the questions that must now be asked. Their promise is clear. We stand to learn, not only about all the extra Jesuses, but about all the extra energies early Christians invested in the creation of a novel persuasion. Come to think of it, that might make an even more interesting picture than the one we have had in mind.

WORKS CONSULTED

Mack, Burton L.
   1988   *A Myth of Innocence: Mark and Christian Origins.* Philadelphia: Fortress.

Robinson, James M.
   1982   "Jesus: From Easter to Valentinus (or to the Apostles' Creed)." *JBL* 101: 5–37.

www.ingramcontent.com/pod-product-compliance
Lightning Source LLC
Chambersburg PA
CBHW032256150426
43195CB00008BA/480